UFOs Are Here!

UFOs Are Here!

Unmasking the Greatest Conspiracy of Our Time

Brad Steiger and
Sherry Hansen Steiger

Citadel Press
Kensington Publishing Corp.
www.kensingtonbooks.com

Contents

"Our Planet Doesn't Belong to Us Anymore!"

The former NASA scientist really got our attention when he told us about underground UFO bases in which large storage vats were filled with human body parts waiting to be blended with the fluid that extraterrestrial aliens used for food.

Earlier that evening we had listened with great interest when the engineer—who over the years had worked with numerous government projects—told us how pieces of crashed flying saucers were an integral element in developing the Stealth's ability to baffle enemy radar. Because of the boost our aeronautical science was given by alien technology, he said, our new generation of jet fighters would look remarkably like some eye witness descriptions of UFOs.

We also listened with rapt attention to the former Air Force Intelligence officer who repeated details of a secret deal that a shadow group within our government had made with the aliens— in which the ETIs (extraterrestrial intelligences) traded their advanced technology for the right to abduct humans for a variety of biological experiments.

All of these astonishing allegations were made on a warm July night in 1988, during a session of the UFO discussion group that met at our Phoenix home. An open invitation to visiting UFO researchers to attend these informal meetings had—on this particular evening—attracted a number of new individuals who not only produced documentation of their identities, but also detailed accounts of alleged alien activities that bordered on either bad science fiction or everyone's worst nightmare. In fact, from that meeting onward, we christened our informal gatherings "paranoia nights."

We have engaged in UFO research for thirty years and are quite familiar with accounts of alleged flying saucer hostility, crashed UFOs and scattered alien bodies, UFO kidnappings and abductions, the diverse men and women claiming to communicate directly with extraterrestrial beings, and an entire encyclopedia of UFO accounts ranging from believable and somewhat bizarre to unbelievable and far out.

But these secret government deals with aliens in underground bases and collaboration on the invasion of our planet—although not unheard of in the past—were now being told by individuals who appeared to be former NASA scientists, military intelligence officers, and government project engineers. They relayed these frightening tales with a sense of urgency and desperation that we had rarely encountered before. Theirs was a warning that aliens were not only coming, but that they are *here*—and very much in control of things.

As one of the former intelligence officers phrased it: "This planet is no longer ours. Earth no longer belongs to us!"

From the beginning of UFO investigation in the late 1940s, there have been cries of conspiracy and complaints of attempts by government agencies to silence witnesses of flying saucer encounters. Thousands of men and women have persistently charged that our presidents, military, and top scientists have been in on the secret of the UFO.

As our paranoia nights continued, we discussed such matters as the following:

GENERAL MACARTHUR'S WARNING TO THE NATIONS OF EARTH

On October 9, 1955, the United States' indomitable "old soldier" General Douglas MacArthur issued a warning to the nations of the world that they had no choice other than to unite. As quoted in the *New York Times*, MacArthur expressed his sincere opinion that the nations of Earth must soon "make a common front against attack by people from other planets." The next war, he warned, would be an interplanetary one.

MacArthur returned to the theme of an invasion from outer

space again and again. In 1962 while addressing the graduating class at West Point, he stated: *"We deal now not with things of this world alone. We deal now with the ultimate conflict between a united human race and the sinister forces of some other planetary galaxy."*

Did General MacArthur really know something about the truth behind the flying saucer controversy that the public did not? In his speeches of 1955 and 1962, was he attempting to alert the citizenry of the United States to the threat of an invasion from outer space?

Unfortunately for the denizens of Earth, it would seem that by the time General MacArthur issued his warnings to beware of "sinister forces" from some other galaxy, it was already too late to halt an alien invasion of our planet.

THE BETRAYAL OF EARTH BY THE SECRET GOVERNMENTS

By 1954 covert branches within the U.S. government and the governing structures of other superpowers had cut a deal with representatives of extraterrestrial intelligences (ETIs) to barter superior alien scientific and technological knowledge in exchange for access to certain of our planet's mineral deposits. In addition, the aliens were given *carte blanche* to conduct various types of experiments on humans.

During one of our paranoia nights, a physicist described the grisly chamber of horrors a colleague of his had discovered in a tunnel below an abandoned military base. According to his friend, the tunnel contained the skeletal remains of several hundred young males. In his opinion the aliens were using street people, runaways, and stray kids who supposedly just disappeared, but were rarely missed, in ghastly, unknown experiments.

THE PHILADELPHIA EXPERIMENT

In 1943 Project Rainbow was implemented as an attempt to render our Navy's warships invisible to enemy radar. Some investigators of the incident insist that the experiment was so successful that it not only made the *Eldridge*, a DE 173 destroyer, disappear . . . it dematerialized it—and simultaneously ripped open a hole in the space-time continuum.

This aspect of Project Rainbow was the famous Philadelphia

Experiment, in which the U.S. Navy allegedly teleported a warship from Philadelphia to its dock near Norfolk by successfully applying what would come to be known as Einstein's Unified Field theory.

According to the accounts of supposed eyewitnesses, the project ended in disaster when several crewmen burst into flame during the transfer. Other seamen continued to lapse into partial invisibility during shore leave.

NAZI UFOS

It has been theorized that ETIs first established a regular pattern of interaction with certain German scientists in the mid-1930s. A number of these scientists left their homeland shortly after the Nazis took power. Many immigrated to the United States and were employed by the U.S. military's Project Rainbow.

Throughout the war ETI craft were frequency sighted pacing Allied bombers and smaller aircraft over European cities and landscapes. At first the Allied pilots feared that the fierce Nazi war machine had perfected manned rocketry, but when the strange saucer-shaped objects made no hostile moves toward them, the Yanks and the Brits dubbed the things "Foo Fighters."

THE TOP-SECRET GROUP KNOWN AS MAJESTIC-12

Majestic-12 (MJ-12) is an alleged conspiracy of U.S. military leaders that was said to have been established September 24, 1947, by special classified order of President Harry S. Truman to enforce a lid of security on UFOs. According to certain documents [still under examination], Admiral Roscoe Hillenkoetter prepared a report on November 18, 1952, to brief President-elect Eisenhower on a saucer crash near Roswell, New Mexico, in which four smallish, large-headed, reptilian beings were discovered near the wreckage.

MJ-12 described how all military and civilian eyewitnesses to the downed UFO and its crew were debriefed, and a cover story of an errant weather balloon was fabricated to satisfy the press. A strenuous program was established to discredit any individual who might later attempt to declare the reality of the crashed UFO and its strange occupants.

A UFO PROGRAM OF HUMAN ABDUCTIONS

But by far the most shocking allegation made by our informants was that circa 1954 a shadow group within the U.S. government made a deal with the ETIs that permitted mutilation of cattle and abduction of humans in exchange for advanced alien technology.

The ETIs offered assurances that the human abductions would merely be ongoing examinations designed to enable them to monitor a developing civilization. Regarding the cattle mutilations, the ETIs explained that their own evolutionary ascent had left them with a genetic disorder that rendered their digestive systems severely dysfunctional. The ETIs would best be able to sustain themselves on Earth by ingesting an enzyme, or hormonal secretion, most readily obtained from the tongues and throats of cattle.

THE "GRAYS"

In the jargon of UFOlogy, a number of researchers began to refer to the smallish ETIs as the "Grays," a collective term that incorporated their bug-eyed, reptilian appearance and slate-gray complexion.

UNDERGROUND BASES

A proponent of an alien network of underground bases told us that after the initial agreement between the secret government and the reptilian ETIs, a number of test centers and military bases were built to include huge underground facilities. These cavernous installations were constructed with the assistance of the ETIs and the promised technology was set in place. However, the Grays would permit the technology to be operated only under their aegis.

SECRET GOVERNMENT PROJECTS IN ESP AND MIND CONTROL

Beginning about 1966 bright young people, in a bizarre kind of brain drain, were drawn into secret government projects in ESP, mind control, and mind manipulation—all of which had been designed for implementation by the Grays, the ETIs.

According to alleged eyewitnesses of the experiments, the insidious machinations of the ETIs sucked some of our best and most brilliant young people into a program designed to create a new world of the Grays' own choosing.

THE DEAL WITH THE GRAYS BEGINS TO GO SOUR

By 1982 it became increasingly apparent to the more aware members of the secret government that things were simply not going as planned. Far more people were being abducted than were acknowledged on the "official" abduction list the Grays provided to their partners in the shadow government.

ALIEN-IMPLANTED PREGNANCIES IN HUMAN MOTHERS

MJ-12 began receiving reports of steadily rising numbers of women who described the advent of unusual pregnancies as an unwelcome by-product of their abduction experiences. In certain instances these pregnancies were terminated by the removal of the fetuses in subsequent abductions. In other cases the women were monitored during their pregnancy and the birth of their "starchildren."

After receiving several reports in which males reported the removal of semen during abduction encounters, MJ-12 was forced to conclude that—among other violations of their agreement—the ETIs were performing crossbreeding experiments between humans and Grays.

THE SECRET GOVERNMENT FINDS ITSELF OUTSMARTED

What occurred circa 1983, according to our informants, is that those avaricious, power-hungry individuals in the secret government discovered that they had been outsmarted. Believing they could trust these aliens, they were dismayed to find the ETIs had been using them to achieve their own hidden agenda.

By 1984, MJ-12 realized the terrible mistake they had made in accepting the deal with the Grays. MJ-12 had promoted the motion pictures *Close Encounters of the Third Kind* and *E.T.* to help condition the public to accept odd or ugly aliens as compassionate, benevolent beings concerned about the welfare of planet

Earth. The secret government had helped to sell the reptilian aliens to the masses, and now they were faced with the frightening fact that some of these particular ETIs were far from loving beings.

At about the same time (1985-87), conscientious military intelligence officers, as well as veterans of NATO (North Atlantic Treaty Organization) and SHAPE (Supreme Headquarters, Allied Powers, Europe), unearthed evidence of the betrayal of our planet by the secret government, and began to sound the alarm that a mass alien invasion of Earth was imminent. This would have already taken place in 1987 but for the intervention of other, more benevolent, extraterrestrial beings who are doing what they can to halt the invasion of Earth and to right the wrongs that have already been dealt to humans.

NOT ALL THE ALIENS ARE BAD GUYS

Based on the experiences of our informants, it seems that our human species has received the focused attention of representatives of at least two extraterrestrial or multidimensional worlds. Apparently some ETIs are concerned about our welfare and right to evolve as our own species, but some seem largely indifferent to our species' longevity and integrity.

There exists some kind of "Interplanetary Council," which has decreed that a planet's biological and technological evolution should not be interfered with in any way. The fact that a maverick group of extraterrestrial entities made a bargain with self-serving representatives of Earth's governments to exchange scientific knowledge for minerals, water, raw products—and even for human beings to be used in biological experiments—totally and blatantly violates the council's dictum that a planet's natural evolution should not be accelerated or altered in any way.

OUR PLANET IS THE PRIZE IN A WAR OF THE WORLDS

The thought that we and our planet may be pawns in some greater intergalactic struggle is by far more ego-deflating to our species than Galileo's revelations that Earth was not the center of the universe. It might well be that our beautiful oasis in space could serve as the prize in a war between worlds.

FLYING SAUCERS ARE THE PRODUCT OF A TERRESTRIAL SECRET SOCIETY

Certain researchers who attended our paranoia nights expressed their opinion that the extraterrestrial hypothesis was a hoax perpetuated by an ancient secret society here on Earth that had perfected space travel centuries ago and propagandized the belief in ETs in order to force the nations of the planet to band together and accept the New World Order.

How much of the above may we believe? Have alien beings from some extraterrestrial world truly invaded our planet?

Has our planet been sold out by greedy individuals who comprise secret governments and who direct top-secret military projects? (None of our informants has suggested that the *entire* government or any particular administration has betrayed us. It is the "secret government," perhaps the more powerful of the two, that has bartered with the aliens to benefit themselves at our collective expense.)

Are we the victims of a colossal hoax perpetrated by members of a secret society who wish to rule the planet?

The avowed purpose of this book is to explore these questions—and many more—to the best of our abilities and to seek to ascertain whether or not we must prepare ourselves for a war of the worlds that may leave us in complete servitude to alien masters.

CHAPTER 1

Close Encounters: Hostile and Benevolent

A wealth of evidence exists to document human encounters with aliens. Some of those encounters involve overtly hostile acts such as kidnapping, assaults, mutilation, burnings, paralysis, mind control, mysterious cremations, and destruction of automobiles and machinery. Others are strangely benign during which people experience miraculous cures from illness or acquire special powers.

However, as the following examples will show, contact with UFOs and their occupants changes the lives of the people involved forever.

The incident occurred while Bill English, the son of an Arizona state legislator, was serving as a Green Beret captain in Laos in 1969–71:

"My ten-man team was sent to investigate a B-52 bomber that had gone down in thick jungle territory," English said. "According to the information that we had received, communications had been received from the bomber before it went down. The essence of the message was that the B-52 was being attacked by a large light, a UFO."

English and his men found the plane intact in the jungle. There was no crushed swath of vegetation to indicate a crash landing. Only the bottom of the fuselage showed any damage.

"Although the plane was intact," English said, "the crew was dead. We found them sitting in their safety harnesses. They were all mutilated. Their anuses had been cored out to their colons.

Corkscrew patches of skin had been sliced from their necks and jaws. Their eyes and genitalia had been removed by extremely precise surgery—yet no blood had been spilled anywhere.''

On April 12, 1965, James Flynn, a rancher of East Fort Myers, Florida, claimed that a beam of light had shot out from under the bottom of a UFO and struck him in the forehead while he was on a camping trip in the Everglades. Flynn said that he had instantly lost consciousness. When he awakened, he was blind in his right eye and left with only partial vision in his left eye. Dimly, the rancher could see a symmetrical circle of scorched ground where the cone-shaped UFO had been hovering. A number of cypress trees had been burned at their tops.

Not until Flynn walked into the office of Dr. Paul Brown did he realize that he had been unconscious for twenty-four hours. Dr. Brown was very concerned about his patient's loss of vision. Due to hemorrhaging in the anterior chamber of the eye, Flynn's right eye looked like a bright red marble. His forehead and the area around his eyes were inflamed and swollen. He was almost completely blind.

Because of the rancher's solid reputation, his story of being struck down by a ray from the interior of a UFO made the national wire services. Whether or not the physical evidence— the scorched cypress, the burned circle of grass—constituted proof of the UFO's hostile act to every skeptical inquirer, Flynn was left with cloudy vision in his right eye and a depressed spot of about one centimeter in the skull area above the same eye.

Braniff Airways' Flight 542, a Lockheed Electra turboprop airliner, took off from Houston, Texas, en route to New York City at 10:37 P.M., September 29, 1959. Flight 542 carried twenty-eight passengers and six crew members, and its flight plan called for it to travel over the Buffalo, Texas, area, 68 miles southeast of Waco. The sky was partly cloudy as Flight 542 neared Buffalo at an altitude of 15,000 feet and an air speed of 275 knots.

At the same time that Flight 542 was approaching Buffalo, Major R. O. Braswell was flying a C-47 at 6,500 feet between Shreveport, Louisiana, and Lufkin, Texas, which is east-northeast of Buffalo. It was there that Major Braswell first saw the "thing," colored "like a large red fire," looking like some kind of "atomic cloud," a "massive thing" at about 15,000 feet.

Billie Guyton of Centerville, Texas, was observing the aerial phenomenon from the ground at the same time as Major Braswell. Guyton reported that he watched an object emerge from the firey red cloud.

Jackie J. Cox, a thirty-nine-year-old schoolteacher, was driving toward Buffalo when he heard a noise overhead and looked up to see "a bright light in the sky that spread to cover the entire sky, as if phosphorus or magnesium were burning."

W. S. Webb of Buffalo had just gone to bed when he happened to glance out the window and see "a ball of fire, that looked like a star, shoot through the sky."

Farmer Richard White and his wife had just turned off the television set and gone to bed. White had decided to sleep on the breezeway that night in an effort to beat the summer heat. As he lay gazing at the summer stars, he noticed a brilliant light high in the southern sky: "The whole sky seemed to be lit up by a huge fireball passing overhead, only to be followed by a tremendous explosion, so violent it seemed to shake the ground itself."

Seconds later the quiet countryside was shattered by the sound of shrill whistles as falling debris tore through the still summer night. The giant turboprop airliner had been torn into thousands of fragments.

A Braniff official investigating the wreckage of Flight 542 said that he had never seen a crash "where the plane was so thoroughly demolished, the wreckage so widely scattered, and the people so horribly mangled. And there was nothing among the wreckage to indicate a fire or a bomb aboard the plane."

An investigation and a thorough inquiry produced such uncomfortable facts as the following: (1) There had been no fire or explosion aboard the airliner while it was in flight or after it crashed. (2) Scorch marks found on glass window ports, the rear of the fuselage, and across the parting of the tail showed signs of having been exposed to tremendous *exterior* heat. (3) The force that caused the airliner to disintegrate had not come from within the plane.

The testimony of the residents of Buffalo, Texas—who saw a

UFO launch a fireball at the airliner moments before it disintegrated—remains the only logical explanation for the disaster.

In a more recent case of flying saucer hostility toward humans attempting to share airspace with alien craft, two police officers on a helicopter patrol over Louisville, Kentucky, were attacked by fireballs from a UFO on a late spring night in 1993.

Officers Graham and Downs were already airborne when they received a call around midnight about a break-in. On their way to check out a possible theft, they spotted what they at first believed to be a large bonfire on the ground. But when Downs directed the powerful chopper spotlight down toward the alleged bonfire, he thought that what he now saw below them was more like a kind of balloon.

Perhaps activated in some way by the brilliant spotlight, the object now began drifting back and forth as it ascended.

The glowing object slowly rose until it hovered at an altitude of 500 feet, the same height as the police helicopter. As it hovered near them for a few seconds, the officers could see that they had engaged a strange, glowing, pear-shaped object.

Then the UFO took off at a speed that Officer Downs said he "had never seen before."

The object circled the police helicopter twice, then began to move up on it from behind.

Officer Graham was afraid that the thing was going to ram his tail rotor, so he pushed the chopper to 100 miles per hour in an attempt to evade their mysterious pursuer.

To Graham's complete astonishment, the UFO easily moved past them at an even faster speed, then shot hundreds of feet up into the air.

Baffled by the object's maneuvers—and by its intent—the officers were horrified when the UFO blasted three fireballs at them.

Officer Graham expertly banked the chopper to avoid being struck by the fireballs, but by the time they circled and returned, the UFO had disappeared.

According to journalist Louise Milton, the extraordinary encounter of Officers Graham and Downs was confirmed by two other police officers who witnessed the aerial dogfight from the ground.

Officer Mike Smith said that he watched the UFO for about

a minute and saw it shoot three fireballs at the police helicopter. Smith's partner, Joe Smolenski, said that the bizarre encounter over Louisville constituted "the closest I've come to something I couldn't explain."

On June 29, 1964, a Wellford, South Carolina, businessman was returning home from Adanta, Georgia, when he claimed that a UFO swooped down over his automobile, burned his arm, and blistered the paint on the car roof.

"I saw the object so clearly, I believe that I could build one of the things," B. E. Parham said. "It came hissing down and stopped in the air right over my car [as he was traveling on the highway]."

Parham said that he had been driving about sixty-five to seventy miles per hour, but when the UFO approached, the car's engine began to slow down. Parham, the district manager for a Spartanburg, South Carolina, firm, said the object made three passes at his vehicle. It had come from high in the sky, then swooshed over the top of the car, leaving behind an odor something like embalming fluid. Parham said the UFO gave off "terrific" heat and had a number of holes and openings in its sides.

When an Air Force analysis of the incident stated that Parham had been "frightened by ball lightning," the indignant businessman fumed that there was not a cloud in the sky when the object swooped down on him. In addition, he said, "Lightning wouldn't rotate at the top and the bottom, as this object did. Lightning would not stand still."

Parham also felt that he had more than adequate physical evidence to substantiate his claims: (1) His arm was badly burned. (2) The paint on the roof of his automobile was blistered and coated with an oily substance. (3) The radiator and other parts of his late-model car began to deteriorate as a result of the close approach of the UFO.

On April 24, 1966, Mrs. Viola Swartwood was admitted to Memorial Hospital in Auburn, New York, for treatment of electrical shock after a UFO swooped down at the automobile in which she had been riding. Physicians at the hospital said that Mrs.

Swartwood's right side looked as if it had been subjected to an electrical shock, but she had no burns on her body.

Mrs. Charles F. Jones was nearly blinded by a brilliant light that flashed from a UFO as she was driving her grandson to a doctor's office in Merrill, Michigan, on April 25, 1966.

Describing the object as triangular, with no wings and a "stubby nose," Mrs. Jones said the UFO "seemed to be gliding southeast, but then it stopped over the trees and dropped straight down."

On June 17, 1966, a UFO splattered a late-model car with some unknown chemical substance when a Brampton, Ontario, housewife was passing through the outskirts of Georgetown on Highway 7 at 12:30 A.M. Suddenly a bright, round, silver object flew in front of her car and crossed from right to left.

"I watched it for about three seconds," said the woman [who wishes to remain anonymous]. "The object itself looked huge. I stopped my car, and another car in front of me stopped as well. The experience frightened me dreadfully."

The next morning when she and her husband examined the car in the sunlight, they were shocked to find the entire front part of the roof blemished by tiny, hard, transparent chemical blisters. The unknown substance had set rock hard in thousands of bubbles over the fenders, grill, and hood.

Professor Felipe Machado Carrion issued a report in the December 1971 issue of the French journal *Phenomenes Satiaux* (later reprinted in the March–April 1973 issue of *British Flying Saucer Review*) that told of a grisly incident involving a healthy, robust farmer in Sao Paulo, Brazil.

According to Professor Carrion, forty-year-old Joao Prestes Filho was stunned and knocked to the ground by a mysterious beam of light from the sky. He managed to make his way to the home of his sister, where numerous friends and neighbors came to his aid.

Eyewitnesses later told authorities that Prestes showed no trace whatever of burns, but within a matter of hours, the once vigorous farmer literally began to deteriorate before the eyes of his startled friends and family.

Although at no time did he appear to feel any pain, "Prestes' insides began to show, and the flesh started to look as though it had been cooked for many hours in boiling water. The flesh began to come away from the bones, falling in lumps from his jaws, his chest, his arms, his hands, his fingers . . . . Soon every part of Prestes had reached a state of deterioration beyond imagination. His teeth and his bones . . . stood revealed, utterly bare of flesh . . . his nose and ears fell off. . .''

Six hours after Prestes had been struck by the terrible beam of light, he was dead. The rapidly disintegrating man had not even been able to reach a hospital before he was nothing more than a grotesque skeleton. He died attempting to communicate details of his awful experience.

On February 7, 1969, hundreds of people in the area of Pirassununga, Brazil, watched a strange, circular aerial vehicle swoop low over the town, then settle in a nearby valley on tripod legs. Nineteen-year-old Tiago Machado was nearest the mysterious craft when it landed, and he began cautiously walking toward the object.

As he later explained his terrifying experience to the press, Tiago said that the craft "seemed made of a material similar to aluminum, but it was luminous.'' The teenager described the UFO's rim as "spinning around the center.'' According to him, "It never stopped whirling.''

Tiago said that the center section of the vehicle was stationary and appeared to be constructed of a transparent substance. "I could see what seemed to be shadowy figures in the cabin, gathering around what looked like an instrument panel.''

The teenager said that he crept to within thirty feet of the UFO. He was aware that dozens of people had gathered on the distant hills to watch him approach the craft.

The next thing Tiago knew, a bright beam of light shot out from the disc and struck him in the legs. He toppled over, partially stunned and paralyzed, as the UFO suddenly rose into the air and soared into the sky at an incredible rate of speed. Within moments it had disappeared from the view of the gathered crowd.

Tiago Machado's legs turned bright red, and it was obvious to all the witnesses that his legs were painfully swollen.

Although many thought that Tiago's injuries resembled an electrical burn, Dr. Henrique Reis, who attended to Tiago at a local hospital, found no visible wounds or marks to account for the bright red swelling.

On September 16, 1962, Telemaco Xavier is said to have been kidnapped by three aliens from a UFO. According to witnesses, Xavier was last seen walking home along a dark jungle trail after attending a soccer match in Vila Conceicao in northern Brazil.

A workman at a nearby rubber plantation told authorities that he had seen a round, glowing object fall from the sky and land in a clearing. Three occupants emerged from the UFO and grabbed a man who was walking along the jungle trail. According to the workman, the victim managed to put up a brief struggle before he was dragged off to the fiery vehicle.

Rio de Janeiro newspapers quoted authorities who had discovered "signs of a struggle where the worker said the fight had taken place." To the Brazilian newspapers it seemed evident that "Mr. Telemaco Xavier was kidnapped by a flying disc."

With all the attention in recent years directed toward horror author Whitley Streiber's abduction experience, as detailed in his book *Communion,* and the research of artist Budd Hopkins in his works *The Intruders* and *Missing Time,* few people remember the prototypical UFO kidnapping that occurred to Betty and Barney Hill on September 19, 1961. The Hills, a couple in their forties, were returning from a brief Canadian vacation to their home in New Hampshire when they noticed a bright object in the night sky. Barney stopped the car and used a pair of binoculars to get a better look at the light, which soon showed the well-defined shape of a disclike object that moved in an irregular pattern across the moonlit sky.

Intrigued by what he saw, Barney walked into a field to get a better look at the object. Through the binoculars, he was able to observe the UFO and to distinguish what appeared to be windows—and from the windows, people looked back at him.

Barney suddenly became terrified by what he had seen. He got back in the car and raced away from the place where they had pulled over. Then—for some inexplicable reason—he drove down a side road where—as if it had all been somehow prearranged—five humanoid beings stood blocking their path. At the sight of the UFOnauts, the Hills were no longer able to control their movements. It was as if they had been placed in some kind of trance, and they permitted the aliens to lead them into the UFO.

Details of the Hills' remarkable encounter were retrieved under hypnosis, for the couple had been programmed to experience a complete loss of memory of the nearly two hours that had passed from the time they initially sighted the light until they were returned to their car. The interrupted journey home would probably never have been brought to light except for the weird dreams both Betty and Barney experienced and the unaccountable two-hour gap in their trip home from Canada.

The Hills were sensible, down-to-earth people. Barney was a mail carrier and Betty was a social worker. What, they both wanted to know, could be causing their bizarre dreams?

Betty sought the help of a psychiatrist friend, who suggested that the memory of their missing two hours would quite likely return within a few months. But in spite of such assurances, the details of their abduction remained lost until the Hills were hypnotized by Boston psychiatrist, Dr. Benjamin Simon.

Under hypnosis the couple freed the memories of what had actually occurred to them on that most remarkable evening in September. The individual accounts of Betty and Barney agreed in most respects, although neither knew what the other had revealed until later.

Both told of being shepherded aboard a UFO and of being well treated by inquisitive aliens from space—much as humane Earth scientists might treat laboratory animals. The nearly two hours aboard the craft consisted primarily of various physical examinations. The Hills were each given a hypnotic suggestion that they would not remember anything that occurred while they were aboard the UFO. Their induced amnesia apparently was broken only when they were hypnotized by Dr. Simon.

When Betty was placed under hypnosis again in 1964, she recalled a detail of their strange adventure which added a great deal of credibility to their experience. The aliens themselves appeared to have been a great deal more humane and considerate than those ETIs depicted in some later accounts of abductions, and Betty's request to take something with her to prove the truth of their experience was nearly granted. Although she was finally not presented with an artifact of their advanced science, she was shown a star map while on board the space vehicle—and she was given to understand that the chart depicted the aliens' place of extraterrestrial origin.

Betty Hill's map concurred with other, professionally drawn star maps—which in itself is quite remarkable, since she had little understanding of astronomy. In addition to her accuracy, researchers discovered a big bonus: Betty's map showed the location of two stars, Zeta 1 and Zeta 2 Reticuli, which allegedly comprised the home base of the space travelers. What is more, the existence of the two stars was not confirmed by astronomers until 1969—eight years after Betty saw the star map aboard an extraterrestrial spaceship. Zeta 1 and Zeta 2 Reticuli, two fifth-magnitude stars, cannot be seen by observers north of Mexico City's latitude. That is to say, the stars would be invisible to anyone viewing the night sky in New Hampshire.

From the village of Torren, Santo Time, Argentina, came the story of UFO occupants who returned on successive evenings in February 1965 in an attempt to kidnap residents of the small farming community.

The first attack came on a dark night, when a UFO landed in full view of a small group of terrified farmers. Two strange entities, about six feet tall, emerged from the craft and walked directly to a farmhouse, where they attempted to drag off the farmer who lived there. Rallying to their friend's defense, the other farmers managed to thwart the aliens' kidnap scheme and drive off the invaders.

On the next night, when the UFO landed to carry out its kidnapping scheme, the angry farmers met it with gunfire. Although the ETIs' space suits appeared to protect them from serious injury from the farmers' bullets, they seemed to weaken physically—and the farmers had little difficulty in discouraging the aliens from any further attempts at seeking human quarry from their village.

No one on either side of the eerie interplanetary brawl seemed to have received any serious injuries; however, the farmer who had the longest physical contact with the cosmic kidnappers was reported to have come down with a strange skin disease.

Charles Hickson, forty-five, and his fishing companion, nineteen-year-old Calvin Parker, were angling for hardhead and croakers from an old pier near the Schaupeter Shipyard in the Pascagoula River on the evening of October 11, 1973. Suddenly, about eight o'clock, a UFO hovered just above them.

"There was me, with just a spinning reel; and Calvin went hysterical on me," Charles Hickson said later. "You can't imagine how it was."

The object was strangely "fish-shaped," and it emitted a bluish haze. The UFO landed, and the two fishermen were ushered aboard the craft by three weird creatures with wrinkled skin, crab-claw hands, and pointed ears. Hickson and Parker claimed they were given some kind of physical examination, then released.

Sheriff Fred Diamond of Pascagoula told investigators that Charlie and Calvin came to him so frightened he was afraid they were both on the verge of a heart attack.

Hickson told Sheriff Diamond that the luminous, oblong craft landed near them. Three alien creatures had paralyzed him, floated him to their craft, placed him in front of an instrument that resembled a big eye, then put him back on the pier.

Parker was not really able to add very much to his friend's report. He fainted when the three weird-looking aliens had approached them, and he said he really didn't know what had happened inside the UFO. Years later Parker revealed that the experience had so completely horrified him that he was pushed to the point of a nervous breakdown.

After a couple of days, the two men refused further interviews with the press—but their story was interesting enough to draw the attention of Dr. J. Allen Hynek of Northwestern University in Chicago, the astronomer who had served as a scientific consultant to the Air Force. Dr. James Harder of the University of

California had also been attracted to the case, and it was he who hypnotized the two fishermen and drew out additional details of their traumatic experiences aboard the UFO.

"These are not unbalanced people," Dr. Harder said after he had evaluated Hickson and Parker. "They are not crackpots. There was definitely something here that was not terrestrial, not of the Earth."

Dr. Hynek told the press that although the two men had been capable of being hypnotized, their experience was so traumatic that it was necessary to progress slowly with them.

Following the report of Hickson and Parker, literally thousands of UFO sightings began cropping up all over the United States, followed by more sightings from every corner of the globe.

Other residents of Pascagoula claimed to have seen a UFO on that same October 11 evening. And a park ranger near Tupelo, Mississippi, claimed that he saw a saucer-shaped UFO with red, green, and yellow blinking lights on October 5, a week before Hickson and Parker had been abducted in Pascagoula.

For more than twenty years, Calvin Parker maintained his silence concerning the strange events which occurred on that eventful day in Pascagoula. But in the summer of 1993, Parker told UFO researcher-author-publisher Timothy Green Beckley that he was now prepared to reveal additional details about the incident:

"Everybody thought that I had remained unconscious for the most part while I was on board the ship," Parker said. "But frankly, I saw absolutely no reason to trust anyone with my experience. There was a lot that went on that night when I was alone with these creatures that I've never spoken about with another living soul. Until recently, most people scoffed at the idea of alien abductions, but now more and more information is being released; and I feel just a little bit calmer about what happened back on October 11, 1973."

Parker told Beckley that he had experienced at least one additional encounter with the same alien beings who originally examined him and that there was one member of the ETI crew in particular who spoke directly with him and who told him a great deal about alien science, philosophy, and the true reason why they are coming to Earth at this point in humankind's history.

Promising to make public such revelations "in the very near

future," Parker said that what he had to say would definitely shock some people. "Many may go away shaking their heads in disbelief, but I have to be aboveboard and tell the truth of what this is all about—even if it is unpleasant!"

On May 20, 1967, Steve Michalak had been out looking at land just north of Falcon Lake, Manitoba, when he was alerted by the cackling of geese. Glancing up, he saw two objects coming from a south-southwesterly direction. The objects were "glaring red," and Michalak was later unable to estimate how fast they were traveling. What was of prime concern to him at that moment was that one of the objects was "cruising about ten feet above the ground"—and then it landed.

Michalak was not about to rush forward with his hands raised in the traditional salute of peace. He watched the grounded UFO for at least half an hour before he approached it.

"It gave off rainbow reflections," he said. "When a door finally opened, all I could see was a brilliant violet color. It seemed to be making a sort of whistling noise, like it was sucking in air or something."

Michalak described the UFO as being about thirty-five feet long, eight feet high, with a three-foot protrusion on top. It appeared to be constructed of stainless steel, and the Canadian said he was awed by "the most perfect joints I've ever seen. I can't understand how it was done. There was no welding, no rivets, no bolting—and when the door closed I could see nothing."

As Michalak approached the object, he could hear voices coming from within the shiny shell. Being multilingual, he addressed the UFO in English, Russian, German, Italian, and Polish.

At the sound of his voice, the door in the side closed, and the object began moving counterclockwise. Before the UFO blasted off, jets of heat came from a pattern of holes in its side, seared Michalak's chest, and burned his clothing.

Michalak's wife told the press at that time that her husband had not been able to retain food since his frightening experience—and she also complained of the strange odor emanating from his body.

In 1993 NBC's popular *Unsolved Mysteries* series with host Robert Stack dramatized Michalak's UFO encounter.

The night of January 6, 1976, will live long in the memories of three Kentucky women who were returning home from a late supper when they were abducted by a crew of UFOnauts and put through a torturous ordeal for more than an hour.

The three women involved in the nightmarish incident had excellent reputations and were regarded to be of the highest moral character. At the time of their abduction, Elaine Thomas and Louise Smith were in their mid-to-late forties; Mona Stafford was thirty-five.

Mrs. Smith was at the wheel as the three women traveled toward their homes in Liberty, Kentucky. They were about a mile from Stanford when they noticed a large aerial disc hurtle into view.

"It was as big as a football field," stated Mrs. Smith. She described the object as metallic gray, with a glowing white dome, a row of red lights around the middle, and three or four yellow lights underneath.

The UFO hovered ahead of them, then circled around behind their car—at which point the automobile suddenly accelerated to eighty-five miles an hour.

The other women screamed at Mrs. Smith to slow down, but she found that she had no control over the car. Some force then halted the car's forward movement and began dragging the vehicle backward. At that point the three women lost consciousness.

The next thing any of them could remember was driving to Louise Smith's home. They should have arrived around midnight. It was 1:30 A.M. At least one hour and twenty minutes was missing from their lives.

Louise found that her neck hurt. When Mona examined it, she discovered a strange red mark about three inches long and an inch wide, which looked like a burn that had not blistered. Elaine's neck had the same type of mark on it.

The frightened women called Lowell Lee, Louise's next-door neighbor, who listened to as much as they could recall of their terrifying adventure. After they completed their group recollections, he asked each of them to go into separate rooms and draw what the strange craft looked like. The three drawings were very much alike.

Although the peculiar burnlike marks were gone in about two days, the three women still could not account for the time loss— nor could they recall anything from the time the car was being pulled backward until they were driving on the highway about eight miles from where they had first spotted the UFO.

Later, under hypnosis, their separate hidden memories began to shape a bizarre scenario.

Elaine Thomas recalled that when she first regained consciousness, she was lying on her back in a long, narrow incubatorlike chamber—and she was surrounded by small dark figures, which she estimated to be about four feet tall. While something circled her throat, one of the figures pressed some kind of blunt instrument hard against her chest. Each time she attempted to speak, she remembered, it was as if she were being choked.

Under hypnosis Louise Smith said that she had been brought to a dark, hot place, and something had been fitted over her face. She begged the UFOnauts to let her see—but when they did, she immediately closed her eyes, for the scene before her was too frightening to observe.

Although Mrs. Smith was unable to provide a description of the UFO occupants, she recalled that the interior of the craft was dark and she had been very frightened. She remembered praying to God for help and pleading with the beings to let her go unharmed.

She had a distinct memory of crying out, "I'm so weak I want to die!"—and the next thing she knew, she was looking at a streetlight.

Mona Stafford had an unpleasant recollection of having regained consciousness in what appeared to be an operating room. Her right arm was pinned down by some invisible force while three or four figures dressed in white gowns sat around her bed.

In Mrs. Stafford's memory it was as if the UFOnauts were torturing her. Her eyes felt as though they were being pulled out of her skull. At another time it seemed as if her stomach was being blown up like a balloon.

And then the occupants began pulling at her feet, bending

them backward and twisting them until she cried out that she couldn't take any more.

Following the individual hypnotic sessions, the three women were given polygraph tests by Detective James Young of the Lexington Police Department. Young, in a sworn statement, said, "It is my opinion that these women actually believe they did experience an encounter [with a UFO]."

Dr. R. Leo Sprinkle, a professor at the University of Wyoming and an experienced hypnotist, expressed his opinion that Elaine Thomas, Louise Smith, and Mona Stafford had specific impressions that indicated to them that they had been observed and handled by strange beings. He believed it would have been impossible for them to have faked their reactions to such an ordeal, and he commented that their experience during the time loss was common to numerous reports provided by UFO percipients who had reported similar experiences.

Sheriff Bill Norris of Lincoln County, Kentucky, stated that there had been a number of UFO sightings in the county that January.

On July 1, 1965, while working his field near Valensole, France, Maurice Masse was startled to see an object that looked like a giant rugby ball standing among his plants.

As Masse approached the object, which he described as being "about the size of a Dauphin car," he saw two small "men" investigating one of his lavender plants. Aside from their shortness ("about the size of eight-year-old children"), their large heads (three times the size of a normal adult's head), and their lipless mouths, Masse contended that the beings appeared humanlike.

The farmer continued to approach the little men, intent on conversing with them. When they suddenly noticed him, however, one of the aliens pointed a tube at Masse and immobilized him completely.

Freed of further distractions, the two little creatures continued to chatter among themselves in a strange language and to examine the plants.

Although they sent an occasional glance toward the immobilized Frenchman, at no time did he feel that these strange little men wished to do him any kind of harm. Nor did he feel any pain or discomfort in his paralyzed condition. He continued to observe the bizarre intruders without his mental faculties in any way impaired.

It was not until about a quarter of an hour after the spacecraft left his field that Masse was able to move again. A cafe owner and the local police substantiated the farmer's tale by telling journalists that they had seen the strange tracks the little men had left and the holes made by their vehicle's six-legged landing gear. Masse enjoyed a solid reputation in the mountain village, and a *gendarme* informed news personnel that the police would not regard the incident as a hoax, joke, or lie.

On May 11, 1966, eleven-year-old Margaret Switzer was burned on her face by a beam of light emitted from a UFO while she stood in the doorway of her family's ranch house outside a small town in New Mexico. Apparently the facial burns had far greater implications than the doctors realized when they released Margaret from the hospital, for in the four weeks that followed, the girl grew four and one half inches and gained twenty-two pounds.

When Margaret sighted the UFO over the ranch just after dark on that night in May, she had been four feet, eight inches tall and weighed eighty-five pounds. Four weeks later she stood nearly five feet, two inches tall and weighed nearly 110 pounds. The eleven-year-old girl quickly outgrew all her clothing and rapidly stretched out of her newest dresses and largest shoes.

A confused Mrs. Switzer said that just a month ago her daughter had been a normal child who liked to play with dolls. "Now she is suddenly grown-up, cooks meals by herself, cleans house, and takes care of the younger children. And she's had a nearly complete change of personality and habits."

Although Margaret had recovered from the burns around her eyes, she still needed to wear dark glasses in sunlight and could read only a few paragraphs before her eyes began to sting. In reply to queries about her remarkable growth spurt and her personal health, the eleven-year-old could only say that she "just felt funny."

"We know that she definitely saw something in the sky over the ranch that night," Mrs. Switzer said. "We don't know what she saw or what it did to her, but I wish I had kept her inside the house.''

Dr. John Salter, Jr., chairman of American Indian Studies at the University of North Dakota, and his twenty-three-year-old son, John III, say that they were abducted by humanoid aliens while driving on central Wisconsin's Highway 14 on March 20, 1988. After being moved off the highway by an unseen force, the Salters found themselves in the company of numerous entities about four to four and one half feet tall with thin bodies and limbs and comparatively large heads and large slanted eyes. A much taller humanoid guided the father and son through the woods to an alien spacecraft. Communication between Earthlings and ETIs was telepathic.

The senior Salter recalled receiving a couple of injections from the aliens while they were in a brightly lighted room aboard the UFO, but he has nothing negative to say about the results.

"My immunity is heightened," he told nuclear physicist and UFO investigator Dr. Franklin R. Ruehl. "Cuts and scratches now clot immediately and heal rapidly. My head hair, fingernails, and toenails now grow at three times the normal rate. Some of my age spots have disappeared, and the wrinkles in my face have faded.

"Also, hair has developed all over my arms, legs, stomach, and chest, which previously had been almost hairless," added the university professor, who was fifty-five at the time of his alien encounter. "For the first time in my life, my beard is so thick and dark that I have five o'clock shadow."

Although John III did not experience the same physical changes as his father, he characterized the alien encounter as "the most extraordinary event of my life."

Dr. John Salter is not alone in his reaping of positive benefits from a close encounter with UFO aliens. Over the past thirty years of UFO research, we have gathered such intriguing accounts of "miracle cures" attributed to ETIs as the following:

1. In 1983 a farmwife from Illinois injured her hand while helping her husband load livestock for sale. Within a few days she developed an infection that necessitated a visit to the family doctor. Although the doctor gave her antibiotics, he said the swollen hand would require several weeks to heal.

The following morning she was walking in a field near their house when she saw a luminous, egg-shaped object seeming to approach her from the sky.

The next thing she knew, she was in a brilliantly lighted room filled with high-tech equipment. Three small creatures surrounded her, each wearing a surgical mask.

The farmwife lapsed into unconsciousness; when she awakened back in the field, she discovered that her hand was completely healed.

2. In 1973 a toothless, eighty-year-old farmer from Brazil was pleasantly surprised to find that he had new teeth growing in his jaws within two months after his abduction by four small men in a silver, circular-shaped craft.

3. A native of Finland had an enlarged liver ever since his birth, and he had been told repeatedly that it could never become normal.

A few years ago, however, as he was skiing down a remote slope, he was caught in a white beam of light from an egg-shaped UFO.

Disturbed by having experienced missing time as a result of his alien encounter, the man went to a doctor and underwent a complete physical examination. During this examination the doctors found that his liver had been reduced to a normal size.

4. One evening in 1986 wheelchair-bound Richard T. was enjoying the solitude of a beach near La Jolla, California, when a 100-foot-long, torpedo-shaped UFO appeared from out of nowhere to hover above him.

Later Richard said that it was as if he entered a light trance, and somehow both he and his wheelchair were lifted into the spacecraft.

He remembered being examined by smallish humanoids with

large heads and enormously large, slanted eyes. He felt no fear, but rather, a kind of euphoria and peace.

In what seemed like a matter of minutes—but was more likely several hours—Richard awakened seated inside his van, his wheelchair neatly tucked away in the back.

Amazingly, over the next few weeks, his condition began to reverse itself—until he was finally able to walk again with the help of a cane.

5. Mae, a sixty-year-old waitress who worked at a truck stop in Mississippi, saw a bright light overhead as she drove home about 4:00 A.M. on December 15, 1989. She doesn't remember pulling over to the side of the road, but she has a fleeting memory of being on her back in some kind of doctor's examination room.

Two very small "doctors or nurses" stood at her side, while the main "doctor" passed some kind of rod over her body again and again.

Mae had been about to put in her notice at work and enter what would have been a penurious retirement due to the ever-increasing agony caused by her arthritis. When she awakened back in her car at 6:00 A.M., she found that her arthritis miseries were gone. All the pain in her wrist, knee, and finger joints has since remained in remission.

One of our correspondents in Chile sent us her translation of this remarkable account, which seems to bear witness to a grand-scale experiment in which ETIs sought to tamper with the weather and the growing season in a localized area of Chile.

The phenomena began July 10, 1968, on the hill of La Nariz in the coastal zone of the province of Maule, when all of the cars that traveled there were stopped without reason. Drivers and their passengers were forced to remain in their stalled vehicles all night until, suddenly, toward dawn, the cars came back to life on their own and began to move.

To add to the strange event, one of the stalled vehicles was mysteriously drawn backward up a hill for a distance of about 120 feet until it stopped next to the roadbank.

On July 14 the inhabitants of Cauquenes began to experience a preternatural raising of the temperature in the area. Jose Bolosin, the owner of the Curanipe Hotel, said that at 6:30 A.M., even before the sun came up, one could feel a strange heat wave in the area.

Since the normal temperature in that zone at that time of year is below zero, the residents of Cauquenes became very concerned when the unusual increase in heat raised the temperature to around seventy-eight degrees.

"As a witness to the fact of the unusually warm weather," our translator wrote, "this morning [July 15, 1968] the peach trees of Curanipe appeared completely in bloom, before season, because of the hot wind which has prevailed in the last hours. It must also be mentioned that residents in Cauquenes claim to have seen flying saucers in the last few days."

CHAPTER 2

Aliens and Secret Societies

In November and December 1896—after thousands of years of surreptitiously playing the roles of boogey men or magicians for innumerable generations of humans—the ETI's aeons of observing the intellectual evolution of our species indicated to them that they might begin to show themselves in a clearer, more accurate, more technological manner than ever before in recorded human history.

The "airships," as they were called, were first sighted in the skies over various cities in California. They were described as cigar-shaped, apparently metallic objects, with various appendages such as wings, propellers, and fins. At night the airships occasionally swept the ground beneath them with brilliant searchlights.

Although many reliable witnesses, including the mayor of San Francisco, sighted the metallic aircraft at their strange maneuvers, astronomers shrugged off the initial reports and issued official statements that the bedazzled citizenry were no doubt seeing the planet Venus, then unusually bright in the evening sky.

In spite of the scientific debunking of the aircraft, people in California, Washington, and Arizona continued sighting the objects throughout November and December.

The first two months of 1897 were devoid of airship sightings, but in mid-March reports began coming in from Kansas, Nebraska, and Iowa—all describing the same type of mysterious airship that had baffled Californians four months earlier. From the first week in April until mid-May, nearly the entire area east of the Rocky Mountains appeared to be under the scrutiny of the aerial machines.

Quoting from a newspaper account which appeared in the Algona, Iowa, *Republican,* dated April 7, 1897:

"Good reliable citizens of Wesley, Iowa, declared upon their honor that on last Friday evening they saw in the heavens what they supposed to be an airship. . . . It had the appearance of a cone in shape with window in the side through which shone bright lights. . . . They were not able to see in what manner the ship was propelled or what sustained it in the air . . .

"When first sighted it did not have the appearance of being more than a few hundred feet above the ground. . . . It traveled quite slowly at times, and again would move quite fast. . . . Some had an idea they could hear a noise coming from the ship. Some went so far as to say it was human voices, while others thought it was the sound of machinery.

"It has not taken a close reading of current scientific periodicals to note that there is a great deal of activity among inventors in the line of practical aerial navigation, and that the old notion is wrong that man is by laws of nature . . . to be . . . confined strictly to the surface of the globe. . . . So it is entirely possible that the brief glimpses such as the Wesley people have had, are practicable."

[Readers should be reminded that the German Count Ferdinand von Zeppelin did not build his gas-filled dirigible until 1898, and that Orville and Wilbur Wright did not make their historic flight in a powered airplane until 1903.]

Two farmhands from Springfield, Illinois—Adolph Winkle and John Hulle—came upon a landed airship two miles north of Springfield on April 15. Three occupants, appearing to the farmers as two normal human men and a woman, explained that they had landed to repair their electrical equipment and their searchlight. They went on to inform the astonished Winkle and Hulle that their airship had flown from Quincy to Springfield, a distance of approximately ninety miles, in thirty minutes (roughly a speed of 180 miles per hour).

As if the claim of such speed wasn't enough to boggle the

farmhands' minds, Winkle and Hulle must have been left completely baffled by the occupants' claim that they were on a mission to free Cuba from the Spanish and that they would be making a complete report to the government upon the successful completion of their assignment. The Spanish-American War over Cuba did not erupt until the following year—in 1898—and unless Winkle and Hulle were astute students of political events in the making, it is unlikely that they would have the slightest idea why the airship would be flying to Cuba. This is but one of many incidents in which the aliens seem slightly "out of sync" with events occurring in linear time.

"WE COME FROM 'ANYWHERE' "

When John Barclay of Rockland, Texas, was awakened by his barking dog and a peculiar whining sound, he went to the door of his home to see what was creating such a disturbance at eleven o'clock at night.

Barclay's report stated that he saw "an airship . . . with a peculiar-shaped body, oblong-shaped, with wings and side attachments of various sizes and shapes. There were brilliant lights, which appeared much brighter than electric lights. . . . It seemed perfectly stationary about five yards from the ground."

After Barclay watched the airship gradually descend to the ground in a pasture near his house, he picked up his Winchester rifle and went down to investigate.

Within about thirty yards of the airship, the Texan was met by an ordinary appearing man who identified himself as "Mr. Smith," who requested that Barclay set down his weapon, as no harm was intended.

Then, remarkably, Mr. Smith asked Barclay to run an errand for him which seemed designed solely to convince the Texan that the occupants were flying some kind of new invention of definite terrestrial origin. He handed Barclay a ten-dollar bill and requested that he purchase some lubricating oil, a couple of cold chisels, and some bluestone.

When the obliging Texan returned with everything on the shopping list except the bluestone, Mr. Smith thanked him and asked him not to follow him back to the vessel.

"But where are you from . . . and where are you going?" Barclay called after his mysterious visitor.

The airship occupant turned to reply: "We are from anywhere, but we will be in Greece the day after tomorrow."

Once the stranger was back on board the airship, Barclay stated, "It was gone . . . like a shot out of a gun!"

About two hours after the airship made contact with John M. Barclay in Rockland, Texas, the aerial visitor settled back to solid ground near Harrisburg, Arkansas. Whether or not it was the same airship that had risen from Texas soil so brief a time before cannot be precisely determined—for this time the occupants revealed themselves to a Mr. Harris, a former senator, as a bearded inventor accompanied by two young men and a woman.

The April 23, 1897, edition of the Harrisburg, Arkansas, *Modern News*, provided the astounding details of Mr. Harris's other-worldly experience.

Awakened about one o'clock in the night by an unfamiliar noise, Harris was astonished to observe an airship settling down just a short distance from his home. By the time he went to investigate, Harris surprised the crew taking on a supply of fresh water from his well.

The crew was composed of a man with jet-black eyes who appeared elderly, yet whose waist-length whiskers were dark and almost silken, and two young men and a woman who scurried back on board the airship without uttering a sound.

Once the bearded man recovered from the surprise of "finding anyone out at such an hour of the night," he promised to reveal the secret of the airship to Mr. Harris, "everything, except how the effect is produced."

His uncle, so declared the occupant, was a brilliant scientist who had conquered the laws of gravity. He had received offers of huge sums of money from syndicates in New York City, Paris, and London—but he refused them all and managed to lock his secrets alway in a vault shortly before becoming violently ill and dying.

According to the mysterious bearded man, it had taken him another nineteen years before he had been able to master his uncle's formula and to devise an airship that was almost perfection. Almost, but not quite—which was why the inventor and his crew traveled mainly at night, to avoid being detected.

"I must continue to experiment," he told Harris. "I will visit the planet Mars before I put my airship on public exhibition."

At this point the bearded inventor made another peculiar slip in pinpointing linear time. As he explained that weight was no object to his antigravity device, he informed Harris that the crew had on board "a four-ton improved Hotchkiss gun, besides about ten tons of ammunition."

And why was the airship so heavily armed? "We made these preparations to go over to Cuba and kill out the Spanish army if the hostilities had not ceased." [Remember, the hostilities had not yet *begun.*] And now, according to the airship occupant, since the war in Cuba was over, they "might go to the aid of the Armenians," who in 1896 were being massacred in Constantinople by the Turks.

The bearded man boasted that their "improved Hotchkiss" could fire "63,000 times a minute."

Noting that Mr. Harris was impressed by such technology, the man added that his crew could remove the Capitol building from Washington, D.C., and put it down in Harrisburg if they wished. He also let Harris know that he and his crew could take breakfast in Arkansas, do some shopping in Paris, and be back in Harrisburg for dinner "without inconvenience."

In spite of the promise of personally observing such modem wonders, Harris declined the man's invitation to go for a ride in the marvelous craft.

"In that case," the bearded inventor said, "we had better be off before we disturb anyone else."

A few seconds after he bid Mr. Harris adieu, the airship drifted "to a place among the stars and in a few seconds was hid beyond the darkness of the night."

Although the airship was always portrayed by its occupants to be a secret invention, its crew seemed eager that as many people witness its activities as possible. It is also interesting to note that whenever the occupants—most often described as an elderly man with a long dark beard, a young man, and a woman—chose to make verbal contact with a witness, that individual was invariably characterized in the local press as being a person of "undoubted integrity." The airship occupants seemed to single out judges, senators, constables, Texas rangers, sheriffs, and prominent farmers and ranchers to hear their story of a brilliant inventor with his secret factory in Iowa, who promised to have the airships "in general use around the country" within a year. In a couple of reports from Iowa, however, the mysterious airship factory was said to be hidden in a small town in Texas.

Throughout most of the summer of 1897, airship reports continued from places such as Reynolds, Michigan; Belle Plaine, Iowa; Carlinville, Illinois; Flint, Michigan; Atchinson, Kansas; and Hot Springs, Arkansas.

In apparent proof of the airship occupants' boast that they could eat breakfast in Kansas and shop that afternoon in Paris, sightings began to come in from European countries. On July 17, 1897, a small town in Sweden sighted the airship, describing it as resembling some kind of balloon with drag ropes and a net. One occupant was visible in the object's "gondola."

On August 13 a mysterious airship was reported over Vancouver, British Columbia, and at three or four different points in Manitoba and the other Canadian "territories" as the vessel traveled eastward—terminating its flight, or so it would seem, off the coast of Norway, where the crew of the steamer *Kong Halfdan* spotted it. If it was the same airship that was sighted in these widely separated reports, the craft was traveling at a great rate of speed.

The airship was sighted over Ontario, Canada, once again on August 16, then made what seems to have been its final appearance for that particular flap on September 26 over Ustyug, Russia. There, at 2:30 A.M., an engineer sighted the object moving rapidly southeast over the town of Yakolevskaya. He described the unknown craft as having an electric or phosphorescent sheen.

The mysterious inventor in the small Iowa town did not make good his promise to have the wonderful airships available to the general public by 1898.

To the contrary the remarkable aerial vehicle seemed to disappear from the skies completely until March 23, 1909, when Constable P. C. Kettle in the town of Peterborough sighted a "mysterious airship." The unknown object made a sound "similar to that of a motor car," was oblong in shape, and "traveled as fast as an express train" as it directed a powerful searchlight toward the ground.

On May 18 Mr. C. Lethbridge of Cardiff, Wales, came upon the airship while traversing Caerphilly Mountain. According to the witness he had reached the top of the mountain at about 11 P.M. when he was surprised to see a "long tube-shaped affair lying on the grass with two men busily engaged with something nearby." Lethbridge admitted that he was rather frightened of the strangers, who were dressed in "heavy fur coats and fur caps tightly fitted over their heads."

When the noise of Lethbridge's cart alerted them to his presence, the men "jumped up and jabbered furiously in a strange lingo." At the same time the long thing on the ground began to rise, and the two fur-coated occupants jumped into "a kind of carriage" that "rose into the air in a zigzag fashion."

Other citizens of Cardiff also spotted the strange nocturnal visitors, and the Cardiff *Mail* described the object as "very large, with two lights, one at each end."

About the same time residents of Dublin, Ireland, reported a large, cigar-shaped craft "with two clear lights in front and traveling at a considerable pace across the sky."

The London *Weekly Dispatch* listed twenty-two locations where the airship had been reported during the week preceding May 23, plus nineteen earlier reports during March and May.

By July 1909 the residents of New Zealand were visited with a six-week airship flap.

On July 24 a brightly lighted object was seen zigzagging "in the direction of D'Urville Island ... across the bay until it appeared quite close to Motueka, then it changed its course and traveled in the direction of Farewell Split, where it was lost sight of ..."

An object "shaped like a boat with a flat top" was sighted at Kauroo Hill and Maheno on the evening of July 28.

Passengers on a train bound for Greymouth gazed in awe at a light that came in from the ocean on the night of July 29. It was observed to rise and fall occasionally, finally moving off toward Point Elizabeth, traveling against a strong wind.

Airship occupants were reported by a resident of Waipawa who sighted the craft over Kaikora. He stated that the machine was gray and torpedo-shaped, with three men aboard, one of whom shouted at him in an unintelligible language.

Other sightings were reported during the first week in August over Otago, North Auckland, Hawkes Bay, Kaihu, and Clive. The New Zealanders dubbed their mysterious airborne visitor an "Aerialite."

Although a mysterious aerial light was reported in the New England area on September 8, 1909, the airship sightings in the United States did not really get under way until December. Although this time the majority of the sightings occurred in the northeastern states, there were a few notable excursions to Arkansas, one of the areas most favored during the 1897 aerial displays.

On the night of December 21, observers in Potowomut and Providence, Rhode Island, saw an object bedecked with red lights that soon disappeared on the southern horizon.

Thousands of people in various cities throughout Rhode Island and Massachusetts saw an airship grace their skies on the evening of December 22. In Worcester crowds observed the object maneuvering over their city for more than fifteen minutes. Witnesses estimated the vehicle was traveling at speeds up to forty miles an hour, and at the same time "sweeping the heavens with a searchlight of tremendous power."

Thousands more witnesses observed the mystery skyship moving across the states of Massachusetts and Connecticut on the night of December 23. Most of those who observed the vehicle were able to watch it for as long as ten minutes before it moved away rapidly to the southeast.

On Christmas Eve so many people filed reports of the awesome airship that the Providence *Journal* was led to comment that its readership was obviously suffering from severe attacks of "airship-itis," wishing every star to be an airship, every light in the sky to be an airplane.

Again, we wish to remind our readers that in 1909 the status of human-controlled, heavier-than-air flying craft was not really a great deal different from what it was in 1897. The only aircraft known to orthodox science at that time were early models of the Wright brothers and gas-inflated dirigibles of Count von Zeppelin—and none of the creations of the Wrights or the German count were capable of the flight patterns and aerial maneuvers of the mystery airships. The Wright brothers' primitive craft were still hop, skipping, and jumping in New Jersey fields; and zeppelins had such a restricted flying range that great difficulties were experienced in making flights from Germany to England.

It was during the period of great excitement caused by the unknown aircraft in December 1909, however, that a mysterious gentleman who identified himself as Wallace E. Tillinghast claimed to be the inventor of the "secret aeroplanes." It was he, Tillinghast announced, who was responsible for the mysterious light that was seen in sections of the Northeast on the night of September 8. On that very evening he made a nonstop flight from Worcester to New York City, down to Boston, then back to Worcester—an overall distance of about 600 miles.

Identifying himself as a "businessman of good standing," and an "experienced mechanic" of the highest degree, Tillinghast modified his bravado by declaring that in his own good time he would prove his statements concerning the airworthiness of his magnificent flying machine. So far as it is known, the mysterious Tillinghast never did find his "own good time" to demonstrate his "aeroplane" and its remarkable capabilities, and he disappeared from public scrutiny as suddenly as he had burst into the headlines.

The genuine article, however, just kept on flying without any assistance from Wallace E. Tillinghast or anyone else. The airship was seen over Huntington, West Virginia, early on the morning of December 31, 1909, then seemed to go into seclusion for a few days.

At 9 A.M. on the morning of January 12, 1910, the mystery aircraft was sighted over Chattanooga, Tennessee. Thousands saw the vehicle and heard the sound of its engines. Later that same day it was seen over Huntsville, Alabama, traveling at a great rate of speed.

On the morning of January 13, it was back over Chattanooga, this time around 11 A.M. The airship crossed the city about ten times, and witnesses spotted an occupant on board the craft before it disappeared into heavy fog along the Tennessee River.

Yet a third trip was made over Chattanooga around noon on January 14—and then the airship visited Paragould, Arkansas, on the evening of January 15. Witnesses on the ground were able to see three or four occupants in the brilliantly lighted craft.

The last reported airship sighting before the occupants decided to return to the secret factory in Iowa, their base on the Moon, or "anywhere," appears to have been logged on January 20, when a number of witnesses saw a craft over Memphis, Tennessee. The airship was said to be high in the air and was traveling quickly. Witnesses stated that it crossed the Mississippi River into Arkansas, veered slightly to the south, then rapidly disappeared.

Whatever the mysterious airship of 1897 was, and whoever was actually piloting the craft, the fact remains that the reported vehicle was many years in advance of the known terrestrial science of the day. On the other hand, many aspects of the enigmatic airships make them appear to be terrestrial in origin. Their engines made a whirring noise, for example; or in some cases sounded like motorcars. Could they *really* have been the inspired product of some technological genius who manufactured the aeroplanes in his secret factory?

It seems unlikely that such a scientific marvel could have remained undeveloped and unexploited if, in fact, some eccentric inventor in Iowa or Texas had mastered antigravity and fashioned some remarkable propulsion system in 1897.

But what if the terrestrial inventor belonged to some secret society, perhaps one that had been in touch with extraterrestrial intelligences (ETIs)—or their records and artifacts—for thousands of years?

Evidence disinterred from musty libraries in Europe indicates that certain medieval and Renaissance alchemists conducted experiments with photography, radio transmission, phonography, and aerial flight, as well as their traditional quest to transmute lead into gold. What is more, quite a bit of additional evidence indicates that a good many of their experiments with so-called advanced technology were successful.

William Cooper, a former Naval Intelligence officer, saw certain government documents that proved to him that UFOs are real and that an official cover-up of monumental proportions had been set in motion. In addition, he found subsequent evidence indicating that certain secret societies had been interacting with UFO intelligences for thousands of years.

"If it is true that UFOs have been visiting Earth for thousands of years now, as history seems to indicate, then they are really in control," Cooper told us. "Certain societies behind our terrestrial power structures have been communicating with them and getting their guidance from them. Every major improvement in our culture, our science, our technology . . . every major turn which we have taken throughout history would have been because of them."

Cooper has focused a great deal of his research upon a hidden society generally known as the Illuminati.

"The Illuminati was a very well-organized group that was supposedly founded in Bavaria in 1776 by a German law professor named Adam Weishaupt," Cooper explained. "But I have been able to trace the history of this group all the way back to the ancient Temple of Wisdom in Cairo, long before the birth of Christ. Weishaupt did not begin the Illuminati. He merely headed one chapter of it.

"The Illuminati exists today under many names and many different occupations. They are extremely powerful, very wealthy men, who believe themselves to be the guardians of the secrets of the ages."

And it would appear that if such secret societies as the Illuminati have also been carefully guarding certain technological gifts of the ETIs, they would have become very powerful, indeed. From time to time, perhaps, this alliance between the ETIs and the hidden society elects to make one of its secret technologies known to the general terrestrial population. Such intervention in the affairs of the "outside world" may be accomplished by carefully feeding certain fragments of research to an "outside" scientist whose work and attitude have somehow made him acceptable to the society.

Some UFO researchers have gone back over the list of the "witnesses of integrity" to the 1897 airship sightings and suggested it was all a hoax of gigantic proportions. In a couple of cases, according to some investigators of the airship phenomenon, descendants of those senators, judges, mayors, and law enforcement officers—who gave such vivid accounts to the newspapers in 1897—confessed in their later days that they had told fibs, jokes, and lies.

Well, maybe some of those "witnesses of integrity" may have possessed some dubious motive for hoodwinking their peers and constituents with remarkable tales of flying machines. And maybe some of those prominent gentlemen, deciding they had had enough of pomp and propriety, thought they would obtain some relief from all those years of prim and proper behavior by perpetrating one devilishly good hoax before senility set in. On the other hand, maybe some of their descendants are embarrassed by a grandfather's or an uncle's "wild story" and have decided to confess for them.

We don't know. None of those witnesses are alive today to confirm the validity of their sightings or to admit to having pulled the legs of their friends and neighbors.

But if they were telling fibs, then we can wonder about the motives of these respected and generally wealthy men for having done so, and we can speculate as to their possible motives for engineering an international hoax at this particular time in world history.

If, indeed, such a secret society as the Illuminati does exist—and if it has been slowly feeding us technology according to its own hidden agenda—then as long ago as 1897 it may well have been to the society's advantage to begin to promulgate a "war of the worlds" mind-set among the outsiders on planet Earth. If the society's long-range purpose is to establish a New World Order with its own hierarchy in control of world governments, then the society would have done well to have begun the threat of alien invasion at the beginning of the twentieth century, so that they might be in the ultimate positions of power for the advent of the millennium.

As William Cooper states, "Whether the extraterrestrials are real or not, their alleged existence is being used to help bring about a one-world government. The menace of extraterrestrials provides the existing governments of Earth with the 'external threat' that will force a one-world government to come into existence.

"It seems as though there is evidence to suggest that extraterrestrials are real, but the alleged threat of ETs could also be the greatest hoax ever perpetuated in the history of the world in order to bring us all together to fight the alleged invaders from outer space and make us all dupes for the so-called 'illumined ones' to place completely under their domination.''

And, of course, as long as we are speculating, it may be that the illumined ones, this secret occult society, made their deal with the extraterrestrials centuries ago.

And if this secret society is as powerful as some investigators believe it to be, then its ideas and concepts have infiltrated every level of our own larger society. It is interesting to review former president Ronald Reagan's comments concerning how advantageous it would be to the various governing bodies of the world if there could be a threat of an invasion from an external, extraterrestrial source. Was Reagan inadvertently leaking information concerning the deal already made by our government with alien representatives? Or was he proposing a concept that had been set in motion by "witnesses of integrity" in 1897?

At a conference in 1993, Dr. M. M. Agrest of the former Soviet Union told us that back in 1959—when he became the first scientist to suggest that Earth may have been visited by extraterrestrials in ancient times—he was more highly criticized by his Communist colleagues for having read the Bible and other holy works to arrive at certain conclusions than he was for issuing provocative statements about our planet's unknown history.

The diminutive, white-haired, soft-spoken Dr. Agrest pointed out that sacred Hindu texts contain many descriptions of airships appearing in the sky at the "beginning of time." The *Manusola Purva* tells of "an iron thunderbolt," a gigantic messenger of death that reduced to ashes the entire race of the Vrishnis and the Andhakas. The corpses were so burned as to be unrecognizable. Those who survived the initial blast had their hair and nails fall out. Pottery broke without any apparent cause, and the birds turned white. After a few hours all foodstuffs were infected. "The thunderbolt was reduced to fine dust."

In Dr. Agrest's opinion the above is a poetic, yet explicit, description of an atomic blast with its resultant deadly fallout.

Another Hindu text records the destruction of three cities by "a single projectile charged with all the power of the universe. An incandescent column of smoke and flame, as bright as ten thousand suns, rose in all its splendor . . ."

In the late 1950s a series of excavations conducted in Mongolia, Scandinavia, and Ceylon unearthed artifacts that archaeologists assessed as being very similar to those found among Eskimos. The Smithsonian Institution, sponsors of the study, concluded that 10,000 years ago the people who became the Eskimos had inhabited Central Asia, especially the warm, tropical paradise of Ceylon.

One immediately wonders how, in ancient times, people from a veritable Garden of Eden would travel thousands of miles to settle in bleak, northern wastes. One cannot also help wondering *why* they would choose to exchange their lush forests for snow and ice.

The Eskimos themselves, however, have had an answer for generations, an answer that has never received more than a patronizing smile from anthropologists and missionaries. The Eskimo tradition says that they were *deported* to the frozen north-land by a flock of giant *metallic* birds.

In the late 1960s sixteen stone disks were found in a cave in the Bayan-Kara-Ula Mountains on the China-Tibet border. One Chinese expert has theorized that the groove writing found on the disks relates to spaceships that landed there 12,000 years ago. He believes that the frail tribe of four-foot tall people who inhabit the area—and who hitherto have defied ethnic classification— are descendants of those space colonizers.

Although official Communist party pronouncements from Peking banned the Chinese professor's paper, Moscow scientists conducted investigations of their own. One leak to the West asserted that hieroglyphics on one of the stone disks told of beings called "Dropas" that came down from the clouds on gliders. It was also claimed that Russian investigators discovered that the disks contained large amounts of cobalt and that they vibrated in an unusual rhythm, as if they carried an electrical charge or were part of an electrical circuit. In nearby caves Soviet archaeologists allegedly found 12,000-year-old vestiges of graves containing the remains of beings with huge craniums and under-developed skeletons.

* * *

Certain excavations indicate that the massive cities located on the high plateaus of Peru and Bolivia were once inhabited by a race of giants who constituted a highly advanced civilization over 30,000 years ago. Irrigation works and housing accommodations of this ancient culture are built of huge blocks of stone, each weighing as much as forty or fifty tons. The scope of these mammoth, sprawling cities high in the Andes Mountains would quite likely still lie beyond the accomplishments of our most modern electric turbodrills or our most rugged construction machines.

Even those archaeologists who steadfastly refuse to acknowledge the existence of vanished advanced technologies in ancient times are hard pressed to explain why the known inhabitants of Peru—those Incas who met the Spanish conquistadores—had built such an enormous and complex system of paved roads *before* they had invented the wheel.

In *The Morning of the Magicians,* Louis Pauwels and Jacques Bergier speculate that if in the far distant past there have existed great civilizations built on a system of specialized knowledge, then there must have been textbooks or some record of this advanced technology: "It may well be that some of these textbooks, or fragments of them, have been found and piously preserved and copied over and over again by monks whose duty it was not so much to understand them as to hold them in safekeeping."

And as other investigators have suggested, perhaps enlightened members of some ancient secret society discovered those marvelous texts centuries ago and have been making practical use of them for thousands of years, keeping alive a link with the advanced technical perfection of a vanished terrestrial culture or an extraterrestrial colony.

The disturbing part of the theory of such researchers as William Cooper is the suggestion that perhaps this secret society of illumined ones is no longer content with merely coexisting with other overt societies. Perhaps they have decided that the time is now to begin to set in motion their plans for world domination.

CHAPTER 3

Nazi UFOs

In his controversial presentation *UFO Secrets of the Third Reich*, Vladimir Terziski draws a connection between alien beings and such German secret societies as the Tempelhoff, the Thule, the Vrill, and the Black Sun. Terziski tells of an "alien tutor race" that secretly began cooperating with certain German scientists in the late 1920s in underground bases and began to introduce their concepts of philosophical, cultural, and technological progress.

With help from extraterrestrial intelligences, Terziski postulates, the Nazis mastered antigravity space flight, established space stations, accomplished time travel, and developed their spacecraft to warp speeds. At the same time the aliens "spread their Mephistophelean ideas" into the wider German population through the Thule and Vrill societies.

Terziski maintains that antigravity research began in Germany in the 1920s with the first hybrid antigravity circular craft, the RFZ-1, constructed by the secret Vrill society. In 1942–43 a series of antigravity machines culminated in the giant 350-foot-long, cigar-shaped Andromeda space station, which was constructed in old zeppelin hangars near Berlin by E4, the research and development arm of the SS.

While Terziski is not alone in making such claims regarding ETIs and Nazi interaction, other researchers scoff at them as pure fantasy. It remains for us to attempt to ferret out the details of what may be another massive cover-up of the international shadow governments—or at least to reveal what facts seem to be generally known about certain German scientists' passion for space travel.

Shortly before the Third Reich collapsed in 1945, Wernher von Braun, Hermann Oberth, and about eighty other top scientists were smuggled out of Nazi Germany by the Allies.

The allies also captured various documents, files, plans, photographs, and designs. However, one specific file, containing discoid-shaped aircraft disappeared.

"At the same time, 130 crack Nazi designers of specialized aircraft also disappeared," said UFO researcher Jammie A. Romee. "The mysterious disappearance of that vital file, together with over one hundred technologists, must be added to the following list of oddities which took place shortly before and after the fall of Adolf Hitler's Third Reich:

"1. The unexplained disappearance of several German freight U-boats, each capable of transporting up to 850 metric tons;

"2. The disappearance from Tempelhof Air Base of several long-distance planes with flight plans to Spain and South America;

"3. The disappearance of several tens of millions of marks in hard currency, gold bullion, and precious stones from the Reichsbank;

"4. The fact that UFOs were, and continue to be, sighted in great numbers over areas of South America in which many Nazis [and members of secret societies] are known to be hidden."

In 1938 Hitler's aide, Martin Bormann, had ordered the careful mapping of all mountain passes, caves, bridges, and highways and began selecting sites for underground factories, munitions dumps, and food caches. Giant underground workshops and launching pads, known as "U-plants," were established in which top German scientists would be assigned the task of creating secret weapons. A slave-labor force of 250,000 was required to complete work on such fortresses. Networks of tunnels and assembly plants were fashioned in Austria, Bavaria, and northern Italy. Allied intelligence had learned of work at the Luftwaffe experimental center near Oberammergau, Bavaria, to create Project *Feuerball* (Fireball), an aerial device designed to confuse Allied radar and interrupt electromagnetic currents. Efforts were accelerated to perfect the craft in 1944, but work seemed to have been shifted to the development of the *Kugelblitz* (Round Lightning), a round, symmetrical airplane, quite unlike any previous flying object known in terrestrial aviation history.

In May 1945, after the Nazi surrender, British agents—searching the files of some underground factories in the Black Forest—located a number of documents describing important experiments concerning the development of "new turbine engines capable of developing extraordinary power."

A friend of ours—who once worked as a design engineer at the De Havilland aircraft plant in Canada—told us that Canadian intelligence had taken plans for an advanced circular aircraft that had been found at Peenemuende, site of the Nazi rocket-experimental complex from 1937 to 1945, and presented them as a challenge to the scientists at De Havilland.

"We actually made the 'flying saucer' fly—for a while," our friend said. "We never mastered the complete techniques of the propulsion system to keep the bloody thing in the air for very long at a time."

The fascination of German science with rockets began in 1923 with Dr. Hermann Oberth's book *By Rocket to Interplanetary Space*. There were many other books that advanced the cause of spacecraft development that appeared in Germany in the mid-1920s.

In 1927 the *Verein Fuer Raumschiffahrt* (Society for Space Travel) was organized, with Wernher von Braun and Willy Ley among its members. The VFR produced the world's first rocket-powered automobile, the Opel-Rak 1, with Fritz von Opel in 1928. Further experiments were made with railway cars, rocket sleds, crude vertical takeoff and landing aircraft, and some successful rocket launches from the *Rakentenflugplatz* (rocket air-field) near Berlin.

When Adolf Hitler seized power in Germany in 1933, the Nazi party took over all rocket and aircraft development, and all astronautical societies were nationalized. In 1937 the Peene-muende group was formed under the direction of Walter Dorn-berger and Wernher von Braun.

But what if there could have been primitive prototypes of terrestrial flying saucers flown as early as 1942 by an ultrasecret group of Nazi scientists working under extraterrestrial guidance? These initial Nazi UFOs may still have been basically low-altitude craft—and while they may have been capable of flying distances far greater than any conventional aircraft, the antigravity devices were not yet perfected to the point where they could circle the globe indefinitely.

A U.S. Army Air Corps major who claimed over fifty missions as a B-17 pilot told of encountering "Foo Fighters" over Berlin circa 1944:

"These things [unknown circular craft] popped up out of nowhere. Suddenly they'd be on our wing, six or eight of them, flying perfect formation.

"You'd turn and bank; they'd turn and bank. You would climb; they would climb. You dive; they dive. You just couldn't shake them. Little, dirty, gray aluminum things, ten or twelve feet in diameter, shaped just like saucers; no cockpits, no windows, no sign of life."

Did they ever try to shoot down any Allied craft?

"As far as I know, when the things got sick of the cat-and-mouse game, they would just take off into space and disappear, flying at the most incredible speeds—maybe 5,000 miles per hour or more!"

What do you think the craft were?

"Some of the guys thought that they were more of Hitler's V-weapons, something the Nazis were only able to get up in the closing days of the war. Some of the boys thought they were Russian. Some even believed the things must have been from outer space because they maneuvered so uncannily and flew at such superhuman speeds."

* * *

A man who had been a "belly gunner" on several bombing raids over Germany told us of his encounters with the strange, saucer-shaped aerial objects:

"I suppose that I felt especially nervous and vulnerable because I sometimes seemed so all alone in my little capsule under the bomber. Anyway, these things, 'Foo Fighters' we called them most of the time, would zip right up beside our 'flying fortress' like they came from out of nowhere. Usually, they would just pace us, like they were observing us. Sometimes I felt that I could feel eyes inside the craft, watching my every move; but I could-never see into the things or figure out how *they* saw anything.

"I personally saw the objects half a dozen or more times. I thought at first that they were some new kind of buzz bomb that the Nazi supermen had dreamed up, and I expected them to attack us and try to blast us out of the skies. I never heard of any of the things making any aggressive move toward any Allied aircraft."

An officer in Paris recalled reports of unidentified flying objects that had harassed Allied bombing missions during the last days of World War II:

"There were any number of them, very well attested. They were considered so secret they were in the 'eyes only' file. That means you couldn't make a copy of the papers.

"You want to know something else? Those flying saucer-shaped craft were reported in the closing days of the war over Tokyo, as well as over Berlin."

CHAPTER 4

The Philadelphia Experiment and the Rainbow Conspiracy

If it truly did occur, then the so-called Philadelphia Experiment and its tragic aftermath constitute one of the most bizarre government cover-ups of all. Those who insist that the ill-fated experiment actually took place maintain that in October 1943 the U.S. Navy accomplished the teleportation of a warship from the Philadelphia Naval yard to its dock near Norfolk, Virginia—and at the same time, the procedure caused the warship and its crew to become invisible.

At first the scientists in charge of the experiment were elated with its apparent success, and military officials were jubilant at the thought of being able to convert whole fleets of warships, bombers, and fighter planes into invisible avengers that would deliver sudden havoc and destruction to the Nazi and Japanese forces around the globe. With this new secret weapon of invisibility, World War II would be over within months.

Then, as a terrible by-product of the process of teleportation and invisibility, a number of the crew members reportedly burst into flames in some kind of spontaneous human combustion. Others reportedly lapsed once again into complete or partial states of invisibility in front of their families or in crowded public places—while still others required confinement to psychiatric wards.

Accounts of the Philadelphia Experiment make great yarns, perfect for regaling drinking buddies around the bar or widening the eyes of the kids around a campfire. When we wrote an article on the alleged experiment for *Saga* magazine in the late 1960s, our approach was that it was another of the strange flying saucer mysteries that had attained mythic stature as a result of having become one of the favorite "twicetold tales" of UFOlogy. Therefore we were surprised to receive a great deal of mail from those who claimed some sort of personal involvement in the secret Navy project.

Men who claimed to have been crew members on the *Eldridge*, the warship they named as having been the vessel teleported to Norfolk from Philadelphia, scolded us for writing so matter-of-factly about such a tragic occurrence.

"You would not write of this so objectively if you were forced to live with this horror," said one letter writer.

Others wrote graphically of having seen their buddies burst into flames days after the experiment was supposedly completed. Some said that certain of their fellow crew members had somehow melded directly into the metal of the *Eldridge* during the molecular mixup that had taken place during teleportation.

An anonymous letter writer informed us of witnessing a series of bizarre occurrences in 1947-48, which he believed may have been associated directly with the secret Navy experiment.

During the Second World War his landlady's son had enlisted in the Navy, and our correspondent was led to believe that the young man had subsequently been killed in action. Some years later, however, he met someone of the son's description in the hallway of the rooming house. According to our correspondent the young man greeted him with a friendly "hello"—and then "vanished like a ghost."

After that eerie hallway encounter, the boarder often saw the young man appear, then vanish. On one occasion the strange young man appeared, began to weep despondently, and begged the landlady for something to eat.

The matter became even more confused in the boarder's mind when the young sailor's widow, who had continued to reside with her mother-in-law for many years after her husband's alleged death, moved out after obtaining a *divorce*.

After he read our article in *Saga*, our correspondent began to wonder if his landlady's son might not have been one of those unfortunate seamen aboard the experimental vessel. Had he, even years later, still been lapsing into invisibility and suffering the torments of the damned? Thoughts that he, himself, had seen a ghost or was going insane plagued our anonymous correspondent for many years.

In our own case, in 1967, we received most of the data for our article from a friend named Steve, who, in turn, had acquired the material from a scientist-engineer named Alfred Bielek. We met Bielek himself around 1968, and we became good friends. Although he was a man of many parts with varied interests and an obvious mastery of things electronic, Al continued to be fascinated by all aspects of the Philadelphia Experiment. He had no doubt that the event had actually taken place.

We were probably as startled as the next person when, in September 1989, Al stepped before the large audience gathered in Phoenix for Timothy Green Beckley's UFO–New Age Conference and declared that he had been a participant in the incredible experiment. Al said he had survived time-warping, teleportation, invisibility, electromagnetic bombardment, and a period of brainwashing by an ultrasecret agency to be able to tell his story.

After his mind-boggling speech, we arranged to have several interviews with Al in order to understand more completely what he believed had occurred during the legendary experiment—and the missing years of his life.

Bielek claimed that the initial stages of the experiment had begun in Chicago about 1931 under the aegis of a U.S. Navy-sponsored team of scientists composed of Dr. John Hutchinson, dean of the University of Chicago; the brilliant Nicola Tesla, and Dr. Emil Kurtenauer, an Austrian physicist. In 1933 the operation was moved to the Institute for Advanced Studies at Princeton University. Joining them was Dr. John Eric Von Neumann, who would later become one of Bielek's mentors.

"Von Neumann, born in Budapest, Hungary, had exhibited a genius in mathematics at an early age," Bielek said. "He had been at the University of Berlin and the University of Hamburg when he immigrated to the United States. In 1933 he was invited to join the Institute at Princeton and to become involved in the Navy project, which was known as 'Project Rainbow.' Dr. Albert Einstein, who was also at the Institute, was aware of the project, though he did not participate directly in the nuts and bolts of it."

According to Bielek, the concept of the Philadelphia Experiment was set up by a group of ETIs who had met with President Franklin Delano Roosevelt in 1934. "FDR met with the aliens somewhere in the mid-Pacific—I believe it was on board the *Pennsylvania*—signed an agreement that would exchange alien technology for certain planetary privileges," Bielek explained.

The treaty, Bielek said, was with extraterrestrials that he labeled the "K-Group," alien life-forms that could pass for humans. "Because their skin has a slightly greenish tint, they often bleach or dye their epidermis in order to pass among us as human beings," he stated.

According to Bielek, the meeting between FDR and the K-Group of ETIs was arranged by Nicola Tesla, who had been in contact with alien intelligences since 1895. "Tesla's communications with extraterrestrials accelerated in the late 1920s and the early 1930s, ever since he created the huge radio receivers for RCA," Bielek explained.

Tesla's initial communications had been with entities from the Pleiades, who appeared to be completely human and who stated that humankind had issued from their original stock. FDR met first with Pleiadean emissaries, then later with the K-Group, a "nearly human" species. Almost immediately after the second meeting, President Roosevelt signed a treaty of mutual noninterference, and our country's sciences enjoyed a remarkable acceleration of theory and application on nearly all levels of material endeavor.

Bielek maintains that a "partially successful," test in invisibility was accomplished by the research group at Princeton in 1936.

"By strange 'coincidence,' a UFO crashed in Germany in 1936," he said. "Since the craft was more or less intact, the artifact greatly stimulated Nazi science. Fortunately for the rest of the world, the Nazi scientists were never able to crack the problem of the UFO's basic drive mechanism."

The initial Navy experiment in invisibility was scheduled to take place on a cold day in March 1942. "All the levers were pulled—and nothing happened!"

Bielek is convinced that Tesla sabotaged that first attempt at placing a warship into a state of invisibility. The electronic genius had protested the presence of a live crew on board the *Eldridge* a DE 173 destroyer, insisting that the experiment should first be tried with the vessel alone. He had also demanded that the scientists be given more time to work out problems.

Tesla left the project at this point, arguing that the experiment was unsuccessful. Ten months later, on January 7, 1943, he was found dead in his New York City hotel room.

Dr. Von Neumann was now in charge of Project Rainbow. At 0900 hours on July 22 [rather than in October as other accounts would have it], the switches were flipped once again. According to Bielek, "for twenty minutes the *Eldridge* was invisible to radar and to visual contact."

The ship returned with most of the crew demented, but in spite of the heavy loss of personnel to hysteria and near-insanity, the scientists and Navy personnel were given twenty-one days to try the experiment once again.

On August 12, with new crew members—and this time trying only for *radar,* rather than *optical,* invisibility—the *Eldridge* was successfully invisible to radar for around seventy seconds.

Then there was a brilliant blue flash—and the warship disappeared . . . for four hours.

"The ETIs had wanted the experiment to take place exactly when it did in August 1943," Bielek said. "They had been making a careful study of Earth's biorhythmic cycles for centuries, so they knew the precise date when they would be able to tear open a massive hole in hyperspace.

"The Philadelphia Experiment was a setup by the humanoid aliens to create an opening in the space-time continuum so the ETIs would have easy access to Earth," Bielek said. "The U.S. Navy, the many scientists assembled, the government officials privy to the secret experiment were all laboring under false assumptions when they believed that the aliens were assisting them to achieve invisibility for U.S. military vessels. Although *we* were working toward the goal of invisibility, the aliens among us had a much larger and more self-serving goal in mind—to tear a massive hole in hyperspace."

When the warship returned to visibility in the Navy yard, four seamen were embedded in various sections of the *Eldridge.* Some had burst into flames. Others were glowing. Most of the rest were insane. Only those, such as Bielek, who had been shielded by steel walls or decking survived unscathed.

"The whole incident was swept under the Navy's rug," Bielek said. "Cover stories were created. Men were placed into asylums. The experiment was classified as research on the atomic bomb.

"Those who might have asked embarrassing questions were too busy with the enormous war effort that was taking place at that time. We were taking our lumps in the South Pacific. The wounded were coming back from everywhere."

UFO researchers themselves are divided as to the authenticity of the Philadelphia Experiment. Some years ago we discussed the matter with John A. Keel, one of the leading UFO investigators. Keel expressed the opinion that the legend may have grown up around a magician's plan to create a new kind of camouflage to make warships appear to vanish from enemy view.

"During the Second World War, the leading magician in the United States was Joseph Dunninger, who was also a master showman," Keel explained. "Dunninger proposed to the U.S. Navy that he would make ships invisible. He may have been talking about some form of camouflage—but in time Dunninger's claim did get publicity. . . . Perhaps a fantasy was built around Dunninger's claim."

Timothy Green Beckley, author, publisher, and long-time student of UFOs is convinced that a daring scientific experiment occurred in the Philadelphia Navy yard circa October 1943: "There have always been creative minds that have sought to recapture the ancient mysteries and apply them to modern technology. I believe the Navy's experiment in invisibility was yet another of those attempts to recapture the super science of the ancients."

Kevin Randle, a former captain in Air Force Intelligence, agrees that something unusual may have taken place that gave birth to the legend of the Philadelphia Experiment—but he does not believe that the experiment occurred in the manner in which it is most often described. He is amenable, however, to the suggestion that the U.S. Navy could well have been working on a radar cloaking device, such as that recently achieved by the Stealth bomber. "Such a device," he acknowledges, "would have been of great benefit to the Navy during World War II."

Other UFO researchers are convinced that *some* kind of secret experiment took place, quite likely dealing with incredibly high voltages of electricity, which may well have burned or scorched seamen—or even delivered a terrible kind of negative "electro-shock" treatment that drove some of the crewmen mad.

Al Bielek claims that in spite of their failures, the Navy tried another experiment with the *Eldridge* sometime around October 27—this time without personnel. Once again the warship disappeared. When the *Eldridge* returned, there was some damage and half of the scientific equipment was missing.

"After this incident the 'powers that be' pronounced that they had had enough of such experiments, and the *Eldridge* was placed on active duty until 1946," Bielek said. "After the warship was removed from duty, she was 'mothballed' until 1951 when she was transferred to the Greek Navy."

Supporters of the Authenticity of the Philadelphia Experiment believe that the hole ripped in the space-time continuum during the ill-fated event permitted the secret mass invasion of Earth in 1954 by the reptilian/amphibian, large-headed, bug-eyed species euphemistically known as the "Grays."

CHAPTER **5**

The U.S. Military and UFOs

In September 1947 Lieutenant General Twining of the Air Material Command (AMC) expressed his opinion that the many
reports of the flying saucers were of sufficient substance to warrant a detailed study. On December 30, 1947, a letter from the
chief of staff directed the AMC to establish a project to collect,
collate, evaluate, and disseminate all information concerning
UFO sightings.

The project was assigned the name "Sign," and the responsibility for the task was delegated to the Air Technical Intelligence
Center. Project Sign became "Project Grudge" in December
1948. In March 1952 the project was given the title "Bluebook"
until its official termination in December 1969.

The late Dr. J. Allen Hynek, who was teaching astronomy at
Ohio State University at Columbus in 1948, was selected to serve
as astronomical consultant to Project Sign and Project Bluebook.
Dr. Hynek was selected both for his professional acumen and
for the fact that he was teaching not far from Wright-Patterson
Air Force Base, where the office of UFO research was established.

When Dr. Hynek came on board, he initially felt that UFOs
were a symptom of postwar nerves, a bizarre kind of fad that
somehow kept people's minds occupied.

"The government was trying like mad to determine whether
[the UFO phenomenon] the Martians or the Russians were
responsible for the elusive discs being tracked in our atmosphere," Dr. Hynek told Timothy Green Beckley. "To put it

bluntly, they needed a competent astronomer to tell them which cases arose out of the misidentification of planets, stars, meteors, and so forth."

At the beginning Dr. Hynek said that he would have taken bets that the "whole mess" would be forgotten by 1952, "at the very latest." He admitted that nobody enjoyed "busting holes in a wild story" and showing off more than he did. "It was a game, and a heck of a lot of fun. . . . Never in my wildest dreams did I suspect that [UFOs] would turn out to be a global phenomenon."

Project Bluebook's staff was assigned to carry out three main functions:

1. To try to find an explanation for all reported sightings of UFOs;

2. To determine whether or not the UFOs pose a security threat to the United States;

3. To determine if UFOs exhibit any advanced technology that the United States could utilize.

A Bluebook officer was to be stationed at every Air Force base in the nation. It would be his responsibility to investigate all reported sightings and to get the reports sent to Bluebook headquarters at Wright-Patterson Air Force Base at Dayton, Ohio.

"The late 1940s were the early days of the Cold War, and for a time the possibility that the 'flying discs' might be Russian in origin, the product of kidnapped German scientists, seemed very real to the Air Force," said Hayden C. Hewes, a long-time UFO researcher. "By the summer of 1948, the Air Force began to consider the possibility that the discs were interplanetary in origin. By the end of 1949, the Air Force had decided there was nothing to the flying saucers that a good dose of ignoring them wouldn't cure. The pesky saucers kept returning, however, and by the fall of 1951, the Air Force was back in the saucer-chasing business once again.

"The summer of 1952 brought the greatest UFO wave of all time," Hewes continued. "Flying saucers were tracked visually and on radar over the White House and the Capitol in Washington. Over 300 UFO reports were made in the month of July alone.

"About this time the Central Intelligence Agency (CIA) became interested in the UFO business for the first time. In January 1953 the CIA convened a panel of eminent scientists who spent four days pouring over the UFO data then available. Named for its chairman, Dr. H. P. Robertson of Cal-Tech, the Robertson Panel concluded that UFOs *themselves* were not a real problem, but that UFO *reports* might be—perhaps even being used by a potential enemy to clog military communications in time of imminent or actual attack.

"The Robertson Panel subsequently recommended that the Air Force Project Bluebook essentially become a palliative to keep those citizens interested in UFOs 'off the backs' of vital channels of military intelligence. Consequently, Bluebook became more public relations than serious investigations from about 1953 until its termination in 1969."

The chaos and confusion of those early days of saucer spotting took a sinister turn with Captain Thomas Mantell's tragic encounter with a UFO over Godman Field Air Base in Kentucky.

The morning of January 7, 1948, Kentucky State Highway Patrol offices received a number of calls inquiring about any unusual aircraft that the Air Force might be testing in the area. Residents at Marysville, Kentucky, had sighted UFOs—or at any rate unfamiliar aircraft—flying over their city.

At 1:15 P.M. the Kentucky highway patrol called the control towers at Godman and asked if they had anything strange aloft that might be flying over Marysville and troubling the city's residents. Godman Field checked with Flight Service at Wright-Patterson and received a negative to their query of test craft in the area.

Within about twenty minutes, however, the highway patrol informed the tower operators at Godman Field that they were now receiving reports of strange aircraft—"circular, about 250 to 300 feet in diameter"—over Owensboro and Irvington.

In another ten minutes the tower operators at Godman were sighting the object for themselves. Once they were satisfied that they were not seeing an airplane or a weather balloon, they put in calls to the base operations officer, the base intelligence officer, and several other high-ranking personnel.

At 2:30 P.M., forty-five minutes later, base personnel were still discussing among themselves what course of action would be best to direct against the UFO. At that time four F-51s were sighted approaching Godman Field from the south. The tower radioed flight leader Captain Thomas Mantell and requested that he take a closer look at the UFO and attempt to identify it or provide a more complete description of the object.

Mantell was still climbing at 10,000 feet when he made his last radio contact with the tower at Godman Field: "It looks metallic and it's tremendous in size. It's above me, and I'm gaining on it. I'm going to 20,000 feet."

Those were Mantell's final words. His wingmen saw him disappear into the stratospheric clouds. A few minutes later Mantell crashed to the earth and was killed.

In those days of official efforts to debunk the reality of the UFO enigma in the eyes of the collective public, the Air Force issued an official explanation that Captain Mantell, experienced though he was as a pilot, had "unfortunately been killed while trying to reach the planet Venus."

Which also meant that in addition to Captain Mantell's tragic misidentification—the crew in the control towers, the base operations officer, the base intelligence officer, and several high-ranking personnel had all been deceived by the planet Venus. Even when Mantell found himself below the object and described it as "metallic and tremendous in size," he was actually aiming his F-51 at a planet that was millions of miles distant in outer space.

On October 1, 1948, George F. Gorman, a twenty-five-year-old second lieutenant in the North Dakota Air National Guard, was waiting his turn to land at Fargo when he was startled by the sudden appearance of a bright light that made a pass at him.

When he called the tower to complain about the errant pilot who had nearly collided with him, he was informed that the only aircraft in the vicinity was a Piper Cub that was just touching down on the landing field and his own F-51.

Baffled, Gorman scanned the skies and found that he could still see the mysterious light off to one side. More than a little irritated by the eccentric pilot's near-fatal misjudgment, he decided to investigate and determine the undeclared aircraft's identity.

Within moments he found himself once again under attack when the strange light put itself into a collision course with his F-51. Gorman had to take his craft into a dive to escape the unswerving globe of light. Then, to his terror, the UFO repeated its charge, and once again he just managed to escape collision.

When the UFO at last disappeared and ceased its passes at his F-51, Gorman was left shaken and convinced that "its maneuvers were controlled by thought or reason."

Throughout our thirty years of UFO research, pilots have been among our staunchest allies. Sam—who served as a fighter pilot during the Korean conflict—has literally been conducting his own private vendetta against UFOs since 1952.

"Here I was, thinking I was God's gift to women, America, and the U.S. Air Force," he recalled. "I was in my F-86A Sabre jet, the ultimate in technology, the cutting edge of aeronautical science and these things ... these so-called flying saucers ... would come swooping out of nowhere and make me look like I was flying a World War I biplane. I mean, they would zoom past me like I was parked in the clouds. It seemed to me as though they were purposely humiliating me."

Although Sam admitted that the rapidly maneuvering objects never made any hostile or aggressive movements toward him, their obvious superiority in the air and the humiliation it caused him was enough to make his temper flare.

"I probably wouldn't have gotten so ticked off if it had not been official Air Force policy back then that these things simply did not exist," he admitted. "It just burned me to be made a fool of by something that officially wasn't there. And what's more, if we even mentioned that we had seen a UFO, we could be in for big trouble and several hours of debriefing. Who needed that after returning to base after a long, stressful mission?"

Today Sam is a "flying farmer" in the Midwest who keeps his twin-engine plane in a hangar next to his barn. Give him a couple hours' notice that there is a UFO sighting in progress anywhere within his flying range, and day or night, rain or shine, Sam will soon be in the air in pursuit of a mysterious adversary that has haunted his dreams for forty years.

On July 26, 1952, UFOs were sighted flying in formations composed of as many as eight to ten craft. It may have been a nervous officer who remembered the "Foo Fighters" of World War II who gave the order to "shoot them down" when he spotted the dozens of flying saucers suddenly converging on Washington, D.C.

Several prominent scientists, including Dr. Albert Einstein, protested the "shoot-to-kill" order to the White House and urged that the command be rescinded at once, not only in the name of future intergalactic peace, but also in the name of self-preservation. If Washington was about to host a fleet of extraterrestrial space travelers—as it appeared was the case—then it would be prudent to welcome them in peace until their actions dictated otherwise. After all, if these beings had the technological ability to travel through space, they might look unfavorably upon being attacked by primitive jet firepower—and they might very well consider such unprovoked aggressive behavior as a license to strike back.

The shoot-them-down order was withdrawn according to White House orders by five o'clock that afternoon. That night official observers puzzled over the mysterious objects observed both on radar screens and by the naked eye, as the UFOs easily outdistanced Air Force jets.

Within another twenty-four hours, the Air Force was flippantly denying that the incredible UFO encounter over Washington, D.C., had ever really taken place. They arrogantly declared that overwrought civilians had mistaken planets and stars for flying saucers.

But it was too late for Air Force officials to lay the blame for the biggest Red Alert since World War II on laypersons' misinterpretations of the planet Venus, migrating flocks of geese, or hallucinations. The national wire services had already sent the word around the world that the large numbers of UFOs over the nation's capitol had made hardened and experienced military officials so jittery that they had issued orders to destroy them.

The accusative cry of "official cover-up" reverberated from coast to coast and around the globe. It was the UFO Red Alert over Washington, D.C., on July 26, 1952, that signaled the beginning of the erosion of confidence in the integrity of the U.S. Air Force over explaining the strangers in our skies.

Although the combined weight of some of the nation's leading scientific and political minds managed to get the order to "shoot them down" rescinded, it would appear that at least one UFO flying over Washington may have been damaged by U.S. firepower during the Red Alert.

The March 1986 issue of *Just Cause*, published by Lawrence Fawcett and Barry Greenwood, carries the copy of a letter from former Navy Rear Adm. Herbert B. Knowles, which states that he was involved in the examination of fragments of a UFO shot down over Washington, D.C., in 1952. The letter was a result of correspondence between Admiral Knowles and Ohio UFOlogist C. W. Fitch, which, in turn, had developed from Fitch's conversation with the Reverend Albert Baller.

In his August 27, 1961, response to Fitch's direct questions, the now-retired Admiral Knowles frankly admitted to having examined a piece of a "small disc" given to him by Wilbert Smith, head of Flying Saucer Research for the Canadian government. To the best of Knowles's recollection, the UFO had been shot down by a jet and had fallen in the "yard of a farmer across the river in Virginia." Several pieces of the UFO had been found.

Admiral Knowles described the piece from the flying disc as a "chunk of amorphous metal-like structure, brownish in color where broken, with a curved edge. . . . The outer surface was smooth, but not polished, and at the broken sections there were obviously iron particles. . . . I would say that the weight was somewhat lighter than if of solid iron, but it was not extremely 'light.' "

According to Wilbert Smith, a chemical analysis made of the piece yielded identification of iron, but "little if anything else could be identified."

Admiral Knowles admitted his firm belief in UFOs and his opinion that the 1952 object could very likely have been a "remotely controlled observation disc" of a type sighted many times "most often in the vicinity of defense installations."

At 4:20 P.M. on January 11, 1965, six Army Signal Corps engineers looked out of the windows of their offices in downtown Washington, D.C., and watched a number of strange, disclike objects zigzagging effortlessly north to south across the sky toward the Capitol building. Suddenly two delta-wing jets burst onto the scene and began chasing the unidentified aircraft, but the discs easily evaded their pursuers.

Although the engineers were hardly alone in their observation of the UFOs, the Defense Department issued an official press release denying that such an incident had occurred. An irate newspaper in the city published the headline: PENTAGON CAN'T SEE SPOTS IN THE SKY.

A man who at the time was serving as a radar operator on board an aircraft carrier told us that he had seen far more than spots on that date—and so had a number of his senior officers. According to our informant, he had watched the mystery objects approach their vessel, carefully plotting their course, until they dropped too low to be monitored. He had wondered where the UFOs could have gone so quickly: "Their proximity to our carrier had been so near that I almost feared a collision as I watched their approach."

Later that day he heard a remarkable account from some of his buddies who had been on deck with a number of officers. "According to them," he told us, "they had all watched the UFOs drawing nearer and nearer our vessel—until the objects seemed to pass right through us! The officers swore all the men to strict secrecy, and said there would be a court-martial for anyone who made a UFO report."

On January 23 two men traveling on U.S. 60 near Williamsburg reported that they had sighted a hovering cone-shaped object. Although the men were in separate cars and were traveling in opposite directions, both of their automobiles had mysteriously stopped as they approached the object.

The cone-shaped UFO was described as aluminum colored. The object hovered over a cornfield near the two stalled motorists for twenty or thirty seconds before it vanished straight up into the air.

Deputy Bruton, chief of Satellite Tracking on NASA's Wallops Island, Virginia, base, was standing in front of his house on January 5, 1965, waiting for the appearance of an artificial Earth satellite, when he sighted a bright object over the southwest horizon. It traveled at tremendous speed and gave off a yellowish-orange glow as it streaked through the sky.

Several residents near the Wallops Island base confirmed Bruton's sighting by independently reporting it to the NASA installation.

On January 25, Woody Darnell, a Marion, Virginia, policeman claimed that he and his family and several fellow officers watched a glowing object that hovered over them for several minutes before it took off in an explosion and a shower of sparks.

Exactly twenty minutes after the Marion sighting, nine persons near Fredericksburg—275 miles from Marion—described a UFO looking like a "Christmas sparkler" as it spun with great velocity and spewed sparks as it glided over the Rappahannock Valley.

On January 26 the UFOs were once again back over Marion, but this time they were seen by many residents. Local radio stations and police were swamped with calls. All sightings were of similar fire-spewing or spark-shooting objects. The craft seemed to eject balls of fire as they accelerated away from the sight of the witnesses.

The Rev. H. Preston Robinson described a UFO that gave off a buzzing sound and had a round bottom from which several lights could be seen.

A fellow UFO researcher told us not long ago that in her analysis of the Washington area sightings of January 1965 that "it seems obvious that many of the UFOs sighted—what with their shooting sparks and buzzing sounds—were early attempts by the technological branch of the shadow government to perfect a flying saucer based on the elements of alien superscience that had been bartered to scientists working in underground bases.

"Anytime you hear reports from those days [circa 1952–67] that describe sparks or 'jet trails' or buzzing sounds issuing from UFOs, you are most likely hearing descriptions of terrestrial, rather than extraterrestrial, saucers. Now when you hear about UFOs in those days being invisible on radar or seeming to penetrate solids, such as your report from the radar operator on board the aircraft carrier, you know that you are hearing about true alien spacecraft."

Which is not to say, however, that the sightings in the Washington, D.C., area in January 1965 did not include a mixed bag of genuine ETI craft together with the early, clunkier UFOs fashioned by MJ-12.

On May 15, 1954, Air Force Chief of Staff Gen. Nathan Twining informed an audience at Amarillo, Texas, that the "best brains in the Air Force" were trying to solve the problem of the flying saucers. "If [the-UFOs] come from Mars," he said, "they are so far ahead of us that we have nothing to be afraid of."

If, as some researchers now accuse, Gen. Twining was privy to the deals and decrees of Majestic-12 and the secret government, then he may have been leaking information to the general public based on his suppositions regarding the ETIs. He may have been parroting what he had been told—that the aliens were benevolent entities who had come to trade their advanced technology and aspects of their superior science for certain mineral rights to the planet Earth.

The general's bland assurances that an ultraadvanced culture from another world would automatically be benign did little to calm an increasingly bewildered and alarmed U.S. public. High-ranking officers in all military branches were beginning to demand a wider exchange of information regarding the UFO controversy, and important senators and congressmen were applying pressure to end the Air Force's policy of secrecy toward flying saucers.

The Air Force's—or some now would say MJ-12's—response to these demands was to issue the controversial Air Force Regulation

(AFR) 200-2 to all Air Force personnel on December 24, 1959. Briefly stated, AFR 200-2 made a flat and direct statement that the Air Force was definitely concerned with the reporting of all UFOs "as a possible threat to the security of the United States."

In the controversial Paragraph 9 of the regulation, the secretary of the Air Force gave specific instructions that Air Force personnel were to release reports of UFOs only "where the object has been definitely identified as a familiar object."

On February 27, 1960, Vice Adm. Robert Hillenkoetter, USN, Retired, former head of the Central Intelligence Agency, stunned the Air Force when he released to the press photostatic copies of AFR 200-2, which warned Air Force Commands to regard the UFOs as "serious business." From the perspective of the current controversy over the secret MJ-I2 group, of which Hillenkoetter was an alleged member, some researchers suggest that Hillenkoetter's conscience had got the better of him and that the press release was his way of alerting the public to certain elements within the Air Force who were playing a dual role in the UFO controversy.

Along with an explanation of the details of AFR 200-2, the press release stated that "unidentified flying objects—sometimes treated lightly by the press and referred to as 'flying saucers'— must be rapidly and accurately identified as serious USAF business. . . . The phenomena or actual objects comprising UFOs will tend to increase with the public more aware of goings-on in space, but still inclined to some apprehension. Technical and defense considerations will continue to exist in this era. . . . What is required is that every UFO sighting be investigated and reported to the Air Technical Intelligence Center at Wright-Patterson AFB and that explanation to the public be realistic and knowledgeable. Normally that explanation will be made *only* by the OSAF Information Officer . . ."

Across the planet curious individuals read the details of Hillenkoetter's press release, and even UFO skeptics had to ask themselves why such a dramatic statement about an unknown phenomenon would be made by an organization that had repeatedly claimed that "flying saucers" were nonexistent, and that anyone who saw one was hallucinating or was abysmally ignorant of natural phenomena.

An intelligent reader could only peruse the contents of the

press release that detailed AFR 200-2 and conclude that the Air Force was obviously very much aware of the physical reality of UFOs and was actively investigating their origins—regardless of official dismissals and denials.

In December 1969 Project Bluebook closed its pages and issued its official conclusions regarding the mysterious objects that continued to traverse the skies overhead:

1. No UFO has ever given any indication of threat to the national security of the United States;

2. There is no evidence that UFOs represent technological developments or principles beyond present-day scientific knowledge;

3. There is no evidence that any UFOs are extraterrestrial vehicles.''

According to one of our informants, a former officer in military intelligence, ''The official conclusion released to the public was exactly what MJ-12 wanted everyone to believe. Sure, there was no threat to the national security, because the deal had already been made with the aliens. A peace treaty, so to speak, had already been signed. The UFO technology was already being developed in full swing in 1969 in several underground bases.

''MJ-12 wanted the 'war of the worlds' mentality to die down. They wanted the masses to stop thinking about the threat of extraterrestrial invaders. They would soon begin their own positive propagandizing with such films as *Close Encounters of the Third Kind* and *E.T.* to popularize the cute-ugly, but friendly, aliens soon to emerge openly on the planet. MJ-12 had controlled the Air Force investigations of UFOs since 1947.''

CHAPTER 6

Soviet Encounters with UFOs

Dr. Lev Chulkov, a professor of mechanics and applied mathematics, is the author of *The Sons of the Stars,* the first book in Russia to promulgate the extraterrestrial concept of UFOs. In the March 1993 issue of the journal *AURA-Z,* Dr. Chulkov detailed the strenuous censorship that the former Soviet regime had directed toward any discussion—academic or otherwise—of flying saucers. Even though Joseph Stalin had expressed an interest in the phenomenon in the early 1950s, military and civilian authorities made UFO research impossible.

On May 17, 1967, the courageous Dr. Felix Zigel, a professor at the Moscow Aviation Institute, formed an unofficial body of some of the Soviet Union's top scientists and cosmonauts to investigate UFO reports in their sprawling nation. Dr. Zigel—who had quietly been conducting his own research since 1955—pointed out that in 1967 there had been 200 reports of UFOs from southern Russia alone.

In October 1967, Maj. Gen. L. Reino offered his assistance in establishing the UFO Department of the All-Union Committee of Cosmonautics. Although 350 enthusiastic individuals attended the first session of the department on October 18, by late November the group had been disbanded by order of Army Gen. A. Ghetman. Before the end of the year, the Department of General and Applied Physics had condemned UFO research in the Soviet Union.

However, as Dr. Chulkov duly noted, the censors committed

many slips, such as the following item carried by the newspaper *Trud* on January 30, 1985, which reported a massive UFO that was seen following a TU-134A passenger plane until it landed in Tallinn.

At about the same time, according to *Trud,* another TU-134 was flying from Leningrad to Tbilisi when the control tower informed its crew that a UFO was fast on their course. When first pilot V. Gotsiridze, the commander of the Tbilisi plane, spotted the object, he decided to take a closer look at their pursuer. His decision proved to be fatal.

The UFO shot a "scanning ray," which struck first pilot Gotsiridze and partially enveloped second pilot Kabachnikov. A few days later Gotsiridze died in a hospital of a disease resembling skin cancer. Kabachnikov was made an invalid for life.

The startling newspaper account was documented with the medical conclusions of the attending physicians. Dr. Chulkov states that soon after the article appeared, its author, the science editor, and the editor in chief were "sacked," with rumors of their "severe punishment" dissuading other journalists from covering UFO reports.

According to Russian informants who have been freed from censorship by the recent disintegration of the USSR, in 1985 two Soviet MIG fighter pilots intercepted a UFO in a remote region of Azarbaijan and shot it down.

Although the Russian pilots had intended only an intercept and a warning to an unidentified craft in their airspace, the unknown object proved to be from no known terrestrial state. When the UFO accelerated into a collision course toward one of the MIGs, the Russian pilots felt they had no choice other than to open fire.

Wreckage of the alleged extraterrestrial craft was found by two unwary mushroom pickers, who, according to the informants, died later from apparent radiation exposure. Soviet military authorities arrived on the scene of the crash, took numerous photographs of the wreckage, and filed extensive reports on the incident.

In 1989 two Soviet jets scrambled over Borisov, Byelorussia [now Belarus] after a large flying disc with five beams of light emanating from it had been observed hovering over the city. Ground Control had instructed one of the MIG-24 Foxbat interceptors to approach the UFO. As the MIG drew near, the large disc aimed one of its beams at the approaching fighter, illuminating its cockpit.

Both the pilot and the copilot reported the sensation of extreme heat, but only the copilot was able to manage a partial shielding from the brilliant light that blasted their cockpit.

Within a few months, according to Russian UFO researchers, the pilot had died of cancer resulting from extreme doses of radiation, and the copilot had been removed from duty due to prolonged periods in which he suffered loss of consciousness.

While on a regular, scheduled flight across the central plains of Russia in 1961, a mail plane with four passengers on board was snatched from the skies by a UFO.

According to Italian science writer Alberto Fenoglio [translated by Robert Pinotti, May 1966, *Flying Saucers*]: "The machine was found intact two days later near Tobelak [Siberia]. Everything on board . . . was in perfect order. The tanks contained fuel for two hours of flight. *The four passengers had vanished without a trace.* At a distance of 100 meters from the aircraft there was a huge, clearly defined circle, 30 meters wide, on which the grass was all scorched and the earth depressed. A 'flying saucer' had been there."

On April 24, 1970, a Soviet supersonic bomber heading from Moscow to Vladivostok—on what was described only as a secret mission—disappeared without a trace over Siberia. The pilot had been talking by radio to the ground base when his transmission was suddenly cut off.

An intensive search was conducted, with over 200 aircraft meticulously criss-crossing the area of the bomber's last known location. Although they never found any trace of the supersonic bomber, many of the pilots involved in the rescue mission reported that they had not been alone in the skies while they searched for their comrades. They described "very large dirigible-type objects" or "luminous discs" soaring above them.

One pilot radioed to base that the objects were "the biggest things" he had ever seen. "But they're too high. We can't get near them."

On October 16, 1981, a globe-shaped UFO blasted open the underbelly of a Soviet fighter plane over the Baltic Sea, knocked out the jet's instruments and engine, and nearly caused it to crash. Lieutenant Boris Korotkov was flying back to base after a training exercise when he encountered a UFO. Before he could adequately respond to the shocking sight, he felt his rocket-equipped fighter being rocked by an explosion.

According to the Russian Army newspaper *Red Star*, Korotkov immediately radioed his base that he had been hit and that his engine had ceased to function. When the base asked for specifics concerning his attacker, Korotkov replied that he had never seen anything like it.

"It is globe-shaped, perhaps sixteen feet in diameter," he said.

In a later interview with the Soviet magazine *Technology & Youth*, Korotkov described first sighting the UFO. It looked, he said, like "a huge, bluish ball" whose flickering color reminded him "of the base of the flame of a match." He added that the object had a ring in its center about three feet in diameter and six inches thick.

The UFO maneuvered to a scant twenty feet in front of Korotkov's fighter and maintained that distance, as though it were "guiding" him. "It was as if we had become one," Korotkov tried to explain.

Then the object disappeared—and an instant later Korotkov heard an explosion and felt his fighter being rocked by the concussion.

When Korotkov discovered that his engine was dead, his base radioed him to bail out and jettison the fighter. When he tried one last time to start the engine, however, it flamed back into life—and he made it back to the air base.

Although the official explanation of Lieutenant Korotkov's harrowing experience was listed as an incident with "ball lightning," Russian astrophysicist Dr. Vladimir Azhazha scoffed and expressed his opinion that the fighter pilot had encountered an extraterrestrial craft.

On August 26, 1983, Soviet radar picked up an undeclared aircraft over their top-secret submarine base at Ventspils on the Baltic Seacoast in Soviet Latvia. Six jet fighter planes equipped with heat-seeking missiles were dispatched with orders to attack and destroy the spying intruder.

When the Soviet fighters found the UFO at an altitude of about 9,000 feet, they fired their missiles. Incredibly, according to Russian UFO researcher Dr. Eduard Naumov, the missiles exploded almost the instant they were launched, "thus destroying the very planes that fired them. All but one plane fell into the sea, and the one that returned was badly crippled and barely made it."

Soviet news accounts mentioned neither the UFO nor the five jets that were sent crashing into the Baltic Sea. Rather, the official reports focused on the survivor, Sen. Lt. Mikhail Anisimov, who, according to the cover story, was on a "routine defensive mission" when "something huge crashed into the fighter head-on in a collision of incredible force."

That "something huge" was once again officially declared to be "ball lightning."

Dr. Naumov rejects the official account, stating that serious researchers who examined the case laughed at the explanation. "How many times can the government say it was ball lightning?" he asked rhetorically.

From the onset of UFO activity in the modern era, the former Soviet Union—with all of its atomic installations, airfields, missile bases, war plants, power stations, and active space program—seemed to be as closely under surveillance by the ETIs as was the United States and other nations of the West.

In the spring of 1959, UFOs brought near-panic to Soviet radar and Air Force personnel by hovering and circling for more than twenty-four hours above Sverdlovak, headquarters of a Tactical Missile Command. Red fighter pilots sent aloft to chase away the UFOs reported that the alien objects easily outmaneuvered their jets and zigzagged to avoid their machine-gun fire.

In the summer of 1961, a mammoth, cigar-shaped UFO and a number of smaller saucers took up positions above Moscow. They appeared to be observing the construction of new rocket batteries being set up as a part of the Soviet defense network.

A nervous battery commander panicked and gave the order to fire a salvo at the giant "mother ship." The missiles were fired, but they all exploded at an estimated distance of two kilometers from their intended target. A second volley of missiles were fired with the same result. The third salvo was never launched, for at this point the smaller UFOs swooped down closer to the rocket batteries and stalled the electrical system of the entire missile base.

When the smaller saucers and the larger aerial object moved on, the base's electrical apparatus was once again found to be in working order.

According to one informant the Soviets received another graphic and frightening demonstration of the UFOs' ability to interfere with and to control activities on Earth late in 1961 when a mysterious explosion occurred in a factory manufacturing heavy armored tanks.

At first Soviet authorities sought to pin the blame on U.S. espionage agents. However, several witnesses said that at daybreak a ball of fire had descended toward the factory just before the violent explosion occurred.

When the great cloud of smoke cleared, a UFO was seen hovering overhead for several minutes, as if making certain that the job had been accomplished. At the approach of fighter planes, the UFO took off at a tremendous rate of speed.

The area of the factory that seemed to be the focal point for the hovering UFO was now a rubble-filled crater—where a few minutes before had stood a department in which a special automatic device for atomic cannon was being manufactured.

But the greatest mystery of all, according to the Russian informant, was that no one was injured in the blast.

It seems that the factory's alarm siren had sounded only a few minutes before the explosion, and all the workers had taken shelter. At a subsequent inquiry it was established that no human hand had touched the alarm—a fact demonstrated by the position of the interrupter switch.

For some reason, the UFOs that destroyed the section of the tank factory that either offended their peaceful sensibilities or potentially threatened their proposed domination of the planet saw fit to provide the Russian workers with a warning before launching the deadly fireball.

CHAPTER 7

UFOs and Commercial Aviation

While military pilots around the world have steadily filed reports of UFO sightings, we will never have any way of knowing how many pilots did not report their sightings due to the fear of official reprisal. For many years AFR 200-2 prohibited any member of the Air Force from even discussing UFOs.

The same was true of commercial pilots. In 1968 a pilot who flew for one of the major airlines told us that he could be "black-balled for life" if he talked about UFOs.

"But I know that I've seen many things in the sky that I have to say were beyond our present stage of technology," he said. "We pilots get together in informal groups and talk shop just like anyone else. It would be my educated guess that over half the pilots for this airline see UFOs regularly."

As early as 1959 John Lester of the Newark *Star-Ledger* reported his survey of a group of more than fifty airline pilots, all of whom had more than fifteen years of experience. At the time of Lester's survey, the Air Force had astonishingly extended its censorship policies to the airlines, a situation the pilots found not only intolerable, but absolutely ridiculous. Each pilot who spoke to Lester claimed to have seen at least one UFO—and all the pilots had been interrogated by the Air Force.

"What it was really all about," an airline pilot told us during an off-the-record interview in 1968, "was not to acquire research data and to analyze our reports, but to shut us up!

"At first these guys who claimed to be Air Force Intelligence tried to put the fear of God into us. Then they put some real teeth into their threats when they announced that any pilot who did not maintain maximum secrecy after sighting a UFO would be subject to a possible ten years in prison and a fine of $10,000!" Needless to say, the airline pilots were totally disgusted with Air Force procedures and policies. As one pilot who complained to John Lester phrased it: "We are ordered to report all UFO sightings. But when we do, we are usually treated like incompetents and told to keep our mouths shut."

Weary of playing the fool to Air Force interrogators, in the mid-1960s commercial pilots formed the Volunteer Flight Officers Network (VFON) comprised of almost 30,000 flight crew members who flew almost two million miles of routes. Sixty-eight airlines made up the network, fifty of which were outside the United States. VFON intended to get all flight crew members in the habit of carrying cameras so that photographic evidence of UFOs might be amassed for the most skeptical of analysts.

VFON was able to circulate current reports of UFOs, re-entering space debris, satellites, meteors, and fireballs by using the teletype linkup that already connected most of the world's major airlines. But even the support of an efficiently operating network of 30,000 observers was not able to absorb completely the shock effect of an encounter between a UFO and an airliner. No amount of discussion and preparation could appreciably minimize the knee-buckling, stomach-tingling, sweat-producing trauma that occurs during the "moment of truth" when faced with an object that seems clearly to be the result of an alien technology.

On September 10, 1967, the crew of a Douglas DC-6 bringing ninety-six vacationers back to Great Britain from Majorca, Spain, sighted a cone-shaped alien craft while flying at 16,000 feet.

"It was fantastic," said Captain Fred Underhill. "I saw the UFO for three minutes, and it was like nothing that I had seen before."

Captain Underhill, First Officer Patrick Hope, and Flight Engineer Brian Dunlop saw the UFO cross their path at supersonic speed about forty miles ahead of their DC-6. While they watched, the strange cone-shaped object slowed, changed direction, and began moving toward them.

"In my business you get used to seeing other aircraft moving in the sky," Captain Underhill said, "but this thing was going very fast. At first it was just a silver dot that seemed to be moving directly across our path. I estimate that in the first minute that I watched, the UFO must have traveled about sixty miles. This puts the speed at about 3,500 miles per hour, faster than any aircraft I have ever seen before."

It was about 5 P.M. when the crew members made the sighting. Visibility was good, and the sun was shining on one side of the UFO. The DC-6 was about eighty miles northwest of Barcelona, cruising at a speed of 300 miles per hour.

As the three flight officers watched the incredibly fast-moving UFO ahead of them, they became a bit uncomfortable when it slowed down and turned in their direction. Its sudden approach did, however, give them a chance to get a close look at the mysterious interloper.

"It was about 100 feet high and 80 feet wide," said First Officer Hope, who made a sketch of the object to send to the Denver, Colorado, headquarters of VFON. "It was shaped like an ice cream cone pointed upward. It was apparently made of silver metal. The top part was quite clear, but below that it was an indistinct shape lost in some sort of haze."

Captain Underhill noted in his report that there was no sign of portholes, doors, or even a vapor trail. After turning in their direction, the cone-shaped UFO had come alongside the DC-6, veered toward it, then disappeared out of sight below the conventional airliner. It was as if the UFO had tired of pacing the slow-moving, sluggish terrestrial aircraft.

Reinhardt N. Ausmus of Sandusky, Ohio, was one of the earliest U.S. airmen. A member of the Early Birds, an organization composed of aviators who flew before or during World War I, Ausmus was traveling on Route 99 about 6:45 P.M. on January 30, 1967, when he and his wife observed a UFO over the Plum Brook Station of the National Aeronautics and Space Administration (NASA).

Ausmus—who had long been skeptical about the existence

of UFOs—said the object appeared stationary in the sky for more than four minutes.

On July 10, 1968, over Warren, Ohio, Richard Montgomery, a commercial pilot, said that he, his brother, and their dates were chased by a UFO as they flew at an altitude of 4,000 feet. "We were cruising over the west side of Warren about 10:20 P.M. headed east when I noticed an object coming toward us from the direction of Youngstown," Montgomery said. "I swung over to get a closer look when the object began to head directly toward our aircraft. Then it stopped, hung motionless . . . and as our aircraft came closer, the UFO moved swiftly upward and came back at us from another angle."

Montgomery described the UFO as being cylindrical in shape, of metallic composition, with a muffled light beaming from underneath. The object, about ten feet in diameter, kept following Montgomery's craft, even though he sent his airplane "into several maneuvers . . . which simulated a military dogfight."

Tiring of the game, the UFO suddenly sped off "in an easterly direction at amazing speed and was quickly out of sight."

In those earlier days of UFO chaos and confusion, aviation officials, as well as their flight crews, sighted UFOs. During a trip to Brazil in October 1966, James Pfeiffer, a respected aviation industry executive, saw and personally photographed a UFO.

"It was spheroid-shaped," Pfeiffer said, "roughly seventy feet in diameter, very smooth in construction."

The executive reported that the object had hovered at about 1,500 feet above the lagoon-side restaurant where he sat, then zoomed away at a great rate of speed and changed direction. He insisted that the object had not skidded or banked, but executed a flat, ninety-degree right turn.

After this bit of "impossible" maneuvering, Pfeiffer stated that the object settled down in the woods across the water and emitted a high- then low-pitched whining sound that was "noisy enough to bring the restaurant employees outside to watch."

Air Force investigators were especially interested in Pfeiffer's photograph of the object because of the shadow on the left side of the UFO, which suggested that the object had indeed been three-dimensional when sighted.

In March 1988 an aeronautical engineer—we'll call him "Jake"—told us he had discovered that some of his associates had been working with aliens in constructing advanced aircraft.

"That was the reason for the big swap of humans for technology and the reason why the MJ-12 group had cut the deal with the aliens in the first place.

"You know," Jake went on, "we were supposed to have this giant leap for all of humankind at the expense of those of us that the secret government considered expendable. But even though we started using alien technology to build flying craft in the late '50s, I don't think we really came close to getting anything right until the Stealth was perfected."

A number of cases of UFO sightings in the mid-1960s reported vehicles to have left visible exhaust trails and to have made high-pitched whining noises. As any UFO buff could point out, the flying saucer tradition demanded that the things be absolutely noiseless—at most making a low hum—and that they cross our atmosphere without leaving jetlike "tracks" in the sky to mark their passing. Even then we had wondered if those craft were experimental terrestrial versions of UFOs that were being produced by some secret government aviation agency.

"Your suspicions were correct," Jake said. "According to my sources a number of fairly successful prototypes of our own saucers were being flown in the '60s. The trouble was, the aliens were holding back vital aspects of their technology necessary to make exact replicas of their craft. That's why people were spotting vapor trails and hearing whining sounds. Those craft weren't much more than 'super jets,' which satisfied some of the engineers working on the project, but made others suspicious that the aliens were deliberately holding out on them."

We mentioned a specific case from our files dated March 6, 1967. Fred Schott, president of Schott Aviation, was piloting W. A. Vorhees, president of the Electric Wheel Division of Firestone Tire and Rubber Company, to Quincy, Illinois, from a business meeting in Kansas City when the two executives sighted what they deemed a possible UFO.

Schott reported that they had first noticed a long, white exhaust trail that extended straight north. The UFO was not clearly visible, but the two businessmen were able to distinguish a light. Although the sky was clear for the 8 P.M. sighting, the observation of the lighted UFO lasted only about four seconds when the exhaust trail was abruptly cut off.

Pilot Schott told newsmen that he was unaware of any conventional or jet aircraft that could move at the rate of speed at which the "light" had traveled. The aviation executive also observed that the exhaust trail they had seen was totally different from any other he had previously encountered.

"Different," Jake agreed, "but not so different that the pilot couldn't identify that it was some kind of exhaust trail. So back in the 1950s and '60s the aliens let us clunk about in those primitive models, blaming *us* for not getting their technology right. Their standard routine was to explain that they could only guide us. It was up to us to employ correctly the bountiful gifts that they had bequeathed us."

In the meantime, of course, Jake said, alien craft were still zipping through our airspace, making both our conventional aircraft and the newer hybrid alien/human vehicles look like horse-drawn chariots compared with the products of their superior technology.

On April 21, 1991, a cigar-shaped UFO at least fifty feet long buzzed an Alitalia airliner as it was approaching London. Captain Achille Zaghetti immediately informed air controllers at West Drayton, the center for London-bound flights, that the Italian airliner had experienced a near-miss with an unidentified aircraft that soared about 1,000 feet above them at their flying altitude of 20,000 feet.

Radar operators picked up and recorded the UFO. No other aircraft were in the immediate area. In a matter of seconds the UFO had left a ten-mile trail on the radar screen—and disappeared.

An Army spokesman stated that there were no military operations of any kind being conducted in the area. "The area in question is a very busy civilian route," the spokesman pointed out. "We are not allowed to exercise in that area."

A spokesman for Britain's Civil Aviation Authority insisted that they had "checked everything possible for some kind of explanation and cannot find out *what* this object was—it is a complete mystery."

Government officials did their best to clamp a lid of secrecy on the frightening near-miss between a Boeing 747—and its 300 passengers—and a huge, cigar-shaped UFO that appeared to be coming straight at it.

At 1:45 A.M. on August 5, 1992, the United Airlines jumbo jet was on the first leg of its 6,000-mile flight from Los Angeles to London when the stunned pilot—whose identity remains secret—gasped in wide-eyed horror as he sighted the UFO soaring toward his airliner.

The jumbo jet was cruising at 600 miles per hour at an altitude of 23,000 feet. The pilot and crew members estimated the UFO's speed at an incredible 1,800 miles per hour.

The UFO seemed to be coming straight at the jet airliner's nose. Helpless to do anything other than pray, the crew was relieved when the mysterious craft suddenly dropped from its course when it was about 1,000 feet from a collision with the 747.

Government officials from nearby George and Edwards Air Force bases made it very clear that the object that nearly struck the United Airlines jumbo jet was not an out-of-control missile or an experimental aircraft off course.

A number of our informants have stated their somewhat fearful opinions that the aliens are becoming bolder than ever when it comes to buzzing our airliners and frightening both aircrews and passengers.

"It's as if they no longer care that much about maintaining the veil of secrecy that they had put up around their activities on our planet," a former Air Force officer told us. "But strangely enough—when our official agencies make their formal statements to the press—they still continue the pretense of denying the fact that UFOs exist. Either these guys with the Air Force, the FAA, and so forth, are still in the dark—or else the secret government is really putting the clamps to them.

"When I've thought deeply about this enigma of why our government agencies continue to carry on the charade of officially denying the reality of UFOs and the alien bases, I've concluded that the secret government, the MJ-12 types, may still believe that they can somehow best the aliens and restore some kind of equilibrium to the terrible mess that they have created."

CHAPTER 8

Direct Contacts with UFOs over Military Bases and by Military Aircraft

In February 1968 we spoke with Lt. Col. Howard C. Strand, base commander of the Detroit Air National Guard. At that time Lieutenant Colonel Strand had over 7,000 hours of military flying time, more than half in jets. A soft-spoken, gentleman-officer of the old school, Strand impressed us as an honest, straight-from-the-shoulder military man who did not seem the sort of person to fabricate a story.

On a clear late winter day in 1953, Strand encountered a number of UFOs while flying over Detroit. At that time he was on active duty in the Air Force, flying F94-B aircraft and was stationed at Selfridge Air Force Base, Michigan. Prior to that sighting he had not been a believer in flying saucers.

"Approximately 10:00 A.M. one morning in March 1953, I was scrambled on a routine patrol mission," Strand said. "We were expecting the Navy to try to penetrate our air defenses in the local area for practice purposes.

"After about twenty minutes of flight, the radar site controlling our flight gave us a target to our left at about the eight-o'clock position. Upon visual checking, my airborne radar operator and I could see tiny specks in the sky which appeared as a ragged formation of aircraft. Our position at the time was approximately thirty miles northwest of downtown Detroit. The targets appeared to be over the city's central section."

Strand recalled that the objects were a little lower than their aircraft, so they were in a slight downhill run at full military power, without afterburner on the intercept.

"I remember thinking more than once that I should be able to start identifying the aircraft any second—but I couldn't," he said. "Their tails, wings, and aircraft features just didn't seem to 'pop out' as they normally do when you close in on an aircraft to identify its type."

All the while that they were on a quartering head-on intercept, Strand's radar operator in the backseat was trying to pick up the targets on the airborne radar.

"The ground radar had both our aircraft and the unknowns painted as good strong targets," Strand said, "but we were still unable to get any positive identification, and the objects seemed to be getting a little larger all the time.

"About this time my radar operator started receiving some returns on his scope and thought that he was picking up the targets. I was watching the objects until I looked in the cockpit, trying to inch out a little more speed without going into afterburner. When I looked up again—after no more than two to four seconds—*the objects were gone!*"

Strand had estimated the number of unknowns to be between twelve and sixteen. He and his radar operator had expected to see and to identify Navy fighter-type aircraft. But now there was nothing. *Every last one of the objects had disappeared from sight.*

Immediately Strand asked the ground radar controller where the mysterious craft had gone.

"I was told that the targets were still there—loud and clear! We continued to fly the headings given by the controller, right into the center of the targets. We flew and turned in every direction, but there was still nothing in sight."

Gradually the targets disappeared from ground radar after Strand had continued to fly among them for three or four minutes—as close as 2,000 feet, according to radar.

"Our airborne radar had picked up nothing after the initial fleeting contact before the objects disappeared from visual sight," Strand recalled.

No UFO report was submitted by Strand's aircrew for one basic reason: This was the era when the Air Force denied even the possibility of UFOs, and a concentrated effort was made to portray everyone who made such reports as silly or stupid.

In retrospect Lieutenant Colonel Strand told us he had personally come to two conclusions about his sighting.

"Number One: I could not identify the objects as conventional aircraft because they weren't. There were no wings or tails to 'pop' into sight for identification as known aircraft. At the time I had no thoughts of 'flying saucers'; therefore I made no effort to identify them as such. If I had even so much as thought of it at the time, I never would have taken my eyes off them.

"I can say definitely that the objects were *not* conventional or jet aircraft, due to the fact that no aircraft could have turned around or gotten away in the two to four seconds I was looking in the cockpit. Remember, we were bearing down on the objects at approximately 500 miles per hour in a quartering head-on pass.

"Number Two: I now believe that the objects went straight up, out of sight to me and my airborne radar operator, but remained visible as targets on the ground radar. Other sightings have been made where UFOs have gone straight up for tens or hundreds of thousands of feet in one or two seconds, then hovered or moved slowly at that altitude.

"At the time of the sighting," Strand said, "I had 1,700 hours flying time, accrued in nine years. Today I still feel the sighting on that perfectly clear day in 1953 was no figment of the imagination or trick of the eyesight."

According to a former Air Force officer, the international military bases have always been popular spots for cruising UFOs to test their mettle against our aircraft.

On December 16, 1966, three UFOs were spotted over the Naval Auxiliary Air Station near San Diego, California. The objects were observed for nine minutes by fourteen persons. Ensign John Schmidt, a helicopter pilot at Ream Field, reported that he and some friends were leaving through the main gate when they first spotted the UFOs at 9:30 P.M.

"There were three of them," Schmitt said. "They were bright, round yellow objects up about 50,000 feet and flying in a triangular formation. They looked to be about the size of a quarter from where we were."

With the helicopter pilot were Ensign David Coghill, a pilot at Miramar Naval Air Station, and Ensign David Conklin, a North Island Naval Air Station pilot. "We didn't know what they were," Schmitt admitted, serving as spokesman for the trio. "But none of us had ever seen anything like them.

"We agreed that they couldn't be meteors. They would hover, then go forward, then to one side. They were traveling at speeds from about the maximum speed of a bomber to about five times that.

"A fourth one came over the horizon from the east at a terrific speed. It came up to the group of three, stayed near the formaion for a minute, then headed east. It dropped to a lower altitude, and the magnitude of its speed increased. It dropped what appeared to be two spheres of light, which disappeared, then it headed west, and we lost sight of it.

"The other three objects suddenly disappeared. They flew in formations and moved in different directions. We had these objects in sight for about nine minutes."

In May 1993 we received a report from a man who had served as a military policeman with the 591st at Fort Bliss, Texas. According to our correspondent he was assigned to guard duty at one of the radar areas one night in 1956 when a UFO appeared over the base at around midnight.

"There were planes coming and going. And then there was nothing but this bright light in the sky over the base," he said. "It just got bigger and bigger. It got so bright that the area I was guarding seemed as bright as daylight. Then it was gone in the blink of an eye.

"All the time it had hung above the base, there was no sound, no wind. Nothing. The night was clear. No clouds. Few stars.

"This really happened, and it scared me no end. When I think about it, it still bothers me."

"The aliens declared a kind of war against our military bases in 1947 when mysterious green fireballs rained down at White Sands-Holloman and Los Alamos, two of the top-secret military installations in the United States," said one of our informants. "I think the message the extraterrestrial intelligences were broadcasting to the citizens of the world was that all the combined military agencies of Earth could do nothing to stop them if they really wished to conquer the planet.''

Our informant went on to tell us a grim story that he had discovered when he served in the Air Force.

"There were no names or dates listed in the report, but I figured that the incident probably occurred around 1952. According to the report an F-86 jet was sent aloft to investigate a UFO that had been hovering over an Air Force base for about an hour. The horrified radar operator saw the two blips come together over the base. Then there was only one blip left, and that one was shooting off the radar screen at an enormous rate of speed. No trace was ever found of the F-86 or its pilot.''

A similar case, infamous in the annals of UFOlogy, and said to be fully documented by the USAF itself, occurred in 1953 when an F-89 jet interceptor was hijacked over Kinross AFB in Michigan. As in the previous incident with the F-86 fighter, while air defense radar watched helplessly, the two blips merged into one—and the UFO soared away toward Canada. Nothing was ever found of the jet or its two-man crew.

UFO researcher Tom Camella managed to catch M.Sgt. O. D. Hill from the Air Force's Project Bluebook in several moments of candor when he asked him about UFOs and our disappearing military aircraft. "I must confess to you that it is true,'' Master Sergeant Hill answered.

Hill also relayed an account of the 1955 UFO kidnapping of a transport plane with twenty-six persons aboard. The transport was being carefully tracked by a radar station and maintaining constant radio communication with the base when the radar operator suddenly discovered a second blip on his scope. He immediately radioed the transport's pilot and advised him to be cautious of an unidentified object that was rapidly moving toward the aircraft.

In the words of Master Sergeant Hill: "The UFO was traveling at a high rate of speed, about 2,500 miles per hour. It jumped about on the radar scope like a tennis ball. All of a sudden the mysterious blip headed straight for the transport plane and before the radar operator could warn it, the two objects had

united into one on the radar screen. The one remaining blip
sped straight up at a terrific rate of speed."

The transport plane had completely disappeared. A surface
search of the water in the area did not reveal even an oil slick.
The only testimony to the transport's previous existence was the
discovery of a general's briefcase floating on the surface of a
nearby lake.

Around that same time in 1955, a civilian pilot and his friend
were doing some prospecting above the Agua River near Prescott,
Arizona. The two men swore that they saw two brightly luminous
UFOs attack a military plane by directing "some kind of strange
beams" at the craft that caused it to explode.

Even worse, according to the pilot and his prospector friend,
when the airmen jumped free of the burning craft in their para-
chutes, the UFOs swung back and seared the survivors with the
same deadly rays.

On October 3, 1955, a B-47 bomber crashed near Lovington,
New Mexico. One of the crew survived and said that something
had struck their plane in midair.

A witness said that he had seen a "ball of fire" near the plane
before it crashed.

Later that same month another B-47 crashed, this time in
Texas. Once again a witness had spotted a ball of fire near the
craft.

Strong circumstantial evidence exists to support the allegations that on April 30, 1964, a "force from outer space" landed at
the Holloman U.S. Air Force Base near the White Sands Proving
Grounds in New Mexico.

According to Terry Clarke of KALG radio in Alamogordo
[nine miles east of Holloman], he received a telephone call from
an informant who claimed to have monitored the testing range
radio communications that day. As he tapped into the range's
frequency, he heard the loudspeaker at Main Control on the

Holloman Air Force Base/White Sands Proving Ground Integrated Test Range blare the electrifying words: "I've got a UFO!"

The voice of the man who claimed to have encountered a UFO belonged to the pilot of a B-57, who had been flying a routine mission in the vicinity of Stallion Site, a few miles east of San Antonio, New Mexico.

"What does it look like?" the controller asked.

"It's egg-shaped and white," the B-57 pilot answered.

Minutes later, after the big B-57 had made its turn and come in over the area where the UFO was first seen, the pilot contacted Main Control again and shouted excitedly: "It's on the ground! The UFO is on the ground!"

Then, according to Clarke's information source, photo crews were asked to stand by—and then all radio communications ceased. Follow-up telephone calls to the base indicated that a major security clamp down was in effect.

Rumors soon buzzed throughout the area that a UFO had been captured on the ground and was being kept in a Holloman Air Force Base hangar under heavy guard.

"The story was essentially true," one of our informants, a former Air Force officer told us not long ago. "The problem was, though, that the UFO landed at Holloman of its own accord. It wasn't 'captured' at all. It was just another of the carrots that the Grays dangled on a stick to keep the Majestic-12 boys happy while the aliens were following their own secret agenda."

According to alleged eyewitness accounts, President Dwight D. Eisenhower, then only recently resigned as the supreme commander of Allied Forces in Europe, inspected a variety of alien space vehicles on a U.S. Air Force base. Interestingly the supposed incident—in the same manner as accounts of the Philadelphia Experiment—continues to grow, gaining new adherents of its historical validity and adding identities of eyewitnesses who claim to have been present at the shattering review of superior extraterrestrial technology.

Dated April 16, 1954, a letter was written by Gerald Light, Los Angeles, California, to Meade Layne, San Diego, the late director of Borderline Sciences Research Associates:

I have just returned from Muroc [Muroc Dry Lake, located at Edwards Air Force Base, California]. The report is true—devastatingly true! I made the journey in company with Franklin Allen of the Hearst papers and Edwin Nourse of Brookings Institute [President Truman's financial advisor], and Bishop McIntyre of L.A. [confidential names for the present, please].

When we were allowed to enter the restricted section . . . I had the distinct feeling that the world had come to an end. . . . For I have never seen so many human beings in a state of complete collapse and confusion, as they realized that their own world had indeed ended with such finality as to beggar description. The reality of "otherplane" aeroforms is now and forever removed from the realms of speculation and made a rather painful part of the consciousness of every responsible scientific and political group.

During my two days' visit, I saw five separate and distinct types of aircraft being studied and handled by our Air Force officials—with the assistance and permission of the Etherians! I have no words to express my reactions. It has finally happened. It is now a matter of history.

President Eisenhower, as you may already know, was spirited to Muroc one night during his visit to Palm Springs recently. And it is my conviction that he will ignore the terrific conflict between the various "authorities" and go directly to the people via radio and television. . . . From what I could gather, an official statement to the country is being prepared for delivery about the middle of May.

I will leave it to your own excellent powers of deduction to construct a fitting picture of the mental and emotional pandemonium that is now shattering the consciousness of hundreds of our scientific "authorities" and all the pundits of the various specialized knowledges that make up our current physics. In some instances I could not stifle a wave of pity . . . as I watched the pathetic bewilderment of rather brilliant brains struggling to make some sort of rational explanation which would enable them to retain their familiar theories and concepts. . . . I shall never forget those forty-eight hours at Muroc!

The Earl of Clancarty, a member of Great Britain's House of Lords, who has treated the subject of UFOs with extreme seriousness for decades, recently repeated the testimony of a British pilot who had been vacationing in Palm Springs in February 1954 and was summoned to the base by military officials. According to the pilot—a man Lord Clancarty respected as a gentleman of greatest integrity—the aliens disembarked from their space vehicles and approached President Eisenhower and a small group of political and military figures.

The aliens seemed able to breathe the air of Earth without the need of a helmet with breathing apparatus, and the pilot described the ETs as basically humanlike in appearance, about the same height and build as an average man. However, their features were, in his opinion, somewhat misshapen. The aliens spoke English, and the thrust of their dialogue centered on their wish to begin a program of education for the people of Earth that would make all of humanity aware of their presence.

The British pilot recalled that Eisenhower was not in favor of such a program. In a very forthright manner, he told the aliens that he didn't believe the people of the world were ready for the sudden revelation that extraterrestrials were on the planet. Such an announcement, in Eisenhower's assessment, would only cause widespread panic.

The aliens appeared to understand the president's point of view, and they agreed not to institute their proposed program of widespread Earthling awareness of their presence. However, they informed Eisenhower that they would continue to contact isolated humans until more people got used to their being on the planet. The president agreed with a program of limited contact, but he urged the aliens not to do anything that would create panic and confusion among the people of Earth.

Next on the alien agenda, the ETs demonstrated a number of their incredible technical advances. Eisenhower was very uncomfortable when the aliens displayed their ability to become invisible. It was indeed eerie, the pilot agreed. For although the humans assembled for the exhibition knew the aliens were really there, they could not see them.

After the demonstration of controlled invisibility, the aliens boarded their craft and left the air base. Those who had witnessed the historic meeting were sworn to maintain complete secrecy.

Lord Clancarty clarified that although the pilot had kept his vow and had not previously disclosed word of the remarkable events at Edwards Air Force Base, he believed that all the principals who were present in 1954 were now deceased.

Dr. Hank Krastman of Encino, California, revealed in *Unexplained* magazine (Vol. 4, No. 2, 1993) that he had been present that day in 1954 at Edwards Air Force Base as a young sailor in the Royal Dutch Navy. Krastman was trained for internal services dealing with matters concerning the NATO pact and CIA affairs, and at nineteen years of age he was serving as an adjutant to Mr. Rob, the ship's commander.

Krastman remembered that on February 19, 1954, they were briefed about a top security meeting that would take place the following day. The next morning they left Long Beach Navy Base in a van with a military police escort, and they arrived at Edwards Air Force Base at 10 A.M.

Escorted to a hangar at the far west side of the base, Krastman recognized the president of the United States, Dwight D. Eisenhower, and, among others, Albert Einstein, Wernher von Braun, Victor Schauberger, and Howard Hughes.

Krastman wondered what the "two Nazi war criminals" were doing there. To the young Dutch sailor, von Braun, with his work on the V1 and V2 rockets, and Schauberger, who was involved in Hitler's secret V7 flying discs, were two scientists who had been responsible for the deaths of many of his countrymen.

Krastman heard his commander being told that there were five alien ships in the other hangar, and that some of the ETs would demonstrate the capabilities of the craft. Krastman was not allowed to enter the hangar that contained the aliens and their spaceships. When his commander returned, he was very pale and would not give him any information regarding what he had seen.

The next day, Krastman said, various large crates were loaded onto their ship for the return voyage to Holland. He later found out that the crates were destined for a secret underground NATO base—a converted coal mine of great depth—in Limburg, Holland.

In 1959 Krastman returned to the United States as an immigrant, and he has continued to dig into the true meaning of his peculiar experience in February 1954.

We do know that President Eisenhower never called the press conference which Gerald Light had been so certain would take place. Perhaps Eisenhower's rationale for not revealing the truth about flying saucers to the people of Earth was that he truly feared "a state of complete collapse and confusion" a "mental and emotional pandemonium" . . . "pathetic bewilderment" . . . as humankind realized that the world it had known and charted had ended with "such finality as to beggar description."

According to Lawrence Fawcett and Barry Greenwood, authors of *Clear Intent: The Government Cover-up of the UFO Experience*, for two very intense days near the end of October 1975, UFOs defied the efforts of security personnel at Loring Air Force Base in Maine to protect the base's munitions storage area. While the glowing alien craft hovered over the nuclear weapons stockpile, the stymied Air Force defenders could do nothing but maintain an alert.

At last the bizarre UFO dimmed its light and vanished from sight. The helpless Air Force security breathed a collective sigh of relief and draped a cloak of silence over the incident. It was decreed to be imperative that the U.S. public remain totally ignorant of the fact that a UFO had kept one of the nation's most sensitive defense installations on full alert for two days.

Elaine Douglass, associate editor of the *Right to Know Forum* presented an account of three witnesses who, in April 1991, telephoned a radio call-in program on KPFA-FM in Berkeley, California, to report having seen aliens at Edwards Air Force Base and the China Lake Naval Weapons facility.

One of the speakers identified himself as a Vietnam veteran, former Green Beret, a military medal-holder, and a licensed general contractor who had worked on projects at China Lake and at Nellis, Scott, Edwards, and Andrews Air Force bases. He identified the construction projects in which he participated as being "mostly underground," very extensive, and "definitely not normal military structures," with four-foot-thick concrete walls and electronically controlled oval doorways.

In one building at Edwards, it took over five minutes to get from the top to the bottom by elevator—a depth, he estimated, to be thirty stories.

It was here that he saw his first alien. "He was ... I'd say between eight and nine to ten feet tall. He was wearing a lab jacket and talking to two [human] engineers. This [being's] arms were almost down to his knees. It threw me into shock!"

At that point security personnel spotted the witness and told him to leave. The next day he walked off the job.

When the witness was asked if the being he saw could have been an abnormally tall human, he answered: "Definitely not. He had big slanted eyes. A big head. Greenish skin. And his fingers were extremely long."

The witness reported that he and a number of his co-workers had encountered the smallish "Grays" when they were working at the China Lake naval facility. According to his account they were staying late to finish a particular job when one of his co-workers told them to follow him—he had found something that he had to show them.

"We looked in the window and there were these four little gray guys about three feet tall," the witness said. "Right then security saw us and they told us, 'We thought you guys left.' And they escorted us and said, 'You're not allowed around this hangar. This hangar is off-limits to everybody. You'll get yourselves shot.'"

The construction worker said that the sight of the four smallish entities "messed" with his friend's mind so much that he kept sneaking onto the base to observe them: "He finally got caught and was kicked off the base. About three months later they found him mysteriously dead in Orange County."

The witness admitted that his friend's death had "kind of put a scare" into him. He said that he knew when not to mess with something.

"I know what's going on at Edwards is real," he said. "Somebody's playing games with us."

CHAPTER 9

NATO's Secret UFO Agenda

When Bob Dean, a retired Army Command sergeant major, reflects on the matter of UFOs, he says he became involved in the field "through the back door." A veteran of twenty-seven years in the Army, Dean was Infantry Unit commander in combat in Korea, Laos, Cambodia, and North Vietnam. He was also with Special Forces attached to an outfit in South Vietnam known as MAC-V-SOG, or Military Advisory Command Vietnam Special Operations Group.

With that track record it's understandable that Bob Dean has always thought of himself as a no-nonsense, hard-nosed professional soldier. His perception would soon change with his new mission. In the summer of 1963, Bob Dean was assigned as an intelligence analyst to SHAPE headquarters (Supreme Headquarters, Allied Powers, Europe) in Paris. Although this assignment was considered in the military to be a "plum" appointment, little did Bob realize that with the appointment his destiny would be more bizarre than the wildest science fiction scenario.

One of the requirements for Bob's assignment was a top-secret clearance. His "cosmic top-secret" status was the highest given at NATO (North Atlantic Treaty Organization).

Dean, a master sergeant, was assigned to the Operations Division—Supreme Headquarters Operation Center. "This was basically a war room," Dean told us. "SHAPE was the Central Headquarters Command for all Allied forces throughout Europe—from the northern border of Norway clear down to the southern border of Turkey. All the NATO countries with military forces had representation (fifteen countries) at the Paris headquarters."

It wasn't long into the new assignment that Dean became aware of a study that had begun in 1961. Since this topic was extremely sensitive, it was not generally discussed—yet there was gossip about it when occasional boredom would set in at two or three in the morning at the Operations center during long twelve-hour shifts.

At one such time an Air Force controller who was a full colonel happened to mention: "Wait until you hear what we have been doing lately." And he went on to talk about a project that he referred to as an Assessment.

This study had been triggered by an incident in February 1961 involving about thirty to fifty enormously large, circular, disc-shaped, metallic objects flying in formation over Central Europe. Similar circular objects had been sighted many times before—especially throughout the late 1950s. On this particular occasion, however, these UFOs almost caused the Soviets and the Allies to start shooting at each other—each suspecting the other of invading their territory.

These craft would mysteriously appear flying out of the Eastern zone, over Soviet Russia and the Warsaw Pact nations. Flying very high and extremely fast, it was apparent that these objects were under intelligent control. Not only were they physically visible, but they were tracked by every radar installation and station in the area.

For some time the Allied forces and the Soviets believed the mysterious new type of craft to be some military breakthrough by the other side. Dean explained to us that many military personnel at that time did not have a background on UFO information: "The average guys, the tankers, infantrymen, and ground artillery crews really didn't know that much—so they got a little concerned. Only a select few of the Air Force had some inside information about UFOs."

The Deputy Supreme Allied Commander at the time was British Air Marshall Sir Thomas Pike. He was the equivalent of a five-star ranking general and was directly under Bob Dean's boss, four-star American Army Gen. Lyman Lemnitzer, who was with "SACEUR" or Supreme Allied Commander in Europe.

Sir Thomas Pike had tried repeatedly to get information from both London and Washington, D.C., on UFOs. "Every time he tried, he was completely stonewalled," Dean said, explaining that during that time there was a large French spy ring that was operating out of Paris. "London and Washington, D.C., would not let any information go out because just about anything that would be sent went directly to the KGB in Moscow—most often even before it got to us.

Air Marshall Pike decided to order an in-house (NATO/ SHAPE) study to assess the situation involving these incidents of the circular discs and related matter. The study known first as "An Assessment" was later named *The Assessment: An Evaluation of a Possible Military Threat to Allied Forces in Europe.*

"By speaking out about what I saw in the Assessment, I'm violating my National Security oath," Dean admitted. "I'm not an unpatriotic soldier by any means. I've never divulged any of my security secrets—but the implications of everything I saw in the Assessment has caused me for the past thirty-some years to wrestle seriously with my conscience until I'm at the point where I am now. I feel that not only the people in this country—but the people on the entire planet—are being lied to. And I mean that there is a *massive* cover-up.

"In this particular matter, I feel that not only does everybody have the *right* to know—but to use a military term—they have a *need to know* what is really going on. The Cold War is over now, and I think we have all heard that 'we won.' So many things have developed—and come through my own research since the Assessment—that show me that this is a deep, ongoing matter about which everyone needs to know the truth."

The knowledge that Bob Dean came by in reviewing the Assessment over and over prompted him to develop an obsession to study and research history, philosophy, religion, anthropology, archaeology—everything that might fill in the pieces and add to his understanding of the implications of UFO and extraterrestrials on our planet's and our own evolution. He has been working on his own book for over ten years now, detailing his experiences and insight. The book will be called *The Time Has Come, The Greatest Story of All Time Must Now Be Told.*

THE ASSESSMENT
AN EVALUATION OF A POSSIBLE
MILITARY THREAT
TO ALLIED FORCES IN EUROPE

The Assessment, the main document, is an inch and a half thick. The Annex, or the support information to the Assessment material, is over eight inches thick. The official report took three years to complete, and there were only fifteen copies published— one copy for each of the NATO allied countries. Dean told us that the study ended in 1964 with the following conclusions drawn by the researchers involved:

1. Our planet Earth and its inhabitants, the human race, have been under extensive, detailed, in-depth surveillance.

2. This surveillance or monitoring has been going on for a long time—for hundreds or even thousands of years—and was a possible threat to our Allied forces.

3. However, because of the high level of demonstrated technology, whoever or whatever is behind these circular, metallic discs must not be a real danger. By now, if these beings were hostile or malevolent, they could have easily destroyed us. We have virtually *no defense against their advanced technology*. We can only conclude that they must be watching or observing us.

4. There seems to be enough evidence that some kind of a procedure or process—some "plan" on the part of the aliens— seems to be developing. The sightings, landings, and abductions appear to be growing. The visitors seem to be *increasing contact with us in a gradual unfolding of a plan in which they eventually interact with Earth's inhabitants.*

A huge circular, metallic disc thirty meters wide crashed near the Baltic Sea in a little town called Timminsdorf, which was in the British zone. "The Brits put a perimeter around it and somehow figured out how to get inside the disc/craft where they found *twelve little alien bodies*," Dean told us.

"The beings were very strange looking. They were smallish

and gray in color. All of the information I have ever run across indicates that no other UFOs have ever crashed other than those manned by the little gray entities."

Continuing his account of the alien corpses, Dean said that one of the things about the autopsy report that intrigued him the most was the determination that all twelve bodies were absolutely identical. "In fact, they looked so much alike when they were lined up on the autopsy tables that one of the doctors commented that they looked as if they were cut from the same pattern," Dean said.

The autopsy report revealed that the extraterrestrial entities were apparently "living systems." Each one possessed a lung system, a heart system, a blood/circulatory system—yet they had no indication of being either male or female. There was no reproductive system.

MORE CONCLUSIONS FROM THE ASSESSMENT:
FOUR ALIEN RACES ARE VISITING THE EARTH

There are four different and separate groups of aliens visiting our planet. Those groups were classified in the following manner:

Group 1: Referred to as the "Grays," biological androids or clones;

Group 2: Humanoids or humanlike in appearance;

Group 3: Taller Grays—about six feet tall with humanlike heads, but without the big wraparound eyes;

Group 4: Reptilian in appearance—some kind of reptilian connection, but with lizardlike skin. The eyes have vertical pupils.

The researchers determined that if these four groups weren't working together, they at least seemed to be cognizant of what the other groups were doing and were aware of one another's presence.

Dean remembered that what really intrigued the generals the most was that one of the extraterrestrial species looked human.

They looked so much like we do that if one of them sat next to any one of us in a restaurant, dressed as we are, no one could ever possibly tell the difference. That fact so affected the generals that they wondered if these extraterrestrials could be walking the halls of SHAPE undetected—or anywhere else among us for that matter.

"Anyone in the military is paranoid," Dean said. "By the very nature of our work we are trained to be that way. But from then on it was difficult, if not impossible, to know when the humanoid extraterrestrial race would be involved in any activities here on Earth."

There seemed to be no accumulated knowledge in the Assessment of the place of origin of any of the four ET groups. Dean did not recall seeing any reference at all to planets, galaxies, or areas of the universe where these extraterrestrial species came from—in documents nearly a foot thick. Nor did Dean recall reviewing any kind of "official" contact or interaction between any of the alien species with any of our government officials or military officers.

The only contact-type references were of cases like the following three:

One incident that Bob Dean saw reported in the Assessment occurred in the little town of Augsburg in northern Denmark. A commotion in the barnyard over a UFO may have changed the way many in the town, including the police, thought about life—from that day on.

It had been a normal day on the farm, and the Danish farmer and his wife had been enjoying a little time to rest and replenish their energy as they ate their dinner. Suddenly they heard a commotion from the farm animals—mooing, barking, crowing, or neighing—really carrying on as if terrified by something intruding on their territory.

The farmer pushed himself away from his dinner plate and opened the door to see what in the world was going on. He was astonished to see that it was "nothing in the world," but rather a large metallic, circular craft that had landed in his pasture from some other world. The farmer described it as being so shiny and silver that it almost looked as if it were made of aluminum foil.

The Dane just stood there in his doorway in utter amazement as he watched the craft open and lower a ramp, bearing what appeared to be a human being who was smiling directly at him. The strange visitor waved a greeting and started down the ramp. The farmer heard the being ask in perfect Danish if he wanted to see the inside of the ship and go for a ride.

According to the report, Dean said that the old man had a delightful time. He was gone for about two hours or more. In the meantime his wife called the Danish police. She may have been frightened by the whole thing to begin with, but after two hours, she probably had no idea if her husband had been kidnapped or if he was ever coming back—undoubtedly she was upset.

By the time the UFO returned to the Danish farmer's field, it was greeted not only by the farmer's wife, anxiously awaiting her husband's return, but also by the Danish police and the Danish military—as well as friends and family. The reception party watched in astonishment as the UFO again opened up and let down a ramp—this time to let the farmer get off! The old man came running down the ramp, excitedly waving his arms and smiling. He had had a wonderful time.

As soon as the Danish farmer was safely away from the craft, the ramp was taken up, the UFO closed its doors and *vanished* before the entire crowd. Dean said the official report indicated that the farmer did not seem the slightest bit frightened or intimidated by the incident.

Dean told of another incident that reportedly occurred at an Italian NATO Air Base outside of LeBoerno. Just two days before Christmas 1963, a young Italian Air Force sergeant watched as a UFO just "dropped down" out of the sky, landed in front of him, and a humanlike being spoke to him in perfect Italian, asking him if he wanted to go for a ride.

Dean said that the young man was so excited, he wet his pants—and it was an extremely bitter cold day!

"There were many examples like these two cases where everyone could see the UFO," Dean said. "Yet there are many other cases where only some people see it or no one sees it, but it shows up on radar, and so on."

Dean saw that some interesting electromagnetic studies had been done in one of the annex reports of the Assessment. One such case that triggered the research was the following:

At a large NATO Allied Fighter Base in Rammstein, Germany,

a huge object came in and literally hovered over the runway. *Everyone* could see it! It also showed up clearly on radar.

Then all of a sudden, the personnel in radar said, "It's gone! We don't have it anymore!" The men out on the flight line said, "No, it's still here! *We're looking right at it!*"

Dean said the object suddenly "blinked out." It just disappeared. But at that moment the men in the radar shack shouted, "We've got it again!"

"Here's a case where the UFO was first seen *both* on radar as well as physically—hovering over the landing field. Then it was invisible on radar but visible over the field. Then it was invisible over the field, but visible on radar.

"Cases such as these have led us to believe that UFOs possess the capability to cloak themselves so they may be seen when they want to be seen—and remain invisible when they don't want to be seen."

Bob Dean told us, "These UFOs literally made fools out of us. They flew rings around us, constantly. It seems to me that with case after case of these craft being sighted and chased by our military, it was almost as if they were staged incidents just to make the point that they were so advanced that it'd be futile to combat them. Yet it seems apparent that they could have wiped us out long ago, if that was their intention. It's as if they are teasing us gradually, just to let us know they are there and what their capabilities are."

CHAPTER 10

Aliens and the Space Programs

We asked for some form of identification when our informant claimed to be a scientist employed by NASA. His broad smile indicated that he was more than eager to prove his identity, and he soon produced a variety of ID cards that appeared to be official and authentic.

In addition, he pulled out a number of photographs and, in the manner of a proud grandparent showing off pictures of his grandchildren, he pointed out that the beaming fellow posing with several of the more recognizable and well-known astronauts was, indeed, himself.

Once we had satisfied ourselves that our informant could well be exactly who he said he was, we were left with a disturbing question. Should we believe him when he claimed that he and numerous other scientists at NASA were working side by side with extraterrestrials in advancing our space program?

"Oh, yes," he insisted. "I have seen them myself. Some are tall, blond, and blue-eyed—the 'Nordics,' we call them. Others are the small ones that most of us refer to as the 'Grays.' We would never have been able to get to the Moon by 1969 if it hadn't been for the technological assistance of the extraterrestrials who are working among us at NASA."

If the shadow government did in fact make a deal with extraterrestrial intelligences (ETIs) to swap various mineral rights and the freedom to experiment on humans in exchange for advanced alien technology, then it seems to us that the ETIs have not been all that generous in assisting Earth's space program. Unless a secret group such as MJ-12 has their own covert space program operating from some hidden underground base, it would appear that the UFO intelligences have actually been rather busy harassing our space flight centers, as if it is their concerted plan to keep all Earthlings bound to the ground—or, at the very least, to keep our space program under close scrutiny.

According to author-researcher John A. Keel, "A month after the Russians sent the dog Laika into orbit in November 1957, astronomers in Venezuela photographed not only Sputnik II but another unexplained object which was closely following it."

On January 10, 1961, a UFO suddenly appeared from nowhere and took after a Polaris rocket launched from Cape Kennedy. The space center's radar station locked on to the object by mistake and clearly plotted its mysterious course.

The United States' first astronaut, Col. John Glenn, was quoted as saying that he believed "certain reports of flying saucers to be legitimate." On his historic mission on February 20, 1962, Glenn radioed to all of Earth his eerie description of the thousands of greenish-yellow "fireflies" that had approached his space capsule.

While lecturing at a conference in Washington on May 11, 1962, the famous X-15 pilot Joe Walker said that he had recently photographed UFOs while he was in flight. Walker described the five or six objects as cylindrical or discoidal and reported that he had photographed similar objects on a previous flight. *Le Matin* of Paris quoted the pilot as admitting that it was one of his assignments to detect UFOs.

A few months later, on July 17, 1962, Maj. Robert White was flying the X-15 at an altitude of 314,750 feet when he sighted a gray-white object that suddenly appeared alongside his craft and began to pace him. White was astonished when the UFO shot out of sight, for his X-15 was doing 3,832 miles per hour at the time.

The control tower heard Major White shouting excitedly into his radio: "There are things out there! There absolutely are!"

During his fourth pass over Hawaii on May 15, 1963, astronaut Gordon Cooper's transmissions to Ground Control were abruptly interrupted by an "unintelligible foreign language."

NASA officials were both angered and baffled by the unidentified "someone" who had the technology to cut in on the VHF channel reserved for space missions. Language experts were unable to categorize the speech patterns into any known dialect or to derive any sense from the message that NASA technicians had recorded.

It was on that same mission in May 1963 that astronaut Cooper sighted a glowing greenish disc with a red tail closing in on his space capsule.

"He was passing over Australia at the time," recalled John A. Keel. "Personnel at the Muchea Tracking Station scurried outside to take a look. Over two hundred persons clearly saw the object, which was apparently much bigger than Cooper's little space capsule. His description of it was broadcast worldwide on radio and television, but when he returned to the ground he refused to discuss it."

In a later interview astronaut Cooper commented: "As far as I am concerned, there have been too many unexplained examples of UFO sightings around Earth for us to rule out the possibilities that some form of life exists out there beyond our own world."

Four UFOs locked in on an unmanned Gemini capsule on April 8, 1964, and paced it for one complete orbit around the planet.

On December 5, 1964, at 11:06 P.M., just a little more than a week after NASA had launched Mariner IV, UFOs were spotted over Cape Kennedy.

* * *

A month later, on January 5, 1965, the $30,000,000 radar system at Eglin Air Force Base—at that time the only one of its kind in operation—was destroyed by a "mysterious fire" that burned out of control late at night. The unique radar system, constructed by Bendix and turned over to the Air Force on trial, provided an "eye on space" that could have been used to detect, track, and identify objects coming in from outer space. The primary function of the costly radar system was to view all orbiting bodies at least twice a day and to detect UFOs.

The world was amazed on October 12, 1964, when the large Soviet spacecraft Voskhod I, with its three-man crew, came back to earth in Central Asia after only sixteen orbits and twenty-four hours aloft. The Soviet press had boldly proclaimed that the spacecraft would be engaged in a "prolonged flight." What, then, had brought about an abrupt end to the flight of the Voskhod I?

The official word from Moscow was enigmatic. The cosmonauts were quoted as stating that they greatly regretted being brought down so soon, because they had seen "many interesting things and wanted to investigate them more fully."

What may have been the truth was printed in an account in a German newspaper. The author, S. R. Oilinger, claimed that his Moscow sources told him that Voskhod I "was repeatedly overtaken by extremely fast-flying discs which struck the craft violently, shattering blows with their powerful magnetic fields."

On March 18, 1965, Lt. Col. Alexi Leonov stepped from Voskhod II to become the first man from Earth to "walk" in space. Then, for several hours, the Soviet spaceship lost all contact with its control stations on the ground.

Later the downed Voskhod II was found in deep snow near Perm, 873 miles northwest of the area where the cosmonauts had been scheduled to land. The world press carried stories of the spacecraft hurtling toward earth enveloped in flames, its outside antennae burned off, its two-man crew barely escaping with their lives.

A carefully controlled press conference was held with the cosmonauts on March 27. They persistently avoided questions asking them to confirm reports that they had been harassed by a UFO. They admitted having sighted "an unmanned satellite" about a half mile from their spacecraft at 5:12 A.M. on March 19. They also admitted that they had not been able to identify the object and that it had seemingly appeared shortly before they lost contact with their control stations.

UFO investigator John A. Keel recalled the June 1965 flight of U.S. astronauts James McDivitt and Edward White: "They sighted what they termed 'a mysterious object in space' as they orbited over China. Millions heard them describe it live on radio and TV. McDivitt and White reported it as 'a glowing, egg-shaped thing with arms or projections sticking out of it.'"

Keel went on to say that the two astronauts had also reported another UFO over Hawaii during the same mission. Later McDivitt had commented to the press: "I don't know what it was— and so far no one else does either."

At an October 5, 1965, press conference in Dallas, McDivitt confirmed that he and his crewmen had sighted three UFOs on their June 5 orbital flight—and that he had photographed one of them. Later a NASA spokesperson stated that the object remained unidentified.

"They [UFOs] are there without a doubt," McDivitt stated. "But what they are is anybody's guess."

"Astronauts such as McDivitt and others may have been guessing about the true identity of the UFOs," our informant—who claimed to have been a NASA scientist—stated with a broad smile that bordered on arrogance. "But those few of us privy to the machinations of MJ-12 and the deal made with the aliens knew exactly what the astronauts were seeing up there.

"I must admit, however, that many of us were more than a little irritated by some of the maneuvers and what seemed to be deliberate interference by the aliens in our space program," he continued. "After all, they were supposed to help conquer space so that we could join them on a more-or-less equal footing. Sometimes it really seemed as though the ETs actually wanted to keep us earthbound.

"It was true that they had given us a lot of help with the propulsion system and some of the metal alloys during the early days of the space program, but then they started to get stingy with the technology that they were supposed to be sharing with us."

When astronauts James Lovell and Frank Bormann were orbiting aboard GT-7 on December 4, 1965, a massive spherical object slowly crossed in front of them.

When Bormann radioed ground control that they had a "bogey" at ten o'clock high, control technicians suggested that the astronauts might be sighting their booster rocket.

"We know where the booster is," Bormann said coolly. "This is an actual sighting."

On August 26, 1966, B. F. Funk, an aerospace engineer employed at the Huntsville, Alabama, Aero-Astrodynamics Laboratory of the Marshall Space Flight Center, spotted a formation of UFOs near Fort Payne. En route with his wife from Atlanta, Georgia, to Huntsville, Funk spotted the bright objects approaching, with one of the UFOs moving back and forth inside the triangle formed by the other three.

The aerospace engineer reported that the UFOs changed in color from white to orange, were moving at a fantastic rate of speed, and made absolutely no sound as they made a sweeping turn and passed out of sight. Since he was not a layman who had to make a "guess," Funk said that according to his mathematical calculations, the objects were flying at an altitude of 3,000 feet and that they were thirty feet in diameter.

Funk told the *Huntsville News* that he "knew very well what they [the objects] were. They were no ethnical aircraft."

* * *

On June 23, 1966, Julian Sandoval, a flight engineer associated with the Apollo Space Project, sighted a UFO in northwestern New Mexico. Sandoval stated that the object appeared to be suspended above Placitas, a small town north of Albuquerque. He estimated the UFO's length at about 300 feet and said that it disappeared after it increased its speed to a high velocity.

During the Gemini 10 space flight in July 1966, astronauts Collins and Young reported UFOs that were summarily identified and dismissed as fragments of an earlier vehicle's second stage. Later during the same space mission, Collins sighted another UFO over Australia that was moving north to south. NASA officials were unable to identify the object and no further comment was made.

On Wallops Island, Virginia, on September 23, 1966, a space experiment sent a huge multicolored cloud hundreds of miles across the sky. As if the colored cloud had been a red flag waved before a group of angry bulls, the skies were suddenly filled with UFOs from Virginia to Chicago. In the Windy City four pilots at O'Hare International Airport filed a report with the control tower.

On June 7, 1968, when we talked with Lee Katchen, an atmospheric physicist with NASA—who was careful to emphasize that he was speaking as a private citizen—he stated that on the basis of the 7,000 reports that he had examined, he believed UFOs to be extraterrestrial probes.

"UFO sightings are now [1968] so common, the military doesn't have time to worry about them—so they screen them out," Katchen said. "The major defense systems have UFO filters built into them, and when a UFO appears, they simply ignore it."

When asked for specifics, Katchen particularly singled out the radar network employed by SAGE (semiautomatic ground environmental system), the North American tactical air defense system, which tracks all aircraft flights. "The filters cut out all unconventional objects or targets and make no record of UFOs," he said.

"Unconventional targets are ignored, because, apparently, we are interested only in Russian targets, possible enemy targets. Something that hovers in the air, then shoots off at 5,000 miles per hour, doesn't interest us because it can't be the enemy," he said. Katchen added that the only system left that was doing any recording of UFOs was our space tracking system.

"UFOs are picked up by ground and air radar, and they have been photographed by gun cameras all along," he stated. "There are so many UFOs in the sky that the Air Force has had to employ the special radar network to screen them out."

Dr. Vladimir Azhazha, Professor Alexandr Kazantsev, and Dr. Sergei Bozhich, three Russian scientists, insist that Soviet intelligence monitoring the historic Moon landing of the Apollo 11 lunar module on July 20, 1969, revealed that alien spaceships were present to observe the U.S. space mission firsthand.

According to Soviet intelligence reports, Neil Armstrong relayed the message to Mission Control in Houston that two large UFOs were watching the module land on the lunar surface. Buzz Aldrin took pictures of the UFOs from inside the module to support Armstrong's verbal report.

The UFOs set down near the lunar module, but flew away just minutes before Armstrong emerged from the craft on July 21 to make his history-making comment: "one small step for man . . . one giant step for mankind."

The three Russian scientists charge that NASA censored Armstrong's verbal report of the two UFOs on the Moon's surface and immediately placed Aldrin's motion picture film in a top-secret repository after the astronauts returned to Earth on July 24.

Dr. Bozhich said that he was of the opinion that the two alien ships that monitored Armstrong, Aldrin, and Michael Collins were there as a backup, in case something should go wrong with the U.S. Moon landing.

Maurice Chatelain, a former consultant to NASA, has gone

Capt. Edward J. Ruppelt, head of the USAF's Project Bluebook from 1951 to 1953, related an account of the sighting on April 24, 1949, when Commander R. B. McLaughlin, USN, and his crew were preparing to launch a Skyhook research balloon at the White Sands Missile Range in New Mexico.

Suddenly their tracking telescope caught the image of an elliptical object moving at fantastic speeds across its field of view. Computations showed that the object was fifty-six miles high and traveling at a velocity of seven miles per second, which translates to 18,000 miles per hour, i.e., orbital speed—eight years before Sputnik 1.

In July 1952 the Pentagon had become so shaken over the UFO invasion of Washington, D.C., which set off a Red Alert, that a systematic sky search by telescope and camera was ordered and placed under the direction of Dr. Clyde Tombaugh, the famous astronomer who had discovered the planet Pluto. The avowed purpose of Project Skysweep was to search for tiny *natural* satellites of Earth that might be used as platforms in a future space program. At the same time Skysweep personnel were advised to keep an eye out for UFOs.

According to the late science writer Otto O. Binder, "Sometime in 1953 it leaked out that two unknowns had been spied far out in space, circling Earth. They were called 'moonlets' as if they were natural satellites of our planet, but other astronomers failed to verify any such permanent and age-old bodies.

"This discovery really put the Pentagon in a corner, and they never officially admitted that two non-natural satellites had been observed for a short period of time. The mere fact that the unknown satellites later disappeared proved they had moved out of orbit and were therefore powered craft."

In the fall of 1956, almost exactly one year before the Soviet launching of Sputnik 1, one of the engineers at a major electronics firm in Cedar Rapids, Iowa, called our friend Fay Clark and asked if he might bring a tape to Clark's home that had been recorded the night before.

"It appears that they were having their scanning devices going to see if they could pick up any signals from outer space," Fay recalled. "While they were tuned in, a voice started talking that appeared to be emanating from an indeterminate point thousands of miles away from Earth. As I understood the engineer, it would have been impossible for this voice to have originated from our own planet, but it had talked on for nearly two hours.

"The voice appeared to be sexless. It sounded almost mechanical. The material that it was relaying was very high level, very worthwhile. From time to time it sounded like something one expects to find in the *Upanishads*, the biblical book of Proverbs, perhaps Kahlil Gibran's *The Prophet* . . . good material that one might term universal truths." [Fay, who has since passed away, was considered an authority on spiritual and metaphysical matters, and was the owner of Hiawatha Publishing.]

"A few nights later I once again received a call from the electronics firm," Fay said. "The engineer told me the voice was back and said that I should look at approximately 'two o'clock' in the north sky. I saw the object, and it appeared to be about one-third the size of the Moon.

"The object would move across the horizon, stop, remain stationary for a bit, then drop down a little lower, back up rapidly, and move once again across the horizon. It repeated this back and forth process six times before it accelerated and moved out of sight.

"The next morning the radio and papers said that the night before 'an erratic meteor' had caused thousands of telephone problems," Fay concluded his account. "The Cedar Rapids electronics firm had a track on it—and so did stations in Omaha and Davenport. Apparently, as far as they were able to determine, the 'erratic meteor' was about 3,000 miles distant from Earth.

"What they did not publish, of course, was that the 'erratic meteor' was also a talking, metaphysical meteor."

In late July 1957, three months before the Soviet launching of Sputnik 1, Italian astronomers tracked a huge mystery satellite orbiting Earth. Other sources corroborated the astronomers' discovery, and there were even reports of naked-eye sightings of the large object—which was seen to move across the sky in a steady fashion, a pattern that the world would soon come to associate with an orbiting satellite. The satellite disappeared from its orbit of Earth just a few days before Sputnik 1 became our planet's first official satellite.

The *London Times* for November 7, 1957, carried the story of four astronomers at the Commonwealth Observatory near Canberra, Australia, who had been visually tracking both Sputnik 1 and the recently launched Sputnik 2 across the sky when a *third* object suddenly came into the view of their telescopes. The unknown aerial vehicle was a vivid pink and remained in view for two minutes while it seemed to be trailing the Soviet satellites.

"Since the two Russian satellites were the only known vehicles in orbit in 1957 [America's first satellite went up in early 1958] and since both Sputniks had passed by, it could not be argued that the Australian astronomers had mistaken one of the Soviet satellites for the mystery object," Otto O. Binder said. "It was a genuine unknown, for which the U.S. Air Force already had a pigeonhole waiting, labeled 'deny, damn, and deride.' "

Binder stated that the authorities could hardly deny the mystery satellite spotted in late 1959 and 1960, because the Navy tracked it with their SPASUR (space surveillance) radars, which had often assisted NASA in monitoring Earth-launched satellites.

"The most sensational aspect of this unknown satellite was its polar orbit, which neither Russia nor the United States had thus far used in its space program," Binder said. "A big public furor resulted, and the Pentagon was forced to explain the unknown away by stating that they had somehow lost track of the capsule of Discover-5 and it had somehow shifted its orbit to cross directly over the poles.

"There was one big problem with the Pentagon's fairy tale," Binder stated. "On August 23, 1960, a tracking camera of the Grumman Aircraft Company at Bethpage, Long Island, had obtained definitive photos of the mystery satellite and estimated its weight as at least *fifteen tons*. The Discover-5 capsule weighed 1,200 pounds.

"Furthermore, in August 1960, there were only eleven small U.S. satellites in orbit, plus one Soviet satellite remaining out of those that had deorbited. None of ours weighed more than 1,700 pounds. The Soviet vehicle weighed 2,925 pounds. Nothing so huge as the fifteen-ton mystery satellite would come along from either the U.S. or Russian camps for several more years.''

Later in 1960 three mystery objects were tracked not only by NASA's Spacetrack system at Goddard Spaceflight Center, but also by NORAD, the antimissile defense radar network established by the Pentagon with central headquarters at Offutt Air Force Base in Nebraska. As fate would have it, it was a leak through NORAD that led journalists to the story and forced NASA to confess that it had also tracked the unknown objects.

Quick to cover its suddenly exposed backside, NASA insisted that two of the mystery satellites were just bits and pieces of space debris, parts of broken-up satellites and launchers. Only one of the three objects, they maintained, was a respectable size, perhaps comparable to Telstar.

Other data leaks from NORAD indicated that the authorities were once again playing cover-up—and that all three of the unknowns were mammoth.

And since the three mystery satellites remained in orbit, the International Satellite Authority [centered in France], which grants official designations to all satellites launched by any nation on Earth, had no choice other than to add the three unknowns to their list and provide them with catalog numbers.

In 1974 British astronomer Duncan Lunan startled both academic and lay communities when he announced that he had deciphered a message that had been sent to Earth by entities from another solar system. What is more, Lunan made his startling claim in *Space Flight*, the journal of the prestigious British Interplanetary Society.

Lunan's theory postulated that an unmanned "probe" robot satellite, which was placed in orbit around our Moon between 13,000 and 15,000 years ago, has been transmitting a particular message at intermittent periods since the 1920s. According to the British astronomer, the satellite had been placed near Earth by dwellers of a planet orbiting a star called Upsilon Bootes in another solar system. Lunan translated the message as follows:

> Start here. Our home is Upsilon Bootes, which is a double star. We live on the sixth planet of seven, counting outward from the sun, which is the larger of the two. Our sixth planet has one moon. Our fourth planet has three. Our first and third planets each have one. Our probe is in the position of Arcturus, known in our maps.

The executive secretary of the British Interplanetary Society, Leonard Carter, said that Upsilon Bootes is about 103 million light-years from Earth. The robot probe referred to in the message is only about 170,000 miles from Earth, near the Moon, and was placed in orbit about 11,000 B.C.

"Lunan plotted the echoes on a graph," Carter explained. "Oddly, they seemed to make up a series of dots outlining the known constellations, but they were slightly distorted. However, Lunan has gone into the question of this distortion and alteration. And the dots related to the constellations as they were about 13,000 years ago."

Professor Ronald N. Bracewell, one of the leading radio-astronomers in the United States said that in spite of certain reservations regarding Lunan's interpretation of the signals, he would not discount them altogether. In fact, he advocated a similar theory to explain radio echoes noted in 1927, 1928, and 1934.

During the Apollo 7 flight in October 1968, the astronauts were treated to an unscheduled musical program that featured a wide variety of selections, including "Where Angels Fear to Tread."

For the invasion of the astronauts' airspace to have been a hoax of questionable taste would seem to be a complete impossibility. The frequencies used to communicate with the Apollo 7 mission were in the S-Band, which is located around 2,000 megacycles—far away from any terrestrial radio station's standard AM and FM broadcasting bands. In addition, the receivers on the Apollo were too sensitive to receive random signals, and the reflecting layers of the ionosphere would have blocked such signals from ever reaching the spacecraft in the first place.

Although there are some very talented HAM radio operators out there, the cost to any individual or group of radio hobbyists amassing the high-tech sophisticated equipment would be astronomically prohibitive. Some specialist at NASA figured out that to have jammed the astronauts' frequency with a bizarre selection of music would have required a worldwide tracking system, a fifty-foot moveable dish antenna, the combined knowledge of a few PhDs, and the budget of the average billionaire—if he could have managed to get long-term financing.

On the other hand, certain candidates come to mind who would have been able to pull off a little joke on the U.S. space program with relative ease:

1. A secret society that has been collecting wealth for thousands of years;

2. A clandestine agency within a major government with the ability to siphon unlimited funds from the national treasury;

3. A technology developed thousands of years in advance of our terrestrial science that could do whatever it pleased.

On Friday evening, November 14, 1969, observatories all over Europe sighted two bright, flashing UFOs near the path of Apollo 12, which had been launched to place the United States' second team of astronauts on the Moon. As startled astronomers watched through huge telescopes, one UFO appeared to be following the U.S. spacecraft, while the other moved in front of it. On Saturday, November 15, astronauts Pete Conrad, Dick Gordon, and Allan Bean reported to Mission Control in Houston that they had spotted two bogeys tagging along with them 132,000 miles out.

After exchanging several theories back and forth between the spacecraft and Mission Control, "no definite agreement" could be reached concerning "what the crew might have sighted."

"With ground-elapsed time at only thirty-six hours, forty minutes into the flight, the Apollo team had been jolted from what had been scheduled as a 'matter-of-fact' flight," experienced UFO researcher Timothy Green Beckley stated. "Far from being routine, this was to be one of the most bizarre—as well as scientifically revealing—expeditions to date.

"Several times, as the craft sped toward the lunar surface, scientists monitoring the 'chatter' of the command module were stunned to hear unexplainable sounds that were not emanating either from the ground or from the capsule itself. At one point it was suggested that the astronauts 'must be talking to somebody strange now.' "

At 6:45 A.M. on Wednesday, November 19, in the midst of the astronauts' limbering-up exercises on the surface of the Moon, Conrad and Bean told Ground Control that they were receiving weird background noises.

Bean: I keep hearing a whistle.

Conrad: That's what I hear, okay.

Ten minutes later Dick Gordon in the mother ship orbiting the Moon reported to Houston that he kept hearing a constant beeping sound in the background.

Houston, Mission Control: That's affirmative. We've heard it now for about the past forty-five minutes.

Gordon: That's right, so have we. What is it?

Ground Control admitted that it was unable to isolate the source of the mysterious beeping sounds.

In his analysis of the bizarre occurrences during the Apollo 12 Moon landing, Timothy Green Beckley noted that the space-traveling trio had an eerie ending to their ten-day mission.

"As they passed over India at 1 1:47 A.M. on November 24, the spokesman for Apollo 12 reported in a startled voice that they were all watching a bright red object flashing brilliantly against the Earth," Beckley said.

Apollo 12: Looks like it's coming just about out of the center of . . . I would say down from Burma and east of India. . . . I can't imagine what this is.

Mission Control, Houston: We can't either. We're checking the possibilities.

Apollo 12: It's a steady light, and it appears in size to be as big as any of the thunderstorms flashing. . . . It's hard to tell if it is exactly in the center of Earth or not. It's pretty close to being right in the center . . .

* * *

At 11:57 A.M., ten minutes later, Ground Control asked if the bright light was still visible. The astronauts replied that the UFO had disappeared as they continued toward splashdown.

Author-researcher-publisher Beckley agrees that if the ETIs have been assisting the shadow government in perfecting Earth's leap into outer space, they have sometimes been rather callous in flaunting their continued superiority.

"In May 1961 word reached us that two Russian cosmonauts— a male and a female—had lost their lives in space," Beckley said. "They had been launched together in one capsule from Baikonur, near the Aral Sea. Tracking stations in non-Communist nations intercepted and recorded their conversation. Remember the terrible connotations of their last transmission?"

Beckley explained how the cosmonauts desperately radioed Ground Control that they were inexplicably losing control of their capsule. Their last message reads as follows:

The situation becomes critical for us. Something went wrong. We are changing our course. . . . I am talking to the director, do you understand?

If we do not get out . . . the world will not learn of it. . . . You will know what to do. What? What? Here! Here there is something! There is something . . .

"In replaying the taped conversation, one can feel first the excitement and then the shock of the two cosmonauts in their tight quarters," Beckley said. "Those were their last words. Contact was lost at 8 P.M. Moscow time. Was the brave Russian team victim of a close approach of a UFO?

"Indeed, as we stand poised on the threshold of interplanetary travel, we may be thwarted in our attempts by cosmonauts from some far-off world," Beckley stated. "An avalanche of evidence from the earliest days of our space program to today's NASA missions demonstrates that we may well be in the midst of a grand interplanetary espionage game!"

CHAPTER 11

The Sinister UFO Silencers: Air Force, Aliens, or Unknown Agency?

The Air Force got into hot water with civilian UFO researchers from almost the beginning of the modern era of flying saucers in the late 1940s. On numerous occasions, by the time UFO investigators were able to arrive on the scene of a particularly good sighting—perhaps even one in which the object was seen on the ground—they would find that the witnesses had already been silenced by men who claimed to be Air Force personnel or members of some government agency. In certain instances the witnesses stated that they had been threatened, even roughed up, by alleged agents of the U.S. government.

And then the UFO researchers themselves began to complain that sinister voices had whispered threats over their own telephones, issuing stern warnings to stop their investigations immediately.

Photos of UFOs were confiscated. Debris left behind at UFO landing sites was appropriated. Dramatic accounts of interaction with UFO occupants were silenced. Angry civilians began to complain that the United States was not Nazi Germany or Communist Russia. Military personnel simply could not come into the homes of private citizens, confiscate their personal property and leave them in fear for their physical well-being.

It has never been within the line of duty of any government agency to threaten private citizens or to enter their homes without a search warrant. And no government agency is empowered to demand the surrender of private property by any law-abiding citizen.

When the hue and cry reached such proportions that the complaints against Air Force strong-arm tactics could no longer be ignored, Col. George P. Freeman, Pentagon spokesman for Project Bluebook, issued a formal statement that his office had checked a number of cases in which civilians claimed to have been threatened after their UFO sighting. Their research indicated that "these men are not connected with the Air Force in any way."

Colonel Freeman stated that by posing as Air Force officers or as government agents, the UFO silencers—whomever they might be—were committing a federal offense.

Colonel Freeman's official denial had barely been uttered when four bogus Air Force officers assembled the police officers and the civilians who had witnessed heavy UFO activity over the reservoir in Wanaque, New Jersey. Sternly, in no uncertain terms, the people of Wanaque were told that they "hadn't seen a thing," and they were admonished not to discuss their claims of UFO sightings with anyone.

The prototype of what has come to be known in UFO research as the men-in-black (MIB) phenomenon began with the alleged silencing of Albert K. Bender in September 1953. According to the late Gray Barker, who wrote *They Knew Too Much About Flying Saucers* about the case in 1962, Bender had received data convincing him that he had been given remarkable insights into the truth about the origin of flying saucers. He set down his thesis on paper, then sent the report off to a trusted friend. When three men appeared at his door, one of them supposedly held that letter in his hand.

Bender later told his friends that the three men were "pretty rough with him." He was informed that if people were to learn the actual truth about flying saucers, there would be dramatic changes in all things. Science, especially, would suffer a major blow. Political structures would topple. Mass confusion would reign.

In June 1967 two of Bender's closest friends, Dominick Lucchesi and August C. Roberts, told us that Bender had seemed to be a changed man after the three MIB had visited him. "He was scared, and he later suffered from tremendous headaches which he said were controlled by 'them.' Whenever he would think of breaking his silence, one of these terrific headaches would just about knock him out."

Roberts said that Bender dropped all UFO research and went underground, though they knew he was living under another name and managing a motel somewhere in California.

In Lucchesi's opinion the MIB did not come from any known government bureau. "I believe these men and the UFOs come from a civilization that has flourished in secret in some remote area of Earth, such as the Amazon, the North Gobi Desert, or the Himalaya Mountains. It is possible that these are underground civilizations."

Experienced UFO researcher John A. Keel set forth his opinion that the MIB were "the intelligence arm of a large and possibly hostile group." Keel said that he considered the UFO silencers to be professional terrorists assigned the mission of harassing UFO researchers who became too involved in investigations that might reveal too much of the truth.

Keel said that in his own research he had uncovered some extreme cases of personal abuse in which certain UFO contactees and/or UFO investigators had been kidnapped by three men in a black car. "For some reason," Keel noted, "it is almost always *three* men" who subject their victim to some sort of brainwashing that leaves him or her in a state of nausea, mental confusion, or even amnesia—which may last for several days.

When we gathered for the 1967 Congress of Scientific UFOlogists in the old Commodore Hotel in New York City, Keel told of his personal mission to track down the silencers. He said that dark-complexioned mystery men had sometimes silenced saucer sighters even *before* the witnesses had had time to report their sightings. On occasion, Keel said, he had arrived on the scene within moments after the mysterious silencers had departed.

Keel warned that the intelligence behind the UFO controversy did not want people to know their place of origin: "They have been lying to contactees since 1897!" he said, explaining that the first MIB may have appeared in Texas during the airship sightings of 1897. According to newspaper accounts, some "pottery" had fallen from one of the mysterious airships. The next day a dark-suited man of "Oriental complexion" arrived in town and bought up the strange fragments.

On the morning of June 14, 1968. a man representing himself as Air Force Maj. Smedley, a special investigator, called upon Tom, a civilian UFO researcher in Jamestown, New York, and quizzed him about any information he might have acquired from two police officers who had reported a UFO landing outside of Buffalo on June 12.

Tom told us that Major Smedley spoke with a peculiar accent and, strangely enough, did not drive an automobile. After the major left, Tom suffered from an acute headache and could remember nothing of their conversation for about five minutes.

A later check with local Air Force authorities revealed that there was no Major Smedley working out of Jamestown. A more complete inquiry with Air Force Personnel in Boston determined that the U.S. Air Force listed no Major Smedley on their records.

Interestingly the ubiquitous Major Smedley surfaced again in Pennsylvania, alone, on foot, to interrogate a UFO researcher about a case he was investigating. After the bogus officer had left, the UFOlogist became violently ill and had to be confined to his bed for two weeks.

About the same time that Major Smedley was harassing UFO researchers, another bogus Air Force officer, who called himself Captain Munroe, had begun his own campaign of torment in the Pittsburgh area. But the UFO Research Institute of Pittsburgh had an authentic major—Joseph Jenkins, retired—to set on his trail.

Captain Munroe first threatened two youths who had taken a number of pictures of a UFO over Pittsburgh with a Polaroid camera. One of the boys was told by Captain Munroe of the U.S. Air Force that he had better keep his mouth shut about the photographs or "something unpleasant would happen to him." This threat was followed up by another menacing telephone conversation.

* * *

Major Jenkins said that a UFO researcher named Frank was in the midst of an interesting investigation when a series of telephone calls so intimidated him that he dropped "the whole UFO business." According to Jenkins:

"Frank had a visit by three men dressed in black suits that reminded him of the quilted uniforms used by the North Koreans during the Korean War. The three men spoke to him in a strange manner, seemingly out of breath, and never directly mentioned the subject of UFOs. They made very intimidating remarks, referred to some items of his that had recently been stolen, and warned that next time it wouldn't be his 'tangible assets' that would be taken.

"Frank did have the foresight to copy down the license number of their car, but in checking it out found that the number did not exist in the state's files."

Major Jenkins repeated the details of another case in which a man who had taken eleven minutes of color film of a UFO over Vietnam promised to give his fellow researchers in the Pittsburgh area a screening of the object. Prior to his showing the film to Jenkins and others, he received a visit from three men who identified themselves as having come from the Department of Internal Security. These men insisted that the film be turned over to them—which the owner of the footage refused to do unless the men could produce a search warrant. Confused by his adamant denial of their demands, they quickly left. The photographer saw that their automobile had Washington, D.C., plates, but an attempt to further identify the strange visitors met with no success.

The late Ray Palmer, editor of *Flying Saucers* magazine, was one of the most prominent figures on the UFO scene for nearly thirty years. A boy-wonder editor of pulp magazines in the 1940s, Ray had edited numerous periodicals, including *Amazing Stories,* the science-fiction classic, for Ziff-Davis. Cofounder with Curtis Fuller of the unique journal, *Fate,* Palmer ran so many articles and covers on flying saucers that an irritated Air Force officer once accused him of having invented the UFO controversy to sell magazines.

Palmer—who stood four feet, eight inches tall—grew weary of "true believers" gasping upon their first encounter with the UFO maven that he must really be from Mars. His lack of height was due to a crippling childhood accident, not to environmental conditions on some other planet.

During one of our visits with Palmer, he said that he would never have gone further in exploring the flying saucer controversy if the Air Force had not interfered with a special issue of *Amazing Stories* that he had planned in 1948.

"But then they stepped in and tried to halt publication of the magazine," he told us. "That's where they made their first mistake. They convinced me that there really was something to this fantastic story. We had the magazine all ready to go, when Mr. Ziff, the boss, came into my office and told me to kill the issue. Later I saw him talking to seven or eight Air Force men, one a colonel. It was my first experience with military silencing."

Shortly after Kenneth Arnold had made his historic sighting of flying saucers near Mt. Ranier in 1947, Palmer collaborated with the pilot in authoring *The Coming of the Saucers,* the original flying saucer book.

"Almost immediately after the book was released," Palmer said, "Arnold and I were each visited by representatives of the Internal Revenue Service and told that we each owed the government $1,800. There was no room for appeal on our part; we just had to pay the money. Undeclared revenue? No—just their way of letting us know they were unhappy with us."

In later years Palmer claimed regular visits from nearly every known branch of government intelligence. He was accused of printing pornography along with his publications *Search, Space World,* and *Rocket Exchange.* Once he was even investigated for using his presses to print counterfeit money.

Ray Palmer did not hesitate to express his opinion that the Central Intelligence Agency had financed a good many of "the more ridiculous aspects of flying saucers.

"This has been an important part of their plan to discredit serious UFO research," he said. "If the CIA were able to establish UFO investigators as akin to cultists and kooks, then all flying saucer researchers would be guilty by association. The crazier a

UFO contactee [one who claims a direct interaction with a UFO and its occupants] may appear to the general public, the more likely is he to be having his bills picked up by the CIA."

Palmer believed that the Air Force and the government were suppressing knowledge about UFOs, because "the one inescapable fact of history is that the people who are in control want to stay in control."

Although he did not hesitate to declare his belief that there was a "basic reality" behind the UFO controversy, Palmer speculated that the phenomenon might somehow connect with "something within each of us. Perhaps"—he continued his speculation—"those who harnessed this power in the past became the 'masters' who could control time, space, and physical matter."

Palmer may have kept an open mind about all aspects of the UFO phenomenon, but he admitted that he was personally convinced that the answer to the controversy was to be found on our own planet, rather than in outer space: "The supposition that the saucers have an Earth base and may be manned by an older terrestrial race brings the cosmic concept down to reality," he said. "Geographically speaking, our own atmosphere is a heck of lot closer than Alpha Centuri!

"I don't discount the reality of underground cities," he stated. "I do not deny the possible existence of underground cultures. One can find reference to them in the most primitive oral traditions—right up to contemporary accounts.

"Where *do* the flying saucers come from?" Palmer shrugged in response to our direct question. "*What* are they? Well, I'm convinced that they are not 'spaceships' in the literal sense of being craft from some other world. Perhaps they belong in the realm of psychic phenomena. But whatever they are, they must be investigated."

When respected UFO researcher Hayden Hewes and his International UFO Bureau sponsored a symposium on flying saucers in Oklahoma City in 1973, one of his featured speakers, a noted lecturer in the field, became very quiet after he received a telephone call.

"In a few minutes, a long black limo pulled up in front of

our office and two men wearing dark sunglasses and dressed completely in black came to the door and picked up our featured speaker," Hewes said. "The two guys looked like the Blues Brothers in their dark suits and shades. Anyway, they drove off with our speaker, returned him after a couple of hours, but he never said one word regarding where he went or with whom.

"I don't know if they told him what he could or could not say. I don't know if he was one of *them,*" Hewes commented. "I just know that I physically saw them and their limo—and our speaker never said one word to me what it had all been about."

About that same time the International UFO Bureau published two booklets authored by Hewes and illustrated by Hal Crawford—*The Aliens* and *The Intruders*—which graphically depicted alien types and UFO shapes.

"Shortly after publication I received a visit from a man identifying himself as an officer in Naval Intelligence," Hewes said. "He showed me several UFO photographs of the type that I called 'the fuzzies' Pictures of flying saucers fluctuating, as if they were materializing in some kind of force field. You know, like on *Star Trek,* when they are 'beaming up' but haven't quite reached solid form.

"The officer told me, 'We know what these UFOs are, and we don't want you to give them any publicity.'

"I showed him several photos in my own files," Hewes said, "and he quietly acknowledged them. Then he repeated his request, 'Don't give the kind of UFOs in the pictures that I showed you any notoriety, any publicity of any kind whatsoever. We have no problems with your publishing any of the other UFO photographs in your files.'"

Hewes said that the approximately two-hour conversation was very low key. "There were no threats of any kind. I don't know if those were government UFOs or alien craft that they had identified. I do know that such photographs of that kind of 'fuzzy' UFO never crossed my desk."

Author-researcher John W. White, who has investigated the UFO phenomenon from a wide variety of approaches and disciplines also sponsors an annual UFO conference in Connecticut.

In his view the sinister silencers, the MIB, have generated a number of pretty wild reports. White speculates that if the MIB do exist in physical reality, "they may be alien in nature." Pointing out that the silencers work with remarkable speed and efficiency, "it seems that their knowledge is too precise. To get to witnesses as quickly as they do, they have to have been in on the UFO sightings in the first place.

"Also, the MIB are pretty uniformly described as rather short, somewhat Oriental in appearance, and so forth. Perhaps they are entities resulting from crossbreeding between humans and some alien species. There is also an aspect of the MIB that borders on the metaphysical and the supernatural."

Timothy Green Beckley has been pursuing the UFO enigma for thirty-six of his forty-six years. In 1957 at the age of ten, he and his family and neighbors had a dramatic UFO sighting in New Jersey, and Tim wrote to the local newspaper to protest the official analysis of the flying saucer as a weather balloon. By the age of fourteen, he was publishing his own newsletter and making media appearances.

"We have to entertain the possibility that some of these MIB reports are of overzealous CIA operatives," Beckley said. "The Central Intelligence Agency is made up of thousands of individual and independent agents. Within the blanket of the agency are darker, more secretive groups. And there are individual rogue agents, no longer under anyone's control.

"Some of these agents may be going after UFO artifacts a little too aggressively because they happen to be UFO buffs. You know, like passionate art collectors or dealers, they may simply be grabbing up some of the flying saucer memorabilia for themselves."

Beckley has also wondered if some of the MIB might not be representatives of big business or organized religion. "If the complete UFO story should ever be totally revealed, it would have a tremendous impact on all of our civilization—our political structures, religions, business methods. Our social strata and our world would change. And there will always be those who wish to preserve the status quo at all costs."

* * *

Just exactly who comprises the "silence group" that seems so determined to make a sinister battleground of UFO research? We lost a lot of friends and contacts during 1966 to 1972, which seems to have been a particularly active time for MIB harassment of UFO percipients. Some good people whose friendship we had cherished simply could not endure the disturbances on their telephone lines and the bizarre phenomena that had suddenly intruded into their formerly quiet existences as a result of being our friends or of having assisted us with some phase of our research.

And we are still encountering angry individuals who accuse us of having conducted UFO investigations in areas where we have never traveled and of having abused, insulted, and threatened witnesses of UFO activity while we were allegedly there.

In addition, we are frequently told of people who have attended our lectures and seminars in small towns and cities we have never visited. Most often these good folk feed back to us a lot of strange statements that we allegedly made during those phantom lectures—statements that we never would have uttered.

Even though we were actively moving around the United States and Canada investigating UFO phenomena during that period, it seems that persons posing as us were just as active in a negative, often openly hostile, manner.

Certainly as Ray Palmer and many others have suggested, elements of psychic phenomena and the paranormal began to surface in the MIB reports.

A solid, sensible man named Rick sighted a UFO hovering very low overhead. A few days later, he saw three mysterious men in black watching him closely as he entered an airport prior to flying to another city on business. If the sighting and the airport encounter with the three odd fellows were not eerie enough, he was startled to see that they had boarded his flight and were seated in the row in front of him.

Calming himself, he dozed off after a bit. When he awoke, the three men had disappeared, never to return aboard that particular flight.

* * *

A very orthodox farm family had a collective sighting of a UFO over their cornfield one evening. The next day a man claiming to be from a state educational division called at the high school and talked for over an hour with the family's teenaged daughter. The only questions he asked repeatedly concerned whether or not she felt she would be able to recognize a spy. When her suspicious father checked with the school administrators, he was informed that they had no knowledge of such a man nor of such a division within the state educational system.

A few nights later the teenaged daughter began to "channel" messages from the UFO intelligences. The entire family saw UFOs swooping low overhead at night. Eerie lights were seen to dance about in the fields. Beds were rattled at night; mattresses were lifted under sleeping bodies; personal possessions disappeared, then rematerialized in strange locations.

And then the phenomena suddenly ended and life returned pretty much as before—except that the farm family now enjoyed a much larger perspective of the universe and its mysteries.

One of the stranger manifestations of the MIB in our personal sphere occurred to Jim Williams, a close friend who was traveling in England in the summer of 1971 before leaving for Vietnam to visit his son in the Armed Forces.

Jim was walking near a railway station in London when he noticed three men, rather short and somewhat Oriental in appearance, dressed completely in black and openly staring at him.

When our friend, a burly fellow not easily intimidated, returned their collective stare, they approached him and asked him which train they should take for a particular city.

Jim calmly explained that he was a tourist, and it made a great deal more sense to inquire after such data from the gentleman in the information booth just a few feet away from them.

Jim turned on his heel and walked purposefully away from the bizarre trio. A glance over his shoulder showed him that they were still standing there, staring at him, unmindful of checking out anything at the information booth. Suddenly ill at ease, Jim hailed a taxi and went directly to his hotel.

When he got to his room, an uncomfortable sensation prickled the back of his neck, and he glanced out his window. There on the street corner below, staring up directly at his room, were the three odd men.

Baffled by it all, our friend, an extremely composed individual, pushed the strange incident from his mind and went about his business of being a Yankee tourist in Great Britain.

A day or so later, however, Jim found himself in a direct confrontation with the three men when they suddenly blocked his passage on a crowded street.

He was greatly surprised when one of the men asked him in an odd kind of accent if he was a friend of ours. Taken off guard by such an inquiry, Jim nodded his head and acknowledged that he was, indeed, our friend.

When the rather diminutive gentleman in black asked if Jim would deliver a message, he once again nodded his head in affirmation.

The message could be interpreted as being rather innocuous or rather sinister. It was simply that *they would visit us by Christmas.*

Jim had only a peripheral knowledge of the UFO controversy, and it is unlikely that he had ever heard of the MIB or knew anything of their mystique. But he rushed back to his hotel room immediately after the encounter with the three strange men and wrote us a letter with the above details.

To our knowledge we did not host three strangers dressed in black on that Christmas season of 1971. Of course, they did not specify *which* year at Christmas!

Are the UFO silencers horror or hoax? If it is all a hoax, then who is perpetrating it and *why?*

Are the silencers, in spite of all the indignant official denials, human agents from a top-secret U.S. government agency, which knows the answer to the UFO enigma and has been given the mission of keeping the truth from the public?

In some instances we are convinced that the men who identified themselves as Air Force personnel were, indeed, who they claimed to be—i.e., investigating officers who, officially, "weren't really there."

In certain cases we strongly suspect that overzealous civilian researchers, jealously guarding a "really good UFO case," might have been responsible for having made ill-advised threats to UFO witnesses in order to ensure the exclusivity of their investigation.

But in a great many cases, the nagging question seems to demand the answer that the MIB—as some UFO researchers firmly believe—are extraterrestrial aliens who labor to spread confusion and fear among those who have witnessed activities subversive to our species—which the ETIs wish to keep secret.

Or as other investigators insist, are they agents from some ancient secret society that endeavors to guard its clandestine activities for a while longer?

Or could the UFOs and the silencers be coming from a much older terrestrial race—perhaps extraterrestrial in origin—which has survived unnoticed in some remote region of Earth and which has become more scientifically advanced in its self-imposed isolation?

Whoever comprises this persistent silence group either knows—or gives the impression of knowing—a great deal more about the universe than we at our present levels of scientific and technological accomplishments have been able to achieve.

Do the MIB wish us to remain ignorant of the true facts about the UFO controversy because they realize that the more ignorant we are of the true nature of the dangers that face us, the less able we will be to deal with a future crisis situation of overwhelming proportions? The less we are prepared to handle the inevitable confrontation with an alien race, the more rapidly we might allow ourselves, slavelike, to become subject to a society or a species that considers itself superior to us.

If the mysterious silence group should in time prove to be members of a hostile element within an alien species—or citizens of a secret society no longer content with being obscure and benevolent—how much longer will they continue to knock on doors and merely harass us? How much longer will it be before they openly invade our planet?

CHAPTER 12

Secret Underground Bases

George Donald, a California law enforcement officer with ten years' experience, provided us with this report of his family's UFO encounter, which took place at 10:40 A.M. on April 8, 1993. As seems to be true of the vast majority of UFO witnesses, Donald told us that he "didn't believe in flying saucers or the like . . . until now."

Donald, his wife, and four children had been traveling north on Interstate 15 en route to Las Vegas. They were approximately half a mile from the number 27 Henderson turnoff when he glanced ahead and saw that a disturbance had just occurred in front of a mountain on the right-hand side of the road.

"I can only describe this disturbance as an impact/explosion almost half the size of the mountain," Donald said. "I could see a large turbulence that looked like brown dirt mixed with air. As I stared at this huge disturbance, I could see a large reflection rising from it. It was as if someone was holding a giant mirror and shining this reflection into my eyes."

Donald's initial impression was that some kind of construction was taking place by the mountain, but the brilliant reflection had him confused. As he continued to try to focus, he saw that whatever was causing the bright reflection was slowly rising and beginning to assume a clear shape. At the same time the turbulence was settling.

"I could now see a metallic/aluminum disc rising with a white blur beneath it and partially around the side," he said. "As the disc continued to rise, the white blur around it began to disappear. The disc appeared to be taking clear shape, form, and dimension—I could now see the sides of the flying saucer.

"As the massive craft rose and cleared the mountaintop . . . it started to move horizontally with slight upward tilt. Then it disappeared into thin air. It was as if it went into another dimension or it moved so fast that our eyes could not pick it up."

Donald sped up in order to round the mountain and again catch sight of the large UFO. "But there was nothing there. I knew that I had witnessed a UFO, but I still couldn't believe it."

Pooling their collective impressions, Donald found that his family had seen in exact detail the same object that he had just viewed. Two of his children had noticed the UFO before he had, and they described hundreds of small yellow-orange colored lights on the bottom of the craft. In addition, on the front of the UFO, they had observed larger lights colored red, blue, and yellow-orange.

"As I drove into Las Vegas, the reality of what we had just witnessed started to sink in," Donald said. "I had an uncontrollable urge to cry like a baby."

Donald and his family have often reflected on the awesome sight they witnessed. His children draw pictures of the UFO, and they often dream of flying saucers.

As a conscientious law enforcement officer, Donald told us that he had reported the experience to the Las Vegas Police Department and to Nellis Air Force Base. No one, however, seemed interested in following up on his report.

Although there are underground bases in Nevada, Arizona, California, Wisconsin, Colorado, and many other areas, the alleged underground facility outside Dulce, New Mexico, is by far the most notorious. According to many UFO researchers and to men and women who claimed to have worked there side by side with the "Grays," the principal research at Dulce is the study of human genetics and the possibility of crossbreeding the two species and/or developing mutations.

A frequently heard account about Dulce concerns a 1969 confrontation that broke out between the human scientists working there and the aliens. In order to guarantee extended cooperation from the secret government, the Grays took a number of human scientists as hostages.

Crack troops from our Delta Force were sent into the vast underground tunnels to rescue our scientists, but they proved to be no match for the aliens. Estimates of sixty-six to several hundred humans were killed during the violent confrontation.

Because of the sudden realization that the Grays could not always be trusted to follow other than their own secret agenda, the representatives and employees of the secret government withdrew from all joint projects with the Grays for about two years. Eventually a reconciliation occurred, and the alliance between the aliens and the members of the secret government was once again back on course.

Some of the aliens who work in the underground bases consider themselves to be native Earthlings, for they are the crossbred descendants of a reptilian humanoid species—who many thousands of years ago in our planet's prehistory accomplished genetic engineering with early members of *Homo sapiens.*

While some of these crossbred reptilian-human "Terrans" are loyal allies, others of their group have proven to be untrustworthy mercenary agents for the Draco, an extraterrestrial race that is returning to Earth—a planet they consider their ancient outpost.

The Grays are most often described as being under four feet tall, with a disproportionately large head and large slanted eyes. Some of their species appear more sophisticated than others, but they all seem to worship technology at the expense of artistic and creative expression. They also seem devoid of emotion and appear indifferent to the general well-being of humans.

In addition to a number of reported "Hairy Dwarfs" and exceedingly tall alien life-forms, the most commonly mentioned extraterrestrial biological entities (EBEs) next to the Grays are the so-called "Nordics," essentially human in appearance, mostly blond-haired and blue-eyed. Cast in an angelic kind of role in the alien versus human drama, they normally do not violate the intergalactic law of noninterference so they cannot interfere with the grisly machinations of the Grays. Unless, of course, the Grays finally go too far and begin to upset the larger picture of universal balance and order.

* * *

Research scientist Paul Bennewitz claims to have been repeatedly harassed and intimidated by the military after he provided government investigators with proof that he had filmed a formation of UFOs flying over the Manzano Weapons Storage Area and the Coyote Canyon Test Site [where nuclear materials are stored], all part of the Kirtland Air Force Base facilities in Albuquerque, New Mexico. Bennewitz said he saw four saucer-shaped objects lined up beside the outside fence of the air base.

Bennewitz's investigations led him to Dulce, where he spoke with a woman who was kidnapped by aliens after she and her son had witnessed them mutilating a cow. According to the abductee, she and her son were taken inside the Dulce underground base and saw for themselves horrible experiments in which organs and blood were being removed from animals to create a new species of humanoids through gene splicing.

John Lear is the son of the famous aviation pioneer William Lear, who established the Lear Aircraft Company. John himself has earned a well-deserved reputation in aeronautical circles for having test flown over 150 aircraft and having won numerous awards from the Federal Aviation Administration.

A few years ago—before he heard a friend relate a UFO encounter that had taken place in England—Lear had absolutely no interest in such way-out matters. However, as he began to check out the accounts that others were relaying to him, he found to his astonishment that there were mountains of evidence proving that UFOs are real and quite likely from outer space.

Pursuing the subject with his contacts in the CIA and his informants in military intelligence, Lear ascertained that the first UFO crash occurred in Germany shortly before World War II. The Nazis used the technology obtained from the wreckage to initiate the rocketry program that destroyed much of Europe and blitzed the British Isles.

Later, Lear was told, a flying disc crashed near Roswell, New Mexico, and one of the injured aliens on board was kept alive for a short period of time in Hangar 18 in what is now Wright-Patterson Air Force Base.

What shocked Lear was that the government had made secret deals with the aliens, actually exchanging humans for advanced technical data. By 1987 Lear had discovered that the EBEs were putting together a sort of "Frankenstein Army—part alien, part human" in underground facilities in Nevada and New Mexico.

Lear's painstaking research yielded grisly evidence that human, as well as cattle, mutilations had been performed by the aliens as early as 1956. An Air Force major had witnessed the abduction of a sergeant early one morning at the White Sands Missile Test Range. When his body was found three days later, his genitals had been removed, his rectum cored out in a surgically precise plug up to the colon, and his eyes had been removed. His corpse had also been drained of all blood.

"From some of the evidence," Lear said, "it is apparent that such surgery is accomplished in most cases while the victim is still alive."

Information provided Lear by informants concerning the Dulce underground base detailed "large vats with pale meat being agitated in solutions" and large test tubes "with humans in them."

In Lear's assessment the abduction scenario seemed to have at least three purposes: (1) insertion of a tiny probe, approximately three millimeters in size that would monitor and program the abductee; (2) posthypnotic suggestions regarding the abductee's future mission; and (3) genetic crossbreeding between the EBEs and humans.

William Hamilton, author of *Cosmic Top Secret*, first received news of the existence of the secret underground bases in 1979 when an acquaintance who was a government worker revealed the details of military participation in monstrous genetic experiments being conducted with a sinister group of aliens. When his employers discovered that the man had stolen photographs depicting these experiments, his wife and children were "taken into custody" by federal agents as an effective means of regaining the classified material that had been "misplaced."

Hamilton's friend told him that the base at which he had been employed had at least seven subterranean levels. On level four, for example, advanced research in mind control was being

This remarkable photograph of a UFO over San Juan Pueblo, New Mexico, was taken by J.E. Berry in June of 1964.

A sighting over San Francisco looking east on October 10, 1956.
(*Photo by Joe Karska*)

Interceptor jets scrambled and even high-ranking Air Force officers filed UFO reports when a fleet of UFOs were seen over Capitol Hill, Washington, D.C. in 1952.

The UFO landing site near Socorro, Mexico, in the most famous of such UFO touchdowns investigated by the U.S. Air Force. This photograph shows an overall view of the site, facing northwest. The circles indicate a series of alien footprints.

On December 4, 1966, a UFO was seen to touch down on a beach near Brooksville, Florida. This photograph shows one of the four holes that was left by the landing gear of the craft. Each hole was six inches in diameter and the four holes together formed a square which measured ten feet, one inch on all sides.

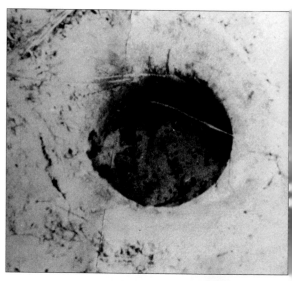

UFO researcher Joan Whitebour discovered a number of peculiar metal "be-be's" near the dumbbell-shaped footprints and the four landing holes at the site of the Brooksville landing. The metallic objects were sent to three separate laboratories but their composition was beyond analysis.

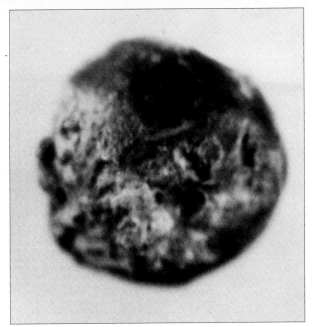

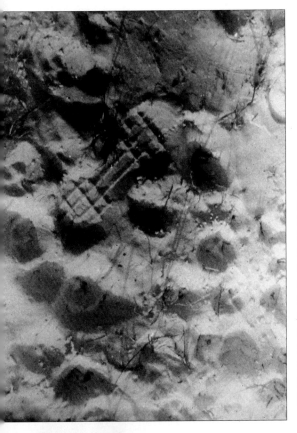

Near the Brooksville landing site were a number of strange, dumbbell-shaped footprints. The prints were eleven inches long, four-and-a-quarter inches wide at the widest part of the foot, and two-and-one-half inches wide at the middle. Researchers estimated that it would have required a body weight of approximately 250 to 275 pounds to have left such impressions.

In the late 1950s, Howard Menger claimed to have made contact with aliens from Venus, including a beautiful blonde crew person who took a personal interest in him. In this photograph, Menger allegedly captured a saucer-like UFO.

...e hundreds of photographs collected by Air Force personnel
...824 taken near Sheffield, England, on March 4, 1962.

...e high school seniors on a biology field trip took these photo-
...s of a UFO on May 26, 1966. The film was processed in the
...Home Central High School photo lab and brought to the office
...cal paper, the *Amherst Bee*, in Amherst, New York.

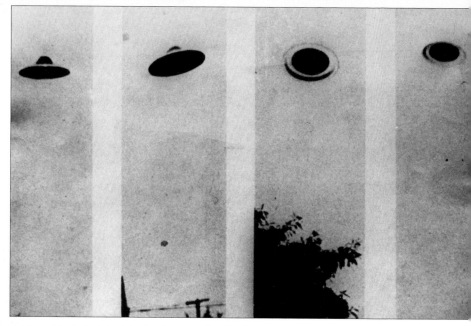

On July 29, 1952, George Stock of Passaic, New Jersey, was working in his backyard when he noticed a mysterious unidentified flying object in the sky. He asked his father to keep an eye on the UFO while he ran into the house to get his box camera. This fascinating series of photographs was the result.

Astronomer J. Allen Hynek (*left*), who for so many years served as the U.S. Air Force's special academic consultant on Project Bluebook, and psychologist James Harder (*right*) were summoned to Pascagoula, Mississippi, in October, 1973 to investigate the stories of Charles Hickson and Calvin Parker, who claimed to have been "floated" aboard a UFO.

This amazing photo was given to us by a UFO researcher who prefers to remain anonymous. According to our informant, this huge piece of unidentified machinery was one of six excavated circa 1990 from a great depth on secret government property in the United States and promptly reburied in that same area. Dwarfing the dumpster of its left side, the surface of this apparatus is covered with peculiar hieroglyphics that appear similar to characters to ancient Hebrew, Arabic, and Sanskrit.

Noted UFO artist Hal Crawford examined a number of old newspaper woodcuts and dozens of contemporary accounts to come up with his impression of the bizarre "airship" that traversed the skies of many southwestern and midwestern states in 1897.
(*Courtesy of Research Department Other Dimensions.*)

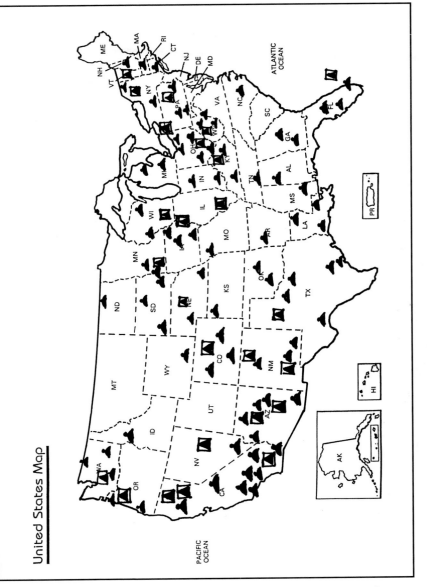

United States Map

The domed-saucer symbol on this map indicates those areas where UFO witnesses have reported the landings of mysterious unidentified aerial craft. The boxed pyramid symbol identifies those areas in which certain investigators and witnesses insist underground or underwater UFO bases are located.

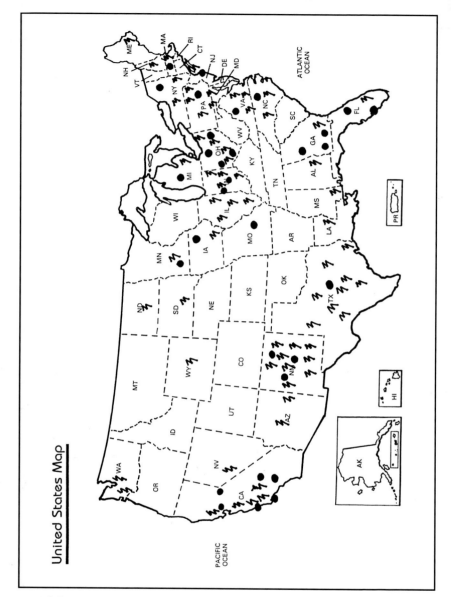

United States Map

While most regions have reported UFO-related electrical interference —blackouts, brownouts, and temporary cessation of automobile engines—the jagged lightning symbol indicates where these types of electromagnetic phenomena have been most frequently reported. The black dot depicts those areas where UFO "debris" such as the Brooksville "be-be," metallic shavings, "angel hair," and other alien materials have been found.

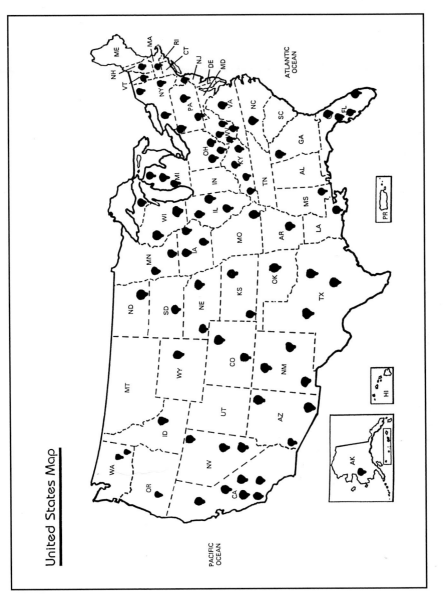

United States Map

Although humanoid UFO occupants and other eerie alien-type entities have been sighted in all fifty states, the little alien skulls on this map depict where such beings have been most frequently reported.

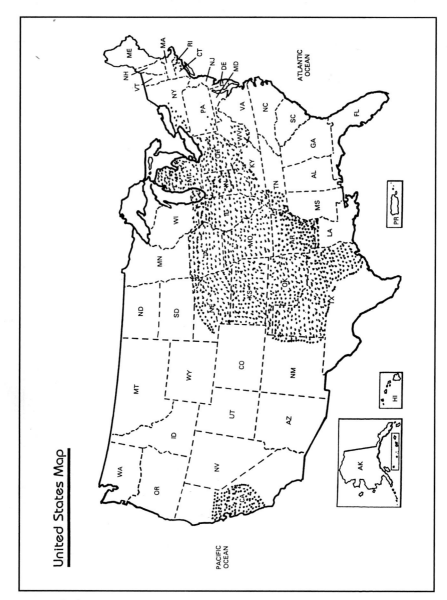

United States Map

Based on contemporary accounts, the shaded areas in this map indicate where the mysterious Airship of 1897 was most often sighted.

conducted. At level six, genetic experiments on animals and humans were in progress. Humans were kept in cages and drugged for some detestable purpose on level seven.

Hamilton's informant had originally been told a false story that the government was conducting special secret tests to cure insanity, but when he realized at last that aliens were actually behind the torturous experiments, he left his post and went into hiding.

In recent years, Hamilton points out, an uncomfortable dilemma has reared its ugly head. A small number of abductees have reported surveillance, intervention, or abduction by people they truly believe to be military personnel. "At first glance, the claims of abductees seem outrageous and paranoid," Hamilton admitted. "But are we to dismiss all of these reports as fabrications of deluded minds?

"Has the military found itself confronting superior intelligence and technology? What if some aliens are friends and others are foes?"

Hamilton feels that the military's role in the UFO controversy seems to argue that we are dealing with actual biological entities and real spacecraft that pose a potential threat to our way of life. Cautioning against panic—"The aliens have been around a long time and have not taken any mass offensive against us to date"— Hamilton states that his greatest concern "is the fact that excessive secrecy [on the part of the government] can lead to a breakdown in our cultural cohesiveness. It can lead to wild rumors and freewheeling speculations. It can lead to ignorance and the disintegration of our society."

Sean David Morton's interest in UFOs came about early in life. "My father was an experimental test pilot with the Navy, flying the SR-71 Blackbird and U-2 spy planes," Morton said. "Dad was stationed at such secret bases as Area 51."

Morton is one of the most avid and articulate proponents of the theory that Area 51, "Dreamland," located in the Nevada desert, is the secret base wherein the government is testing antigravity discs based on alien technology. Sean has visited the area on numerous occasions. He claims to be the first person to discover the mountain peak with the most propitious view of the Groom Lake Area 51 secret base.

What is more, Morton made use of that advantageous mountain peak to videotape the secret Dreamland facility. He provided the film for telecasting on Geraldo Rivera's *Now It Can Be Told* and thereby exposed his accusations of a government cover-up to millions of viewers.

As the son of an Air Force officer, William Cooper was reared on Air Force bases all over the world. Because his father was a pilot, Cooper has heard stories of UFOs and mysterious crashes of craft "not from here" ever since he was a child.

After he graduated from high school in Japan, Cooper joined the Air Force and finished his basic training at Lackland Air Force Base before being assigned to the Strategic Air Command. During his training as an aircraft and missile pneudraulic technician, Cooper remembered that instructors regaled the new men with tales of alien craft that would swoop down on missile silos, paralyze the men on station, then remove the warhead from the missile and disappear at a fantastic speed.

"I met a sergeant who told me that he had been part of a team that had transported a large, crashed disc," Cooper said. "The craft could be moved only at night on back roads, so fences and telephone poles had to be torn down and replaced as the convoy passed."

Cooper listened to all these bizarre stories and wondered what was going on, but he didn't really believe them. When he was discharged from the Air Force in 1965, he decided to continue his adventurous life and immediately enlisted in the Navy. He volunteered for submarines, and he was assigned to the USS *Tiru* (SS-416) at Pearl Harbor, Hawaii.

On a cruise to the Portland-Seattle area, Cooper had his first UFO encounter. "While we were on the surface and I was the port lookout, a UFO the size of an aircraft carrier rose up out of the water and disappeared into the clouds. It descended back down into the water and rose back up into the clouds again several times. It was witnessed by myself, the starboard lookout, the officer of the deck, the captain, and the chief quartermaster, who took pictures of the UFO. We were told never to discuss the incident with anyone ever."

While Cooper was in the Navy, he claims to have come across some highly classified documents pertaining to an alien-government partnership. These documents revealed the details of a secret treaty that had been made with a group of aliens referred to as extraterrestrial biological entities (EBEs). Though at first the government believed that the aliens had only good intentions, it turned out that the EBEs had been responsible for abducting humans, mutilating animals, and conducting weird genetic breeding experiments in deep underground bases. In many instances, Cooper learned, the aliens had actually taken over the underground bases from government agencies, which had built the installations to shelter our president and other high-ranking government officials in case of nuclear attack.

Recently, when we asked Cooper about the underground bases, he replied: "I saw in highly classified documents that there were extraterrestrial underground bases. Whether there really are or not, I don't know. I do know that Nazi Germany perfected the art of building huge underground installations. When the atomic bomb became a reality, underground military installations became not just a reality, but a necessity. I do know that the bases are real, but whether aliens occupy the bases, I don't know.

"These underground bases exist all over the United States," Cooper pointed out. "There is an actual government in-waiting to take over this country in these installations. There are factories, military units, agencies—everything—living underground in actual cities; and they're just waiting to take over.

"If extraterrestrials are real, then I am sure the documents that I read when I was in Naval Intelligence were true. Or, as I have stated, if ETs are not real, then it is an elaborate deception. But some of it had to be real in order to make the deception work. One learns very quickly in any intelligence organization that disinformation cannot work unless it contains an element of truth that will make the public believe it.

"It was over twenty years ago when I saw those documents. I found a lot of elements of truth in what I read then. I have also found some things that have either changed over the years or that may have been deliberate disinformation. The thing is, there is no way to know which is which."

Kevin Randle, a former U.S. Air Force intelligence officer, admitted to us that if the incident of the crashed saucer and the possibility of a surviving alien means that "we've truly got one of theirs," then "all of this stuff about secret underground bases becomes easier to accept." But as of this time, Randle has seen no evidence that convinces him that such bases actually exist.

"Area 51 is real," he said. "It is a government facility where they are developing our next generation of fighter planes. I am not aware of any giant leaps in our technology that suggest we are receiving any assistance from alien scientists in Area 51.

"I've gone to Dulce looking for some evidence of that frequently mentioned secret underground base, but I found nothing to indicate that it did, in fact, exist. If it did, it would seem that our satellites would have picked up some infrared signature or that our military aircraft would have seen some signs of activity on the ground below.

"Unless, of course, it is true that some branch of the secret government is so powerful that it can monitor all such data and censor any evidence proving such bases do exist."

Author-researcher John White believes that there may be a core of truth to the claims about secret underground bases, but dismisses as paranoid fantasy allegations of Delta Force personnel being slaughtered by aliens or the supposed vats filled with human body parts.

"Native Americans in that area have long told of sighting UFOs over the site of the alleged Dulce base," White admitted, "so there may be some kind of UFO activity occurring there.

"Area 51 is no longer any real secret," he said. "The March 1993 issue of *Popular Science* brings the Aurora, our newest 'secret' reconnaissance aircraft 'out of the black' and admits that the Mach 6 spy plane was developed at the closely guarded Air Force test facility at Groom Lake, Nevada."

* * *

UFO investigator and publisher Timothy Green Beckley called our attention to the fact that legends of underground civilizations predate popular accounts of UFOs by many centuries. "One of the most persistent myths of humankind is that of an Elder Race residing within our Inner Earth. Some legends claim the survivors of the lost continent of Atlantis established an underground world.

"There is something within us that makes us repeatedly turn to such mysteries," Beckley said. "And we can't just blame everything on the CIA. Tales of underground bases and societies existing inside Earth may be allegorical, symbolic of something within ourselves. There may truly be something to be learned from these stories that will reveal basic and intriguing factors within the human subconscious."

CHAPTER 13

The Troubling Mystery of UFO Abductions

For nearly thirty years we have participated in the regression of dozens of men and women who claim to have been abducted for brief periods of time by crew members of UFOs. In many cases these abductees claimed to have been given some kind of medical examination. In some instances they were left with peculiar markings and puncture marks in their flesh as physical testimony to the reality of their experience.

Early in 1968, during a hypnotic session with Ashland, Nebraska, city patrolman Herbert Schirmer, we heard him describe his captors:

"They were from four and a half to five and a half feet tall. Their uniforms were silver-gray, very shiny. . . . On the right side of their helmets they had a small antenna, just above where the ear would be. I never did see any of their ears. . . . Their eyes are the one thing that I will never forget. The pupil went up and down, like a slit. When they looked at me, they stared straight into my eyes. They didn't blink. It was real uncomfortable. . . . Their noses were flat. Their mouths looked more like a slit than a regular mouth."

After a detailed description of interior of the craft and the feathered serpent emblems and medallions featured throughout the UFO, Schirmer stated that a spokesperson for the aliens told him that they had been observing us for a long time: "There is some kind of program of breeding analysis. Some people have been picked up and changed so they have agents in our world. They are very smart about the brain and how to change it."

In 1968 we were bombarded with claims by dozens of contactees who said they had been left with an "implant" somewhere in their skulls, usually just behind the left ear. These contactees/ abductees came from a wide variety of occupations, cultural backgrounds, and age groups.

We never found any implants detectable by X rays, but our exhaustive hypnosis sessions produced fascinating, albeit bizarre, information about underground UFO bases, hybrid aliens walking among us, and thousands of humans slowly turning into automatons because of readjusted brain-wave patterns.

During one six-month period in 1969, we encountered as many as twenty-five abductees who gave us the same word-for-word accounts of having received an implant while on board a UFO. In some cases the contactees told us that internal beeping sounds would indicate that a message was about to be received from their alien overlords or that a UFO might be observed.

Since we had repeatedly determined that these implants did not appear to be physical by our earthly definition, what were they? If all this was purely a psychological aberration, how could so many men and women share the identical delusion?

In 1969 we first developed the rudiments of a "cosmic questionnaire" that we began to distribute to people who claimed UFO contactee and abductee encounters, as well as those individuals who had seen ghosts, spirits, elementals, elves and those who claimed illumination, revelatory, or any kind of mystical experience. By 1993 the questionnaire in its various states of development had been distributed worldwide to nearly 30,000 percipients of paranormal or otherworldly phenomena.

From this valuable questionnaire, we have received a seemingly endless variety of reports from those who claim to have been victims of UFO abductions.

Charles of Miami, Florida, is haunted by the memory of lying on a table in a small, metallic room while shadowy figures moved around him in the soft light. He is convinced that during the experience—which he believes to be far more than a vision or a dream—something was implanted in his brain.

"Ever since then," he says, "I feel heat, pain; and I hear a crackling sound in my head, as if some integration process is trying to happen. My perceptions have changed dramatically. I think, now, that the 'graft' has almost taken."

Lila from Memphis, Tennessee, was twenty-two when she made contact with us. She had been communicating telepathically with someone she called "Father" for many years. The entity told her that he was her true male parent, and he had awakened her to the knowledge of who her real parents were and where her home planet is.

Peggy of Dearborn, Michigan, has begun to question the true origin of her daughter Sara and who her child's father might really have been. A single mother, Peggy chose to keep her child when she became pregnant and decided not to marry the man she had been dating.

Because of the accelerated growth of Sara's head, Peggy had the child X-rayed when she was three. The doctor said that although Sara's head was adult-sized, there was no need to worry. Sara had excessively rapid brain development and was an exceptional child with potential genius ability.

When Sara was four or five, she began to draw pictures of spacecraft and an entity she identified as her father. She also began to speak of the lessons that "Daddy" taught her at night. According to Daddy, Sara had come on Earth to show people the way to the Light—before the planet was destroyed.

Mary of New York began having "dreams" of UFO people when she was only five years old. She would see a large ship hovering over her parents' home, and then on a beam of light, entities would come into her room and look at her.

They always seemed to be examining her, as if they were doctors. They never spoke, but their mouths seemed to be fixed in a permanent kind of quizzical smile. She was never alarmed, but, rather, she was fascinated by the procedure.

Shortly after she turned ten, she remembers the entities coming to her, taking her by the hand, and seemingly lifting her out of her body.

She was taken to a lovely pink room where everything was soft, gentle, and loving. Pleasant music was playing. She could not recognize the music, but it relaxed her and made her comfortable. She felt as if she had been taken to a very special nursery.

Mary's most dramatic experience occurred when she was nearly fourteen years old. She was visited in her room by the entities, who stood back in the corner while a more human-appearing figure approached her. In spite of her youth and her inexperience, Mary knew that she and the man were engaging in sexual intercourse. The man caressed her, but did not speak.

Within three months Mary knew that she was pregnant. She was very frightened. She would not turn fourteen for another month. She could not work up the nerve to tell her parents. She considered going to her school counselor with her plight, but she could not bear the shame and humiliation.

In her report to us, Mary swore that she had not had any type of sexual encounter with any boy her own age or any older man. Her only sexual experience had come from the man who entered her room accompanied by the same entities who had been visiting her since she was five years old.

And then Mary told us that the strangest thing happened. She had another dream in which the entities came to her room and once again seemed to examine her. This time she felt a bit of pain, and she remembered that she lay as if paralyzed while they performed some kind of operation on her.

When she awakened the next morning, she found a light smear of blood on her left thigh and a few drops of blood on the bedsheet.

"But I had an inner knowing that I wasn't pregnant anymore," she said. "A short time after the weird dream of surgery, my periods resumed." Several months later Mary had the last of her "UFO dreams." The entities took her aboard their craft, to the beautiful pink nursery.

"This time I was looking at a baby—a beautiful baby boy," she said. "The entities smiled and indicated that I could pick up the baby. I did so, and I had the strongest feeling that I was holding my own child. I caressed him and held him and said, 'I love you.'

"Then everything became hazy. The pink room seemed to get smaller and smaller, and I seemed to be covered with a pink mist. I awakened back in my room, and I have never had another UFO dream of that type."

Christa Tilton said that she first became aware of her abductions in 1975 when she was used in genetic experiments, one of which resulted in a full-term pregnancy of what she believes was a hybrid child.

Hypnotic sessions enabled Christa to remember a series of abduction experiences that began at the age of ten and culminated in her being kidnapped and taken to an underground facility that was jointly run by aliens and the military.

She also recalled the implantation of a device in her left ear when she was very young. "I remember that the alien 'doctor' who implanted the 'tagging device' was more humanlike and a lot nicer than many of the other ETs."

As she grew older, the gentle alien doctor told Christa that they would soon be playing a game with her called "planting a garden." At the time she was certain that he meant the aliens would plant something in the back yard—but that proved not to be the case. A small device was implanted in her abdomen, and she was shown a three-dimensional screen with symbols on it.

In September 1971 Christa was again visited by the same beings. "This time they inserted a long needle from a long tube coming from the instrument panel. I was fairly certain that they were extracting ovum. They examined and changed something in my left ear, then they placed a transparent capsulelike device into the area of my abdomen. When they withdrew the instrument, the capsule was gone. After this examination, I became pregnant—although I had not had sex for eight months."

Sometime in the summer of 1975, when her husband was out of town for a few days on business, Karen of Grand Rapids,

Michigan, dreamed she heard a voice calling her name coming from the hill behind her house. She got up, put on a robe, and walked over the hill.

In the field behind the hill was a very large UFO. She saw three figures standing beside the craft, and she began to walk toward them.

"The aliens were dark complexioned with slightly slanted eyes," she said. "They were small of build and stood about five feet tall. They wore two-piece suits with belts around the waist. On their belt buckles was some sort of symbol, like some kind of bird in flight."

The three aliens informed Karen that they were there because she was one of their kind and they wanted her to bear a child.

"One of the three men came up to me and slowly started slipping off my robe," Karen said. "I tried to move, but I could not. The man on my left stepped forward and started touching me. All I could do was cry. They told me that they would not hurt me, so I should not worry.

"As they helped me with my robe, I could hear them speaking to me. Their mouths were not moving, so I knew that they were using telepathy. The next thing I knew, I was at my patio door."

In her report to us, Karen said that within a few months she knew she was pregnant. Almost nine months to the day of her unusual "UFO dream," her daughter Casey was born.

"Casey is now five years old," Karen wrote. "She has been observed levitating by me and by certain of her playmates. She speaks intimately of relatives, deceased before her birth, and she has already outlined her future as a healer in a hospital."

Estimates presented at a conference on the alien-abduction phenomenon at the Massachusetts Institute of Technology in June 1992 suggested that as many as several hundred thousand to more than three million adults in the United States alone have had abduction experiences. While such a figure seems mind-boggling, some UFO researchers say that the true figure would be much higher.

What are we to make of such incredible claims as those made by UFO abductees?

"I certainly do not deny that there appear to have been actual

UFO abductions throughout history," acknowledged Timothy Green Beckley. "And I certainly like to think that I have an open mind regarding such matters. But I must admit that some of the statistics and claims of the researchers specializing in this area are difficult for me to accept.

"In these troubled times it seems undeniable that thousands of men and women may be experiencing dramatic brushes with the unknown—which they attempt to explain and to deal with in ways they can best understand. Right now the UFO abduction modality is a popular one by which to explain strange and unaccountable experiences.

"I guess I worry most about some of the UFO researchers who hypnotize people who believe they were abducted," Beckley said. "Not only do the abductees feed back pretty much what the researcher already believes, but I cannot help thinking that it could be dangerous to be hypnotized by someone without any real background in medicine, psychology, or counseling. Some of these supposed abductees are allowed to 'remember' some pretty horrible and frightening things, and I worry that some less stable subjects could be emotionally scarred by their hypnosis sessions.

"As a long-time student of the paranormal, as well as UFOlogy," Beckley said, "I cannot help recognizing some old familiar demons of the human psyche emerging in contemporary clothing. The incubus and succubus phenomenon of the Middle Ages—with its emphasis on sexual molestation and the cross-breeding of humans and demons—doesn't seem too far off from the UFO abductors of today.

"And talk of implants and peculiar physical markings on the alleged victims of UFO abductions," he continued, "what about such things as stigmata and the power of suggestion, which can cause bloody wounds to open or close on fanatical or hysterical subjects?

"I am bothered by some UFO researchers claiming as many as fifteen million abductees worldwide," Beckley said. "I mean, why would a bunch of ETs need to examine, fondle, and genetically experiment with millions and millions of people? I suppose it is not impossible, but I cannot help thinking that many of these so-called abductions have to be some kind of symbolic process taking place within the individual abductee."

* * *

Some years ago, after we had interviewed fifty or so alleged abductees, we were struck by the thought that there is something almost primeval in the claims of examinations aboard UFOs. In primitive societies that emphasize pubertal initiations or rites of passage, the young child or the adult supplicant is often snatched away by masked members of a secret society or by stony-faced elders. The initiate is then taken to a place of ordeal or testing, often unconsciously womblike in design or shape. When the initiate has endured the testing process, the rites of initiation, he or she is returned to the village, a new and transformed person.

So, too, is the UFO abductee taken away by secret people whose faces, with their large, expressionless eyes and slitlike mouths, appear masklike. The place of testing and ordeal is not only womblike in appearance, but it is often an egg-shaped enclosure. And after the abductee survives the testing process, he or she is returned to society as a transformed individual.

It may well be that the abductees are having genuine encounters, but of a nature whose true and total significance may be very different from what they suspect.

In his second letter to the Corinthians [12:2-5], the apostle Paul confides to his readers that he was once taken up into Heaven. But even in an age far more tolerant of supernatural occurrences and far less exacting in its scientific requirements than our own, Paul provides a number of qualifying statements that many of our contemporary abductees and contactees would do well to emulate.

When we listen to abductees and UFO researchers telling us about being taken up through ceilings, out through walls, and levitated out windows, might we not just as likely be hearing accounts of experiences that took place in dreams, visions, or astral travel?

If it is possible that the human essence can soar free of the accepted limitations of time and space imposed on it by the physical body and truly engage in astral projection [or the more academic "out-of-body experience"], then it may well be that the paraphysical aspect of humankind may more easily interact with the multidimensional being that we commonly identify as the UFOnaut. Indeed, many accounts that tell of a subject being abducted aboard a UFO might actually be descriptions of a mental/spiritual/nonmaterial experience, rather than an actual physical/material one.

"I was lying on a couch in the living room, and I felt myself being squeezed out of my body," one abductee told us. "It felt like my head was being pulled back and two electric wires were touching the back of my neck.

"Then I became aware of myself in a dome-shaped room. There were machines and computers on each side of me. Smallish entities in colored jackets, like smocks, were operating them. I was unable to move, as if some kind of paralysis had come over me. The beings at the machines turned toward me. Although they seemed almost expressionless, they put me at ease and I felt they were friendly. They told me something that I could not later remember, and I think they put some kind of homing device somewhere in my body."

Another abductee, a policeman from Atlanta, gave us the following report of his experience: "I know that I was not asleep, but I was sitting comfortably in my favorite easy chair, facing the open window and the night sky. An erratically moving light caught my attention.

"Then a strange thing happened. At first I thought I was fainting. My entire being seemed to be rolling up from my feet as if my body were a toothpaste tube and my consciousness was the paste being squeezed from it. Finally my consciousness seemed to burst free and soar through space. The next thing I knew, I was standing inside some kind of craft. I was aware of a lot of smallish people with big heads standing around me, but I could not seem to focus on either their faces or their forms. I was being touched, stroked, poked, and prodded. A voice was speaking to me earnestly, but I cannot seem to recall exactly what he was saying. I know that it had to do with some special mission that I am to perform.

"Then I was aware of my wife shaking my shoulder and telling me that I should come to bed instead of sitting there dozing. I looked at my watch, and I was surprised to see that I had been in that state of consciousness—or whatever it was—for nearly three hours."

Psychic-sensitive Clarisa Bernhardt, who today resides in Canada, has become world famous due to the accuracy of her predictions, especially those regarding the dates of destructive earthquakes. Some years ago, while she was visiting her native Oklahoma, we interviewed her in the company of fellow researcher Hayden Hewes regarding her having been "mentally projected" to an alien spacecraft prior to her physical teleportation.

"On two or three occasions," she said, "they have 'transported' me while my body was still on the bed. They took my consciousness aboard the spaceship. I felt very humble about just getting to go there, so I just listened to them. At the time they gave me some predictions, but they felt that since I was sensitive toward earthquakes, the scientists I worked with would be more impressed if they gave me the dates of the two biggest earthquakes of that year."

One thing that you quickly learn in the UFO field is to stay as eclectic as possible and to avoid focusing your attention on any one theory regarding the modus operandi of the Other, the aliens—whoever they may really be. Just when it would seem that astral projection might allow us to view abduction experiences as being more often nonmaterial experiences than physical ones, we run up against a bizarre case that bends and distorts the laws of physics and the rules of reality as we currently understand them. Although the story is told in greater length in our *Mysteries of Time and Space,* it bears summarizing here.

William, a medical professional associated with one of the largest, most prestigious hospitals in the Midwest, related this account of a most extraordinary incident that occurred in 1968, when he was serving in the Medical Corps and assigned to the military section of a hospital in Hawaii.

One night a bedridden patient in traction and totally unable to move, with pins through his tibiae and femurs, told William that he would be gone that evening for a few hours while he joined his alien friends in a UFO. He said that William might accompany him if he truly believed in UFOs. William declined the invitation, stating that he would be on duty that night.

The patient, a man in his early sixties, was a veteran of World War II. He'd walked in front of a tractor-trailer, broken both his legs in several places, and was completely immobile.

"When I made the initial bed check that night, the patient reminded me that he would be gone for about an hour, and he repeated the invitation that I could come along in the UFO if I wanted to," William said. "I chuckled and walked on to see about the rest of the patients."

The UFO-obsessed patient was in a six-man room, but that night he was alone. William's post was across from his room. When he sat at his desk, he could survey the entire corridor. No one could get on or off the floor without his seeing them. And, of course, at the same time there were nurses, doctors, interns, and MPs walking around.

Later, during a second bed check, William was startled to see that the patient had disappeared from his bed. The traction weights were hanging there; the metal pins were on the bed. But the patient was gone!

An extensive search of the hospital and the surrounding grounds by military police failed to discover any trace of the bedridden man. Other patients said that they had seen a bright light around the time the man in traction had disappeared.

"It would have been impossible for anyone to have pulled the pins out by himself," William said. "You'd just faint from the pain. This guy had been lying in bed with both legs up, his femurs broken. He couldn't move. And if he had fallen out of bed and had tried to crawl, the pain would have been terrible."

When William, other hospital personnel, and MPs next checked the disappearing patient's room, they found that he was back in traction, pins in place. He had been gone for exactly an hour.

A doctor on the floor was completely baffled. He said that

while it might be possible for a man to pull the pins *out*, it would be impossible for anyone to shove them *back in* by himself.

Four MPs grilled the patient for hours, but the man wouldn't reply to their questions. He would only say that he had been with his "friends."

When William was alone with the patient, the man sheepishly reminded him that he could have come along. But since it was apparent that his disappearance had created such a disturbance in the hospital, the next time he went flying with his "friends," he would leave his body there in traction and just go with them in his mind.

As the more discreet UFO investigators have commented, the aliens appear to express an "extraordinary interest in human sexuality." Hypnotic regressions conducted with abductees have produced the somewhat lurid details of a wide variety of means of impregnating Earth females, milking semen from Earth males, and creating a hybrid species.

UFO author-researcher John A. Keel once told us his conclusion that cases of UFO sexual liaisons are actually a variation on the age-old incubus phenomenon. "Induced hallucinations seem to play a major role in these cases," he said. "There may be considerable validity to the theory you expounded in one of your books [*Demon Lovers*]. . . that semen is extracted from human males in some succubi events and that this same semen is then introduced into human females in incubi incidents. The true nature and purpose of this operation is completely concealed behind a screen of deliberately deceptive induced hallucinations. Early fairy lore is filled with identical cases, as you know. And such sexual manipulations are an integral part of witchcraft lore."

Although vividly sensual descriptions of intercourse with demons was wrung from witches during the terrible tortures of the Inquisition by priests seeking confessions of their sins—and the graphic accounts of sexual molestation by alien intruders is wrung from the subconscious of abductees during hypnotic sessions by UFO researchers seeking confirmation of their theories—fair-minded students of either, or both, phenomena would have to concede the enormous number of similarities between being impregnated for Satan's pleasure or being fertilized to produce hybrid soldiers for an alien takeover of Earth. Indeed, according to some researchers, the two violators may be one and the same demonic entity, and the complete domination of Earth may be the identical goal.

Let us briefly consider a parallel between contemporary accounts of UFO abductions and the legends that grew up around the old religion of witchcraft in the mid-1400s. For centuries the Christian Church had officially ignored the practitioners of the ancient ways. But at the dawn of the Age of Enlightenment, when an emerging science was beginning to consider seriously the structure of the universe, certain of the Church hierarchy— the status quo—suddenly became obsessed with devils and their lustful designs upon Earth women.

In his *AntiChrist and the Millenium,* E. R. Chamberlin makes an excellent point that should be kept in mind while considering the ever-increasing reports of UFO abductions, alien impregnations, and sexual molestations by ETs:

"Paradoxically, it was the Christian Church which, seeking with all its powers to combact the practice of satanism, gave that same practice a form. It was necessary to define witchcraft in order to combat it, and by so defining, the Church gave shape to what had been little more than folklore. Most of the elements that eventually went to make up witchcraft had long been abroad in Europe, but for centuries the Church had been content to dismiss them as mere fantasy. The legend of the women who flew by night came in for particular scorn. 'Who is such a fool that he believes that to happen in the body which is done only in the spirit?' Such sturdy common sense was forced to give ground at last to a rising tide of fanaticism."

When it comes to the charges raised by some UFO investigators that the aliens in general—and the Grays in particular— are conducting genetic experiments to alter human evolution, we must speculate—based on our own extensive research— whether the extraterrestrial geneticists might not be completing a centuries-old project, rather than initiating a new one.

Rather than focusing on whether or not the UFO abductors

are conducting genetic experiments with unwilling men and women in 1994, the more powerful query is whether humankind might have been structured by the UFO intelligences from the very beginning of our evolutionary trek.

Our own science has begun the process of engineering the transfer of certain traits from one creature to another, so we will soon be able to create genetically new animals or to transfer a particularly desirable trait within the same species. If we Earthlings are steadily acquiring mastery of such genetic science, where might that place the UFO intelligences, who clearly appear to be aeons ahead of us technologically?

To look at the troubling matter of UFO abductions from the perspective of the ETIs, the process of human evolutionary trial and error might not yet be completed. They may still be monitoring the development of our species through the programmed process of UFO-based examinations.

CHAPTER 14

Crashed Saucers, Alien Corpses, and the Secret Government

One of the most controversial areas of UFO research deals with the assertions of many serious investigators that the mysterious unidentified flying objects—whatever they may be and whomever may pilot them—are far from perfect and crash from time to time.

Long-time UFOlogist Timothy Green Beckley claims to have accounts of 110 crashed saucers around the globe.

Kevin Randle, a former captain in Air Force Intelligence, claims to have unearthed evidence of even more downed UFOs, and he is about to publish this startling information in a book on the history of UFO crashes.

Early in 1993 a bright blue UFO was spotted above Gage County, Nebraska, by numerous witnesses, including two deputy sheriffs and two pilots, who watched it streak across the sky and crash into a wooded area.

A deputy sheriff sew it as he was driving on a gravel road a mile and a half north of Blue Springs about nine thirty in the evening. At first, he said, he thought it was somebody spotlighting for deer—but when he turned off his car lights, he could no longer see the blue glow.

Later, when he drove into the town of Blue Springs, a man told him that he had seen a blue ball streak across the sky at the same time.

By 9:50 P.M. reports of the blue UFO were coming in from the nearby town of Wymore. A number of witnesses there claimed to have seen the object crash-land in the woods.

While he was on duty in his patrol car, a reserve deputy in Liberty reported a blue UFO moving north of town, and he stated that he heard an explosion when the object crashed.

At about the same time, two airborne pilots called the U.S. Weather Service in Lincoln to report the blue UFO they had sighted streaking over Gage County.

"Eerily," stated author-physicist Dr. Franklin Ruehl, "despite two reports of a possible crash from two law enforcement officers and two trained pilots, extensive searches for the downed UFO revealed no signs of wreckage."

Had a UFO crashed into the woods in Gage County, Nebraska?

Reputable witnesses answer in the affirmative.

What, then, happened to the evidence of such a crash?

The simplest explanation is that the witnesses—honest and knowledgeable though they might have been—were mistaken.

Some UFOlogists will insist, however, that highly trained specialists from a secret branch of the government arrived on the scene and spirited away all signs of the incident before local officials could arrange for a proper search of the area.

According to members of the Long Island UFO Network (LIU-FON), a nonprofit research organization, they have evidence that on November 24, 1992 at 7:12 P.M., an alien spacecraft crashed near the area of South Haven Park in Suffolk County close to the residential communities of Shirley and Yaphank, Long Island, New York.

The principal witness, a Mr. Walter Knowles of Mastic Beach, said that he saw the object fall to Earth in a wooded area near South Haven Park along Gerard Road, which borders the western edge of the park.

According to a LIUFON press release, Knowles was driving east on Sunrise Highway while returning home from work around 7 P.M. when he noticed an unusual aerial object to the south of the highway over the stand of trees that separates Sunrise from Montauk Highway. He described the UFO as tubular in shape with two large bright blue lights on each end with a brilliant light in its center. The general color of the object appeared to be a dull, metallic gray.

As Knowles watched the object, it executed a right-angle turn and began to tumble end over end into the woods on the north side of the highway.

He pulled his vehicle over to the right shoulder and got out of the automobile in time to see the object crash to the northwest. Upon impact, Knowles stated, the object emitted a powerful white beam of light, which shot into the night sky.

Later, during the course of their research, LIUFON would learn that the light from the crashed object was seen by residents in the area as far north as Ridge and as far west as Bald Hill in Coram.

Several other motorists joined Knowles at the side of the road, and they all watched as the light subsided into an amber glow—which, in Knowles's opinion, indicated a fire in progress in the wooded area.

Convinced that he had witnessed the crash of a UFO, Knowles decided to leave the area and to continue his drive home. As he was nearing the exit for William Floyd Parkway, he observed a formation of four large, black, military-type helicopters with no visible markings arriving on the crash scene.

A short time later, after he had arrived at his home, Knowles became perplexed when he learned that there was no news coverage of any type of crash—conventional aircraft or UFO—in the area. Knowles asked his brother-in-law to return with him to the area where he had witnessed the tubular-shaped UFO tumbling into the woods.

When they arrived on the scene about twenty-five minutes later, a military roadblock on William Floyd Parkway was detouring traffic west on Sunrise Highway. The military personnel conducting the roadblock were dressed in black jumpsuits, and their vehicles bore no identifying markings.

While Knowles and his brother-in-law were present on the scene, they saw five New York State Police cars being turned back by the black-suited military personnel. Although the state police at West Hampton Barracks later denied Knowles's account, a confidential source from that unit confirmed the incident to a LIUFON investigator.

Finding the side streets of Beatrice, Dawn, and Sunset also

blocked by military personnel dressed in black jumpsuits, Knowles found that he was still able to travel west on Victory Boulevard, and he and his brother-in-law drove up Gerard Road to the second bend in the road where he could see a large fire in progress about 300 yards back in the woods.

He told investigators from LIUFON that there was a strong airborne odor similar to that of burnt insulation and that he could see flames dancing near the top of trees in the park.

LIUFON researchers also received a report from a second eyewitness, a motorist from Brookhaven Hamlet, who sighted an unconventional aircraft while traveling eastbound on Sunrise at around 7:15 P.M. He did not observe the object crash into the park, but he did spot an unusual object in the sky around the time of the reported UFO's firey touchdown in South Haven Park.

Stubbornly investigating this remarkable UFO crash report since December of 1992 when they were first contacted by Walter Knowles, the Long Island UFO Network (P.O. Box 1692, Riverhead, NY 11901), gathered such information as the following:

• All federal, state, and local agencies, including fire departments—which would have been involved in the incident—have denied officially that such an event ever occurred.

• However, on December 20, 1992, LIUFON investigators retrieved fire department equipment from the main fire road in the park that has been identified as being similar to equipment used by the Brookhaven Hamlet Fire Department. Subsequently, LIUFON received confirmation from a Brookhaven Hamlet Fire Department source that their unit was called to the park that night to put out fires caused by something that fell out of the sky. The anonymous source added that fire department personnel were prohibited by federal government orders from speaking about the incident.

• Suffolk County Police sounded a county-wide alert on the night of November 24, 1992, that a UFO had crashed near William Floyd Parkway and all units were to use land lines to receive instruction for emergency mobilization.

• The park itself was closed for several days after the UFO crash, and area residents reported Suffolk police manning roadblocks near the park entrance. At first county officials denied the allegations that the park had been closed, but they later informed the editor of the *South Shore Press* in Mastic Beach that the park had been closed to the general public because of the duck hunting season.

• Numerous area residents reported having heard the object crash on that November night. Others observed the black helicopters hovering over the area for hours.

• A great number of area residents have reported strange electrical problems that seem to stem from the mysterious events of that same November evening. Cable television and home appliances burned out; car batteries suddenly failed; the telephone system malfunctioned; light bulbs burned out with annoying frequency. All of these phenomena, LIUFON researchers suggest, could be the result of a massive electromagnetic pulse effect having occurred in the area.

• LIUFON investigators discovered two areas of flattened and broken trees along Gerard Road. One area over 100 yards long displayed signs of broken and splintered trees. Another spot 200 yards north gave evidence of broken trees and a recent fire.
Trees in the second area gave signs of holding a strong magnetic field after LIUFON researchers tested them with a magnetometer.

• A number of area residents reported to LIUFON that they encountered the same military and police roadblocks that Walter Knowles confronted on the night in question.

• Over seven municipal fire departments responded that night to answer the call to control fires set by the crash of the UFO. In addition, elements of the Brookhaven National Laboratories Fire Department and Emergency Response Team were dispatched to the location since they comprised the only unit on Long Island with the expertise to control a radiological fire.

In June 1993 LIUFON Chairman John Ford received a package in his home mailbox from an anonymous source. The package contained a videotape from a Defense Department systems analyst, who claimed to be a resident of Rocky Point, New York. The video appears to show the recovery of the wreckage of a UFO from an area north of South Haven Park. The tape also contains scenes of what would seem to be bodies and body parts suggestive of belonging to humanoid alien beings.

A complete examination of the tape under the auspices of Preston Nichols and Alan Green, both members of LIUFON, has produced a video enhancement and stop-frame analysis of the tape, which further substantiates the suggestion that the bodies appear to be those of aliens, rather than humans.

The government analyst, who has since contacted LIUFON and identified himself, told Ford that the tape was confiscated from fire department personnel on the scene the night of November 24, 1992.

According to additional information received by LIUFON researchers, the wreckage of the UFO is being stored and studied at Brookhaven National Laboratories.

The official cry of "meteor" went up on December 9, 1965, when, just before sundown, a brilliant orange object crossed the skies from Michigan over Lake Erie, over northeastern Ohio, and crashed in a woods thirty miles south of Pittsburgh, Pennsylvania.

Almost within an hour of the sighting, Dr. Paul Annear of Baldwin-Wallace College had announced his opinion that the object was a meteor. The Pentagon was quick to agree with the professor.

The officially pronounced "meteor" had set grass afire over a 1,000-foot area when it crashed. The object was sighted by several people on the ground and by many experienced commercial and private pilots.

Meteors, of course, do not "fly," but are merely falling through space and become visible when friction with the earth's atmosphere causes them to glow. Meteors are usually first sighted at heights between thirty and sixty miles and "burn out" their glow at about ten miles.

Peculiarly, this particular meteor was charted as having made a 25-degree turn over Cleveland and was clocked at about 1062.5 miles per hour.

Ivan T. Sanderson, writing for the North American Newspaper Alliance, expressed his dissatisfaction with the official analysis of the fiery object:

"So, this object was a meteor; was it? The minimum speed ever recorded for a meteor was 27,000 miles per hour and the maximum was 144,000 per hour, which is to say seven and one-half miles per second and 40 miles per second respectively!

"Since when have meteors or bolides, which is the name now given to meteors that break up in our atmosphere, started ambling along at 1,062.5 miles per hour?"

Sanderson also thought it most peculiar that the military displayed such great interest in the alleged meteor. Bolides crash to Earth nearly every day of the year and are ignored as commonplace by all except those amateur enthusiasts who like to collect hunks of "falling stars."

With this particular meteor, however, "great contingents of specialists from the Armed Forces arrived at the scene of the fall almost as fast as the state police got there."

Nearly thirty years later, area residents who witnessed the "Pittsburgh UFO" and its subsequent crash are still reluctant to accept the official explanations of the object—including a recent theory that maintains what the Pennsylvanians saw was the crash of a top-secret military experimental vehicle.

Journalist Marie Terry quoted James Romansky, a machinist from Derry, as stating that the minute he stumbled upon the wreckage, he knew it was an alien spacecraft.

Claiming that he had stood less than three feet away from the UFO, Romansky described its appearance as resembling a "giant, metallic acorn," with no visible seams, no motors, no portholes or doors.

On a raised circular sleeve of metal, Romansky said that he saw something "that looked like ancient writing or hieroglyphics."

* * *

William Bulebush, a retired truck driver, was the first person to arrive at the crash site. His description of the object exactly matches that of Romansky.

Bulebush said that he could see the UFO arcing on the ground, giving off showers of blue and white sparks. In his opinion the alien craft had "landed gently, nothing like a crashing plane."

According to many area residents, Army officials rushed to the scene of the downed UFO and immediately cordoned off the wooded hillside where it had crashed.

"Later that same night," Romansky said, "a military flatbed truck came in and drove up to where the alien craft was.

"When it drove back through town later, it carried something on the back covered with a tarpaulin. Whatever it was, it was about the size of the UFO.

"The next day the military said that a meteorite had fallen. That's just plain not true."

Long-time UFO researcher Stan Gordon, director of the Pennsylvania Association for the Study of the Unexplained, has expressed his belief that the military secretly hauled the UFO to an Air Force base in Ohio. He has conducted an extensive search for witnesses to the 1965 event who would talk about what they had seen.

According to Gordon, Romansky and Bulebush are independent witnesses who gave him identical accounts of the UFO crash before they ever heard of each other. Gordon remains convinced that the military covered up the truth about what really crashed on a wooded hillside twenty miles south of Pittsburgh on December 9, 1965.

The most controversial alleged UFO crash site of all is the one on which a great deal of the UFOlogy field has been built and the one which has spawned the origins of nearly every UFO conspiracy theory extant today.

According to most accounts, it was on the night of July 2, 1947, that a UFO developed mechanical problems and fell to

Earth on a ranch located about sixty miles north of Roswell, New Mexico.

Major Jesse Marcel—winner of five air combat medals awarded in World War II, intelligence officer for the 509th Bomb Group, a top-security, handpicked unit—was ordered to go to the ranch and salvage the remains of the unknown aircraft reported by Mac Brazel, a rancher who had discovered the debris on his land.

In 1980 retired Lieutenant Marcel told journalists that he and his men found wreckage from the UFO scattered throughout the area of the crash site. He admitted that he had no idea exactly what it was that he and his men were supposed to retrieve—and, forty years later, he still didn't know.

The strange, weightless material discovered by the 509th Bomber Group was difficult to describe. The pieces varied in length from four or five inches to three or four feet. Some fragments had markings that resembled hieroglyphics.

Although the material seemed to be unbreakable, the military investigators thought that it looked more like wood than metal. Marcel put his cigarette lighter to one of the rectangular fragments, but it would not burn. Major Marcel and his crew brought as many pieces of the crashed UFO back to Roswell Army Air Field Base as they could gather.

One of the first civilians who claimed to arrive on the scene following the crash was Barney Barnett, a civil engineer employed by the federal government. Barnett, from Socorro, New Mexico, later told friends that he had seen alien bodies on the ground and inside the spaceship. He described them as small, hairless beings with large heads and round, oddly spaced eyes.

Barnett stated that a military unit had arrived on the scene. An officer had ordered him off the site with the stern admonition that it was his patriotic duty to remain silent about what he had seen.

Nuclear physicist Stanton Friedman has said that he and author-researcher William Moore have now interviewed at least 130 individuals who have firsthand knowledge of the UFO crash at Roswell. Both Friedman and Moore, who is also the coauthor, with Charles Berlitz, of a book on the crash, *The Roswell Incident,* believe that a flying saucer exploded in the area and that the retrieved bits and pieces were shipped off to Wright Field [now Wright-Patterson Air Force Base] in Dayton, Ohio.

Friedman strongly denies the official story that the military had discovered only a downed weather balloon or the debris of a Japanese bomb balloon [known as a "Fugo"] at the crash site. It is his contention that Walter Haut, on direct orders from the base commander, Col. William Blanchard, prepared the official press release from the Roswell Army Air Force Base that initiated the military conspiracy to keep the truth of a crashed UFO from the public.

Friedman states that Maj. Jesse Marcel was very familiar with all kinds of weather or military balloons and that he would not have mistaken such ordinary debris for that of a downed alien spaceship. Nor would any of the military personnel have mistaken alien bodies for those of diminutive human remains.

After the wreckage was properly identified as extraterrestrial in nature, Friedman contends, the official cover-up was instigated at both the Roswell base and at the headquarters of the Eighth Air Force in Fort Worth, Texas, by Eighth Air Force Commander Roger Ramey on direct orders from General Clements McMullen at SAC headquarters in Washington, D.C.

Veteran UFOlogist and respected author-theorist John A. Keel—who has been a journalistic champion of the reality of the UFO mystery for over forty years—astonishes many of his fellow researchers when he often goes on record as completely discounting the allegations that an alien craft crashed near Roswell in July 1947. In his opinion rancher Mac Brazel did indeed find the remains of a Japanese Fugo balloon.

The strange "metal fragments," Keel asserts, were bits of polished rice paper. The strange alien "hieroglyphics" were simple Japanese instructions, such as "insert in slot B."

Remains of Fugo balloons were found in over 300 sites throughout the western states from 1945 onward through the next twenty years. According to Keel, Major Jesse Marcel would have had no trouble identifying the debris as anything other than the pieces of a Japanese balloon bomb.

"During the last days of World War II," Keel said, "Japan launched 9,000 such balloons against the United States. The balloons were quite large, some thirty-three feet in diameter, and were made of the same durable rice paper of which traditional Japanese houses had been constructed for generations.

"The plastic and metal parts formed lightweight gondolas that carried bombs—usually incendiary bombs made from magnesium, a very thin, light metal. The balloons crossed the Pacific on the jet stream—a trip that usually took about three days— and released their bombs at random over the United States.

"In most cases the people who found the debris of crashed Fugo balloons knew what it was, and in many instances the Army retrieved it."

After four decades of researching the mystery of the Roswell flying saucer crash, Keel remains adamant that this particular UFO case presents no real mystery at all. In his opinion the military personnel immediately recognized the debris for what it was and dealt with it accordingly.

"The mystery was created by UFO advocates in the area and ill-informed local military officials who made rash public statements at the peak of the 1947 'flying saucer' wave," Keel said.

In the January 1991 issue of *Fate* magazine, Keel states that the Roswell story is revived every few years by "untrained, inexperienced amateur enthusiasts who are dedicated to trying to prove their personal beliefs in flying saucers."

Although certain researchers may claim that there are as many as 150 "crashed saucer sites," Keel insists that in his over forty years of UFO investigations, he has not been able to accept any proof that these individuals have presented as conclusive evidence of such extraterrestrial aviation accidents. In his opinion not one single crashed UFO story has been verified.

"This is not because of the mythical government suppression," he states firmly, "but simply because of the obvious fact that UFOs are not crashable."

Recently, however, Kevin Randle, together with Don Schmitt, director of the J. Allen Hynek Center for UFO Studies, decided to renew investigation of the Roswell crash. This much-maligned and hashed-over case of an alleged flying saucer and alien bodies still bore many elements of truth and presented more potential for some kind of resolution of the UFO controversy than chasing down hundreds of accounts of lights in the sky.

"If all this fuss was simply about a bunch of ranchers and townspeople finding the debris from a balloon, why did the military seek out those witnesses and threaten to silence them?" Randle asks pointedly. "There is no question that members of the Army were ordered never to talk about what they had seen. And there seems to be substantial evidence to support the claims that military representatives visited the homes of civilian witnesses and silenced them as well.

"Almost at once, UFO researchers believed that something very different from either a weather balloon or a Fugo balloon crashed outside of Roswell," Randle said. "And at the same time there were rumors that one or more of the alien occupants had survived impact. Only recently has there been some confirmation that this allegation may have some validity."

Randle believes that he and Schmitt have found new evidence indicating that the crash occurred on July 4, 1947, rather than July 2, as is commonly stated. It was on July 5, according to Schmitt and Randle, that Mac Brazel visited Sheriff George Wilcox and informed him of the peculiar discovery he had made near his ranch the day before.

The military unit under the command of Maj. Jesse Marcel retrieved the crash debris and alien bodies on July 5. On July 8 Walter Haut, the public affairs officer at Roswell, issued the press release that the Army had captured a flying saucer. Almost immediately thereafter, the official cover story of a collapsed weather balloon falling to Earth in the desert was heavily promoted by the military.

Randle and Schmitt have spent many hours attempting to sift through the claims surrounding the Roswell UFO case. Most accounts speak of five alien bodies found at the impact site north of Roswell and state that four corpses were transported to Wright Field and the fifth to Lowry Field to the USAF mortuary service.

However, numerous secondary accounts of the incident assert that one of the UFOnauts had survived the crash and was still alive when the military arrived on the scene. Some UFO researchers maintain that circa 1986 the alien being was still alive and well treated as a guest of the Air Force at Wright-Patterson.

During an interview with a granddaughter of Sheriff George

Wilcox in March 1991, Schmitt and Randle were told that not only did the sheriff see the debris of a UFO, he also saw "little space beings."

According to the woman, her grandfather had described the entities as having gray complexions and large heads. They were dressed in suits of a silklike material. "Granddaddy thought one of them was still alive."

Later, military men "who were not kidding" visited the sheriff and his wife and warned them that they would be killed if they ever told anyone what Wilcox saw at the crash site. And not only would they be killed, but their children and grandchildren would also be eliminated.

The persistent investigations of Randle and Schmitt located a Ms. Frankie Rowe, who had been twelve years old at the time of the mysterious occurrences outside of Roswell. Her father, a lieutenant with the fire department, had been called to extinguish an early morning fire out north of town. He told his family at dinner that night that he had seen the remains of what he had at first believed to be an airplane, but soon saw was "some kind of ship."

According to her father, he also saw two bodies in body bags and a third alien entity walking around in a daze. He described the beings as about the size of a ten-year-old child. "We don't have any reason to be afraid," he had said. "These [beings] can't hurt us."

A few days later Frankie happened to be at the fire station visiting her father when a New Mexico State Police officer came in with a strange piece of metal that he claimed he had picked from the UFO crash site when no one was looking.

To the astonishment of the firemen, the trooper tossed the object onto a table where it "unfolded itself in a fluid motion," looking not unlike water flowing. Each of the firefighters had a turn examining the alien metal. Even Frankie had her opportunity to touch the stuff, and she remembers being able to crumple it into a ball.

"I couldn't describe what it felt like, because it didn't feel like I had anything in my hand," she told Schmitt and Randle. "It didn't make a sound like aluminum foil or anything like that. . . . It was thinner than the foil [from gum wrappers]. . . .

It wasn't highly polished like sterling . . . but it was lighter than pewter in color."

Later, she said, the firemen got out knives and torches and tried to cut or burn the metal. She was puzzled how the fragment could have become torn in the first place, since none of them could harm it in any way.

Then, according to Frankie, two or three days after the bizarre demonstration in the firehouse, a group of military men arrived at their house and made it clear that they knew all about the fragment of the UFO that the state police officer had stolen from the crash site and displayed to the firemen—and to one twelve-year-old girl.

The leader of the men "didn't mince any words," Frankie recalled for Schmitt and Randle. He told her that if she ever talked about the incident again, her entire family would be taken out in the desert and "no one would ever find us again."

The two UFO researchers also located Glenn Dennis, who had been the Roswell mortician in 1947. Dennis told them that he, too, had been threatened by representatives of the military concerning his knowledge of the presence of alien bodies.

Dennis said that he had "blundered" into the Roswell Army Air Field hospital on the evening that the alien bodies had been recovered. Earlier Dennis had seen some of the debris and had been told about the corpses of smallish beings by a friend.

According to Dennis, a "nasty red-haired officer" confronted him and warned him that if he ever told anyone about the crash or the alien bodies, "they will be picking your bones from the sand."

In Randle's opinion the results of their research prove beyond the shadow of a doubt that aliens exist. And while he and Schmitt do not know conclusively whether or not one of the alien crew survived the crash outside of Roswell, "there is no doubt that something crashed and that it held a crew."

And Randle also insists that "there is no doubt that the crew was not human."

According to UFO researcher and documentary film-maker Jamie Shandera, in December 1984 he received an anonymous packet in the mail containing two rolls of undeveloped 35-mm film. The film, once developed, revealed what appeared to be a briefing report to President-elect Dwight D. Eisenhower, which described details of the recovery, analysis, and official cover-up of the 1947 UFO crash outside of Roswell, New Mexico.

The "official" report also described the recovery of the bodies of four "humanlike beings" that had been found near the wreckage of the downed extraterrestrial spacecraft. According to these documents all four of the entities were dead, and their corpses had been mutilated by desert scavengers and were badly decomposed due to exposure to the elements.

"Although these creatures are humanlike in appearance," the secret report stated, "the biological and evolutionary processes responsible for their development has apparently been quite different from those observed or postulated in *Homo sapiens.*"

The documents that had somehow found their way to Shandera had allegedly been prepared by a group of twelve prestigious and top-secret investigators who worked under the code name of "Operation Majestic-12." Some unknown source had leaked the documents to the filmmaker within weeks of the death of the last member of the original MJ-12 operatives.

We were in attendance at the Twenty-fourth Annual National UFO Conference in Burbank, California, on June 14, 1987, when Shandera, together with Stanton Friedman and William Moore—the two prominent UFO researchers Shandera had enlisted to help him test the truth of the MJ-12 documents—made public their investigations into what purported to be documentary proof of a government cover-up of UFOs that began in 1947. Moore, in fact, had invited us to be seated at the front table when the formal announcement of their startling research was made, promising us that we would be excited by the implications of what was about to be revealed to the gathered audience of UFO enthusiasts.

According to the documents leaked to Shandera, the members of Majestic-12 consisted of the following individuals:

Lloyd V. Berkner, known for scientific achievements in the fields of physics and electronics, numbered among his many posts and positions that of special assistant to the secretary of state in charge of the Military Assistance Program. He was also executive secretary of what is now known as the Research and Development Board of the National Military Establishment.

Detley W. Bronk, a physiologist and biophysicist of international repute, chairman of the National Research Council, and a member of the Medical Advisory Board of the Atomic Energy Commission. Bronk's main field of research lay in measuring changes in nerve cells during the passage of stimuli to the brain.

Vannevar Bush, a brilliant scientist with an almost endless list of credentials, awards, medals, and academic posts held at nearly every major U.S. college, was, from 1947 to 1948, chairman of Research and Development for the National Military Establishment.

Gordon Gray, three times elected to the North Carolina Senate, succeeded Kenneth Royall as secretary of the Army in June 1949. Gray first came to the Pentagon in September 1947 as assistant secretary of the Army.

Dr. Jerome C. Hunsaker, an innovative aeronautical scientist and design engineer, developed the Shenandoah, the first large airship constructed in the United States. Among numerous academic positions, Dr. Hunsaker served as chairman of the National Advisory Committee for Aeronautics.

Robert M. Montague was the Sandia base commander, Albuquerque, New Mexico, from July 1947 to February 1951.

General Nathan F. Twining was in command of the B-29 superfortresses that dropped the atom bombs on Hiroshima and Nagasaki. In December 1945 he was named commanding general of the Air Material Command headquartered at Wright Field. In October 1947 he was appointed commander in chief of the Alaskan Command, remaining in that position until May 1950, when he became acting deputy chief of staff for personnel at Air Force headquarters in Washington, D.C.

Dr. Donald H. Menzel, director of the Harvard Observatory at Cambridge, Massachusetts, was long acknowledged as a leading authority on the solar chromosphere. In 1941, together with Dr. Winfield W. Salisbury, Menzel formulated the initial calculations that led to the first radio contact with the Moon in 1946.

James V. Forrestal served first as undersecretary, then secretary of the Navy for seven years. In September 1947 he became secretary of defense, responsible for coordinating the activities of all U.S. Armed Forces.

Sidney W. Souers, a Naval reservist who rose to the rank of rear admiral, became deputy chief of Naval Intelligence before organizing the Central Intelligence Office in January 1946. In 1944, *Hoyt S. Vandenberg,* a much-decorated Air Force officer, rose to the rank of commanding general of the Ninth U.S. Air Force in France before he was named assistant chief of staff of G-2 (Intelligence) in 1946. In June 1946 he was appointed the director of Central Intelligence.

Rear Adm. Roscoe H. Hillenkoetter was summonèd from the post of naval attache at the American Embassy in Paris to become the first director of the Central Intelligence Agency (CIA), serving from May 1947 to September 1950. [The CIA was the permanent intelligence agency that evolved from the office organized by Souers.]

James W. Moseley—long-time chronicler of the UFO scene, who was also in attendance with us assembled UFO investigators when the research of MJ-12 was "officially" released by Moore, Friedman, and Shandera—was puzzled by many aspects of the alleged documents.

Later, in his monthly newsletter, Moseley speculated that "Document A," which purported to be a letter dated September 24, 1947, from President Harry S. Truman to Secretary of Defense James Forrestal "may be genuine." The problem, Moseley pointed out, was that although Truman did refer to "Operation Majestic Twelve," he did not state the *purpose* of the operation. Therefore, Moseley observes, MJ-12 could have dealt with something far different from covering up a UFO crash in the New Mexico desert.

As an accomplished UFO historian, Moseley was also struck by the fact that Hillenkoetter, then head of the CIA, was listed as the briefing officer of the MJ-12 document. In 1957 the retired Hillenkoetter had joined the board of directors of the UFO research organization [National Investigations Committee of Aerial Phenomena, NICAP] headed by retired Marine Maj. Donald Keyhoe. "If Hillenkoetter already knew that there had been at least one crash involving dead alien bodies," Moseley asked, "why did he play games with NICAP?"

The biggest shocker on the supposed MJ-12 list for Moseley,

and for all of us long-time UFO investigators, was the name of Donald Menzel, the Harvard astronomer, who we all knew was a passionate debunker of UFOs and who had expressed his vehemence toward the subject in three antiUFO books. Moseley had known Dr. Menzel personally. "Did he live a lie [regarding UFOs] for all of his later years?" Moseley asked pointedly. "He would have had to, if he had known since 1947 that dead aliens had been found in New Mexico."

Barry Greenwood, editor of *Just Cause,* mused that his first thoughts upon seeing the list of MJ-12's alleged personnel was that if a UFO *had* crashed and was recovered, this would be the kind of panel that he would want to put together. "All of these individuals were at the top in their respective areas of expertise during the late 1940s and had the added benefit of government experience behind them."

In October 1987 we appeared on a UFO panel at the Whole Life EXPO in Los Angeles, which included Stanton Friedman and William Moore. Although they admitted they were still in the process of validating the MJ-12 documents, they stated they were "reasonably convinced" of their authenticity.

Friedman told the large audience in attendance that one of the principal purposes for the official government coverup of UFOs—as disclosed by the MJ-12 debriefing document—was that there had been "almost a public panic in response to the sightings in 1947."

As of this writing in 1994, the MJ-12 documents remain highly controversial, with UFO researchers divided in their analyses of the investigation of Shandera, Moore, and Friedman.

"I think the MJ-12 documents are clearly false and fradulent," Kevin Randle told us. "A search of the records of the Truman administration reveals no executive order for 'MJ-12.' I think the big giveaway lies in the many incorrect military terms and language used in these alleged 'official' documents. It is clear to me that the creators of the hoax have never served in the military—and neither have the proponents of MJ-12.''

UFO researcher and publisher Timothy Green Beckley has come to believe that the documents themselves are probably not legitimate, but he concedes that ''they may be based on original documents'' that someone leaked so that ''others might benefit from the research.''

Author-researcher John White accepts the documents as genuine until they are proven to be otherwise. ''If the present documents are phoney,'' he says, ''then I believe that *something* very close to this kind of cover-up occurred. I think that [MJ-12] is the genesis of a shadow government, a rogue group, that is capable of making secret deals. I suspect that high levels of our government know about these deals.''

While Beckley is suspicious of the authenticity of the MJ-12 documents, he thinks that whatever crashed in the New Mexico desert in July 1947 was no weather balloon. ''The weather balloon theory is all hot air in my opinion.''

But in the January 15, 1994, issue of his ''nonscheduled newsletter,'' James W. Moseley reprints the telex that was sent by the Air Force to the FBI's Dallas office on July 6, 1947. Submitted by UFO researcher Simone Mendez, the text reads as follows:

Teletype: FBI Dallas; 7-6-47; 6:17 P.M.; Director and SAC Cincinnati, Flying disc, information concerning: [Censored], Headquarters Eighth Air Force telephonically advised this office that an object purporting to be a flying disc was recovered near Roswell, New Mexico, this date. The disc is hexagonal in shape and was suspended by a balloon by cable, which balloon was approximately 20 feet in diameter. [Censored] further advised that the object found resembles a high altitude weather balloon with a radar reflector, but that telephonic conversation between their office and Wright Field had not borne out this belief. Disc and balloon being transported to Wright Field by special plane for examination. Information provided this office because of national interest in case and fact that National Broadcasting Company, Associated Press, and others attempting to break story of location of disc today. [Censored] advised would request Wright Field to advise Cincinnati office results of examination. No further investigation being conducted . . .

Moseley states that the telex indicates that the object retrieved by the military was, indeed, a balloon. The only mystery lay in determining what kind of balloon bore a hexagonal disc suspended by a cable. Of course, Moseley goes on to note, those UFO researchers who champion the reality of an alien space vehicle having crashed near Roswell will perceive the telex as a clear case of the military lying to the FBI as a part of the cover-up process.

On the other hand, in the fall 1992 issue of *UFO Universe,* Judith Willms states in "Close Encounters Update" that retired Gen. Thomas DuBose, who at the time of the Roswell incident was a colonel and chief of staff to Brig. Gen. Roger Ramey, commander of the Eighth Air Force at Fort Worth, Texas, now freely admits that in July 1947 the military investigators had no idea what they had found.

"But the word came down from Air Force headquarters that the story was to be 'contained,' and we came up with this weather balloon story, which I thought was a hell of a good idea. Somebody got [a weather balloon], ran it up a couple of hundred feet and dropped it to make it looked like it had crashed—and that's what we used."

Lewis Rickett, now 82 years old, was a master sergeant and counterintelligence agent stationed at Roswell Air Field, who, with Captain Sheridan Cavitt, another counterintelligence agent, was among those military personnel who were actually at the site.

"It was no weather balloon," Rickett said. "The fragments were no more than six or seven inches long and up to eight to ten inches wide. . . . They were not jagged . . . but curved and flexible. They couldn't be broken."

Rickett and Cavitt collected a bushel basket of fragments, which were sent to Washington classified top secret.

Oliver "Pappy" Henderson, two years before his death, swore at a reunion of his World War II bomber crew that he had flown the remains of four alien bodies out of Roswell Army Field in a C-54 cargo plane in duly 1947.

Don Schmitt and Kevin Randle in their book *UFO Crash At Roswell* include an interview with Brig. Gen. Arthur Exon that, in addition to debris from the wreckage, four tiny alien cadavers were flown to Wright Field: "They [the alien bodies] were all found, apparently, outside the craft itself. . . . The metal and material from the spaceship was unknown to anyone I talked to. . . . Roswell was the recovery of a craft from space."

The controversy surrounding MJ-12 and the Roswell incident is not going to die down until incontrovertible evidence is presented to prove conclusively what really crashed outside of Roswell, New Mexico, in July 1947.

On January 14, 1994, the Associated Press carried the story of New Mexico Congressman Steve Schiff's request to the General Accounting Office (GAO), the investigative arm of Congress, to determine whether or not a government cover-up had been put in place after the 1947 crash of a mysterious object northwest of Roswell.

Schiff said that he had asked the GAO to research the matter after he had received letters from people who claimed to have witnessed the wreckage at the crash site. According to the Republican congressman, as of January 12, the GAO was getting "stonewalled" by the Defense Department—which was only making the congressional investigators "that much more interested" in the case.

CHAPTER 15

UFO Sightings and Cover-Ups that Could Change the World

On July 8, 1984, the headlines of the Toronto *Star* declared: SCIENTISTS AND COMPUTERS ARE HARD AT WORK TO EXPLAIN THOUSANDS OF MYSTERIOUS SIGHTINGS FROM ALL CORNERS OF THE WORLD.

The cover story stated emphatically that the top-secret air bases of Canada and the United States had been innundated with reports of unidentified flying objects that had shown up on radar.

The two-page story named Dr. J. Allen Hynek, the former head of the Department of Astronomy at Northwestern University as the top UFO researcher in North America, according to Canada's own National Research Council and Hynek's own peers. "Canada, surprisingly, has more UFO sightings per capita than anywhere else in the world—I don't know why," said Dr. Hynek.

The Canadian endorsement of Dr. Hynek does not stand alone. *Newsweek* called Hynek "the Galileo of UFO research" and "the WORLD'S ranking expert on the science . . . art of UFOlogy." *Time* magazine said "he was the scientific community's most outspoken investigator of UFOs." Indeed, he was. Dr. Hynek served in the official capacity of scientific advisor for Project Bluebook, the twenty-year top-secret United States Air Force study of unidentified flying objects.

Hynek was so dedicated to trying to find an answer to the UFO controversy that when the Air Force's Bluebook study was terminated, Dr. Hynek founded the nonprofit Center for UFO Studies based in Evanston, Illinois, and in the last few years of his life, he founded a second office, the Center for UFO Research, in Scottsdale, Arizona.

Dr. Hynek investigated over 80,000 reports of unidentified flying objects from over 161 countries worldwide. All 80,000 cases were stored on Northwestern University's giant computer. Hynek, his wife Mimi, and a staff correlated and investigated reports around the world. As many as possible were investigated firsthand, but the sheer volume of the cases and lack of funding for equipment, translations, travel, etc., was a constant frustration.

UFO research has not been the same since his death in 1986. His reputation and respect were well deserved. Dr. Hynek's credentials would be hard to match; his shoes hard to fill. Needless to say, he is missed. He paved the way with his lifelong mission— laying the groundwork for many to follow—including ourselves. We were honored to have worked closely with Dr. Hynek for the last years of his life, serving as his contractual manager and publicist. Through our work with him, we were privy to much information and insight into the incredible and often bizarre field of UFOlogy. Any doubt we might have had into the possibility of conspiracies and cover-ups pertaining to UFOs was quickly put to rest in our own minds.

Hynek told us that the UFO reports which came into Project Bluebook that seemed to have the most substantial information to investigate were removed from his hands. As a matter of fact, he was ordered to make up cover-up stories to steer the public away from any UFO suspicions. In some cases, such as the famous "Michigan" one, so much flurry had already leaked out to the press that when Hynek was ordered to go on record at a press conference to tell the public that all the strange occurrences were attributed to "swamp gas"—many wondered which side Dr. Hynek was on.

The frustration of not having access to the more serious UFO cases wasn't limited to the "nuts and bolts" scientist Hynek. We have already mentioned earlier in this book that former senator Barry Goldwater, and former presidents Carter, Ford, and Reagan were denied access as well.

Of the 80,000 cases in Bluebook files, over 10,000 were "actual UFOs"—or in other words, phenomena that could not be explained away to the public as weather balloons, planes, or a natural phenomenon—they were true unidentified flying objects. In our book 10,000 cases would seem worthy enough to continue the "official" investigations.

Dr. Hynek, who was responsible for categorizing sightings (UFO sightings of the first kind, second kind, third kind, and fourth kind—see Appendix), also was technical advisor to Steven Spielberg's spectacular movie *Close Encounters of the Third Kind*. Dr. Hynek and Spielberg corresponded frequently, and the movie was based on composite cases from the files.

Hynek told us that Canada and the United States shared an exchange program between the two Defense Departments. Many of those cases were not made public until fairly recently when both governments passed Freedom of Information Acts. The story in the *Toronto Star* focused on several of those cases. "You would think that the scientific world would be agog with the phenomenal cases that are coming in, yet Washington or Ottawa file them away," Hynek said.

Dr. Hynek was impressed by the caliber and sincerity of the people who reported the cases he investigated firsthand. "Worldwide, people who report UFOs have *definitely* seen something, but the fact remains that more people do not report what they have seen or experienced for fear of ridicule." Always quick to point out that with the information available, no one has been able to prove whether or not the sightings were alien spaceships or some unknown earthly phenomenon, "the sightings and descriptions display a strange universal consistency that adds to the mystery," Hynek said.

Hynek was keenly aware that the Canadian and U.S. government attitude toward UFOs was not the disinterested one they appeared to have—but in fact was one of the utmost seriousness and secrecy. Declassified documents obtained through the Freedom of Information Act reveal that the "filing away of reports they'd hope would go away" was if anything a *cover* cover story!

In a Canadian Department of Transport memo dated November 21, 1950, Wilbert B. Smith, senior radio engineer, forwarded a proposal to the controller of telecommunications suggesting formal studies of, for example, the use of Earth's own magnetic field as a possible energy source. The subject of UFOs came up in Smith's memo:

I made discreet enquiries through the Canadian Embassy staff in Washington who were able to obtain for me the following information:

a. The matter is the most highly classified subject in the United States Government, rating even higher than the H-bomb.
b. Flying saucers exist.
c. Their modus operandi is unknown but concentrated effort is being made by a small group headed by Vannevar Bush.
d. The entire matter is considered by the United States authorities to be of tremendous significance.

The Smith memo itself was classified top secret.

The "official" closing of Project Bluebook in 1969—with the pronouncement that UFOs don't exist—becomes less believable than Santa Claus to an adult with the evidence that continues to surface.

In her excellent book *The UFO Conspiracy,* respected researcher Jenny Randles makes some powerful observations.

Reports of unidentified flying objects which could affect national security are made in accordance with JANAP 146 or Air Force Manual 55-11 and are not part of the Blue Book system . . . reports of UFOs which could affect national security should continue to be handled through the standard Air Force procedure designed for this purpose.

The above paragraph is from a memo, dated October 20, 1969, signed by Brig. Gen. C. H. Bolender, the USAF deputy director of development. This is what led to the closure of Project Bluebook six weeks later. Yet in 1987 the U.S. government still referred to that closure as marking the end of *all* U.S. Air Force interest in UFOs [note the memo clearly states: *"reports should continue"*]

In all likelihood reports and investigation did continue even if through different channels or the possibility of a "deal having been made" with the aliens—in all good faith, of course—as we've mentioned elsewhere in this book. During 1984, 1985, and

1986 a bizarre sequence of events occurred that resulted in some changes in the field of UFOlogy and its most respected researcher, Dr. Hynek, that to us only confirms the cry of conspiracy and further makes it even more difficult to know or trust the players and their motivations.

Through a series of events, Hynek was led to open a second UFO base in Scottsdale, Arizona. Various complications and disagreements led to severing any possible involvement, alignment, or connection between the Illinois and Arizona locations.

False promises of megadollars had been made to Dr. Hynek from the very beginning to fund a research facility of his dreams based in Scottsdale. Hynek found out that in spite of all the media hype and official releases regarding these promises, once he moved from Evanston, Illinois, to sunny Scottsdale, the funding commitment was as dry as the desert. Hynek, living up to his reputation, took it as a gentleman, made the best of it, and more or less considered it an active retirement. The Evanston Center for UFO Studies remained intact.

Once he was in Arizona, intense discussions ensued between officials at the highest level and Hynek and staff at ICUFOR (the new name given the Arizona UFO Center), regarding the likelihood of the imminent release of the largest batch of classified top-secret files regarding unidentified flying objects that had ever occurred. If the release were to happen, "it would be into the hands of none other than Dr. Hynek himself." Because of Hynek's high standing and reputation, he was considered the most worthy person to whom to entrust the top-secret files.

Promises were made to Hynek to "view" the alleged bodies of aliens and saucer whenever he was ready. After all his intensive pursuit to do so over the years, Hynek wondered, Why now?

A great deal of information was coming in regarding several cases on videotape, as well as substantial witness accounts—thousands of them. Dr. Hynek asked us to view and discuss the videos sent to him, interview people, and discuss with him the most amazing cases, which were building in momentum.

One of these cases is referred to as the Westchester or Hudson Valley incident, which took place in upstate New York. The other was the Westbridge/Rendlesham Forest incident, more commonly referred to as the "Bentwaters Case,' " which occurred over a shared U.S. and U.K. NATO base boundary in Great Britain.

The government was pressured by attorneys and citizens for answers. It appeared that the Freedom of Information Act and the dedication of those in pursuit of truth was about to pay off— but it didn't happen. Instead, some disruptive events took place and Dr. Hynek died of a brain tumor in April 1986.

Whether or not a conspiracy of sorts had taken place to set up Dr. Hynek with false promises and throw him off guard—as many suspect—cannot be proven. Perhaps these "officials" were legitimate and sincere, but the intended release of documents never took place because of the untimely death of Dr. Hynek, the lead "star"—so the play was canceled. Either way the "script" reads like something was going on behind the scenes.

Dr. Hynek was, in fact, working on a book with Philip Imbrogno and Bob Pratt about the Westchester sightings when he died. The book, *Night Siege,* was published in 1987 and is an excellent account of the phenomenal nature of this case.

A few minutes before midnight on New Year's Eve, a retired New York City police officer went out on his deck to uncork a bottle of champagne when he saw incredible bright lights in the sky the shape of a huge boomerang. Convinced that the object was moving much too slowly to be a jet, yet unsure of what else it was, he screamed at his wife to bring the video camera.

It was totally unlike anything they'd ever seen before. The video camera arrived just in time to tape the object as it passed overhead about 500 feet before it vanished behind some trees in the direction of Interstate 84, which was about a mile from their home. Other people recorded the event on videotape as well. Hynek was sent the footage. As we viewed them, the audio portion of one of the tapes captured the spontaneity and betrayed the shock and confusion that seemed to surround all of them. "Oh my God, what the [   ] can that be?" "Look at the size of that!" "Oh [   ]! "I'll tell you this, honey, that isn't like any type of aircraft I've ever seen, what the [   ] is it?"

Analysis of the footage indicated that the lights all seemed to be connected as one object, yet nothing solid seemed visible. The lights would instantly change from white to colored, then to red or blue and back to white. The white lights were so bright they lit up the entire area. The shape mostly appeared as triangular and was as big as a football field.

That was just the beginning. The sightings occurred over a 1,400-square-mile area covering Westchester, Putnam, and Dutchess Counties in New York and neighboring Fairfield, Litchfield, and New Haven Counties in Connecticut. There were so many sightings that the Taconic Parkway and switchboards were jammed for many hours, endangering emergency vehicles, calls, and reports. It was nearly impossible to get through.

There were so many reports that investigators could only concentrate on the "close encounters" where the object came within 500 feet of the witnesses. A conservative estimate was that over 5,000 people saw a triangular or boomerang-shaped object as big as a football field. Sometimes the object shot straight up and disappeared instantly. At times it hovered. Sometimes it shot down beams of light. Other times different colored lights and often no lights at all. Some people reported telepathic communication from the object, some were terrorized; others heard a voice say, "Don't be afraid." Over the years, as the reports were investigated, many people had "missing time" or reported strange occurrences or phenomena, even abductions.

The sightings continued over a period of three years and still continues with random reports and experiences. The sightings were written off as small planes flying in formation. In fact, right after the biggest wave of sightings a group of pilots *did* fly in formation as a joke. Those were the sightings most of the public heard about as they made the headlines.

Some of the same people who videotaped the mystery UFO captured the small planes flying in formation as well. We also saw those tapes. There was no comparison. Not even the skill of pilots flying in formation could duplicate the overhead video of the craft. The engines of the small planes were clearly audible—the craft almost silent.

The FAA denied any craft in the area and said there were absolutely *no* clearances given for landing or take off at the time of all the activity. So, what was it? The Stealth Bomber became public knowledge not too long after that; but no jet could duplicate the strange behavior of the unidentified craft, and certainly the Stealth Bomber is not the size of a football field.

In 1985 Home Box Office did a production with Dr. Hynek and others on UFOs called *America Under-Cover*. With permission, they had one of the videotapes analyzed at the Jet Propulsion Laboratory in Pasadena, California. Dr. Hibbs, a computer-enhancement expert, used the multimillion-dollar equipment used for the Voyager and Viking Space probes. Higgs concluded that the object could not be identified.

Peter Gersten, an attorney with CAUS (Citizens Against UFO Secrecy), Philip Imbrogno, Bob Pratt, and Hynek planned a citizens meeting at a school in Brewster, New York, to bring together as many witnesses as possible. The school auditorium seated 500, but the crowd they expected was somewhere between 100 and 200. The shock was overwhelming when over 1,500 people showed up. The media was there in surprising force as well. More than seventy-five newspaper, radio, and TV crews showed up; even the *Chicago Tribune* sent a reporter. People started arriving at 9 A.M. and stayed all day until midnight.

Many puzzling things happened during the episodes with representatives from the National Security Agency [NSA] and the FBI. Although they said they were not there officially, but because they were "personally" interested, they seemed to know information "instantly" that they could know only if they were "listening in." Evidence from press offices and other facilities with special equipment monitored lines that were indicative of being tapped.

One "representative" from NSA was persistent in wanting to see one of the videotapes of the craft [the Pozzuoli tape]. He'd pop up with facts just learned moments before in conversations he shouldn't have known anything about. Asking if he could meet with Imbrogno and Pratt, he arranged this meeting in a "family" home—which just happened to be near the meeting place they'd just confirmed, moments before on the phone, to meet Connecticut investigator Sheila Sabo.

Upset that they did not have the original tape along, but that it was in a safe place, the NSA agent insisted that Imbrogno hand over that tape in order to have it analyzed. When Imbrogno refused, a most shocking response was given to them. "You know, Phil," the NSA agent said, "the government has done away with people for a lot less."

* * *

We sat in the living room with Dr. Hynek and viewed video-tapes and tried to track down further information on the Bent-waters case in 1984. It took until 1993 for many pieces of what we saw then to come together. We kept what we saw quiet, telling only a few people. Then after talking with one of the witnesses at a conference where we were lecturing, and talking with Jenny Randles and Larry Fawcett and Phil Imbrogno at other times, the pieces of all our information matched. We interviewed Larry Warren, one of the lead witnesses to come forward.

The following is a summary of this most astounding case—perhaps, as Timothy Green Beckley, *UFO Universe,* says, "the most documented close encounter between the military and extrater-restrial intelligence ever made!"

In 1980, on Christmas Day, just after 9:45 P.M. (Greenwich Mean Time), several mysterious lights were sighted in the skies of northern Europe. The lights passed from northern Portugal toward Germany and the southern English counties of Kent and Sussex.

There were many witnesses, including the entire crew of a plane carrying tourists to Spain, witnesses manning air bases and radar monitors at Watton, near the city of Norwich, (southeastern England). Several witnesses in Portugal even developed skin rashes and became ill after watching the lights in the sky that they thought at the time to be "satellite re-entry."

Official explanation of the lights ranged from the atmospheric re-entry of a booster rocket from a Soviet satellite to comets breaking up into small pieces and meteors blazing across the sky. But the lights caused far more commotion than any meteor or falling debris could possibly warrant.

Radar base operators tracked what might have been a UFO that crossed the coast and "landed" near the Rendlesham Forest, where tracking was lost. They phoned facilities in the area to see if any other radar site had tracked the object. They discovered that the object had been seen from the Bentwaters and Woodbridge bases, which were told to retain their radar records for future investigation.

Intelligence officers from the USAF visited the base a few days later, taking these records and telling the staff at Watton that a UFO had come down near Woodbridge Air Base and had been observed by senior military personnel.

Author-researcher Jenny Randles spoke with the radar officer at the base who was present when the intelligence officers visited, and removed the evidence. One radar officer told Jenny that the altitude from which the UFO descended was far above any aircraft's ceiling—so high, in fact, that he could not tell her the altitude because it would reveal details of the radar's limitations, strictly prohibited under Britain's Official Secrets Act.

In spite of "official denial" on the behalf of both the U.S. and British governments, as of this writing in 1993, over twenty-five eyewitnesses have been found and interviewed. CNN ran a series of news reports and *Unsolved Mysteries,* a national TV tabloid show, featured the case two times within one year. Conflicting information from the Air Force, evasive answers from a U.S. senator, and denial of any such incident from the governments indicate that there is a coverup still in effect.

Two British documentaries that were scheduled with the transmission date set were canceled at the last minute. A senior BBC producer told Jenny Randles that wherever he went, people wanted to make a film, but after a few hours, doors slammed shut without explanation. It was "almost as if there is a conspiracy to stop this program being made," he told her.

Many of the firsthand witnesses have experienced ongoing problems dealing with what happened to them during those nights in 1980 and are troubled with nightmares and anxiety. They have been so bothered by the events that despite threats, many of them are talking about what they saw.

It has been through the dedicated effort of many researchers, including Ray Boeche, Jenny Randles, Brenda Butler, Scott Colborn, Larry Fawcett, and Barry Greenwood, as well as Dr. Hynek and the informants that a clearer picture of the scenario is emerging.

As we stated earlier, several tapes were sent to Dr. Hynek in 1985 and 1986 that he had us watch regarding this case. It was stated in those tapes that there were actual photographs, recordings, and video of the UFO and the occupants, soil samples, radioactive readings, etc., that were removed from the officers on duty by an unmarked black jet, to be taken for "official analysis."

The September 1993 issue of *Fate* magazine reported that a "live" tape of UFO arrivals and second night of encounters made in the forest during the study of the landing site was unexpectedly received in August 1984 by investigating UFOlogists in Britain [one copy sent by a USAF colonel who had actually been on the base].

This taped commentary runs for eighteen minutes. A team of officers and airmen were in the forest to investigate the landing site of the "light." They took samples, obtained photographs, and measured traces left on the ground by the initial UFO landing. The following is from that tape:

1:48 A.M. on December 27, 1980. We are hearing . . . strange sounds out of a farmer's barnyard animals . . . very active, making an awful lot of noise . . .

You just saw a light? Where? Slow down. Where?

Right on this position here. Straight ahead . . . between the trees . . . there it is again. Straight ahead of my flashlight beam. There it is.

I see it too. What is it?

We don't know, sir.

At this point the men turn off their flashlights and try to reach the light that they describe as being red—through the trees and clearings. Occasionally the tape recorder is switched on to record what happens. Their voices are very strained and obviously stressed.

We are about 150 to 200 yards from the site. Everything else is just deathly calm. There's no doubt about it, there is some type of strange flashing red light ahead.

Sir, it is yellow.

I saw a yellow tinge in it, too. Weird.

It appears to be moving a little bit this way. It is brighter than it has been. It is definitely coming this way.

Pieces of it are shooting off. There is no doubt about it—this is weird.

For more than an hour the men pursued the craft. Finally

the object stood in front of them and appeared to exhibit an intelligent interest in their presence.

Here he comes from the south. He is coming toward us now.

Now we observe what appears to be a beam coming down toward the ground. This is unreal.

The tape begins to break up at this point with the men's voices "breaking" with the stress of what they are witnessing. "Turning around and heading back toward the base" are the last audible messages on it.

Certain interesting events seemed to link the unfolding of more testimony about the incident. In 1983 *Omni* magazine did a story describing a small craft moving in and out of the trees at Bentwaters and escaping the pursuing USAF. Several witnesses came forward shortly after, one being Larry Warren. In 1983 Warren approached CAUS (Citizens Against UFO Secrecy), and his story matched reports of the incident that Jenny Randles had written about in a UFO journal, which had been the only published statement about the matter until the *Omni* article.

CAUS received a copy of the report submitted by the Bentwaters base to the British Ministry of Defense in London, after using Warren's testimony and British government confirmation to apply the American Freedom of Information Act in order to obtain available documentation.

The document was signed by Lt. Col. Charles Halt, then deputy base commander (later promoted to full base commander). Halt and Moreland confirmed it was real—as did the Defense Ministry in London—after having hidden it for several years.

Copy of Lt. Col. Halt's letter, dated 13 Jan. 81:

SUBJECT: Unexplained Lights
TO: RAF/CC

1. Early in the morning of 27 Dec 80 (approximately 0300L), two USAF security police patrolmen saw unusual lights outside the back gate at RAF Woodbridge. Thinking an aircraft might have crashed or been forced down, they called for permission to go outside the gate to investigate. The on-duty flight chief responded and allowed three patrolmen to proceed on foot. The individuals reported seeing a strange

glowing object in the forest. The object was described as being metallic in appearance and triangular in shape, approximately two to three meters across the base and approximately two meters high. It illuminated the entire forest with a white light. The object itself had a pulsing red light on top and a bank(s) of blue lights underneath. The object was hovering or on legs. As the patrolmen approached the object, it maneuvered through the trees and disappeared. At this time the animals on a nearby farm went into a frenzy. The object was briefly sighted approximately an hour later near the back gate.

2. The next day, three depressions 1 1/2" deep and 7" in diameter were found where the object had been sighted on the ground. The following night (29 Dec 80) the area was checked for radiation. Beta/gamma readings of 0.1 milliroentgens were recorded with peak readings in the three depressions and near the center of the triangle formed by the depressions. A nearby tree had moderate (.05–.07) readings on the side of the tree toward the depressions.

3. Later in the night a red sun-like light was seen through the trees. It moved about and pulsed. At one point it appeared to throw off glowing particles and then broke into five separate white objects that moved rapidly in sharp angular movements and displayed red, green and blue lights. The objects to the north remained in the sky for an hour or more. The object to the south was visible for two or three hours and beamed down a stream of light from time to time. Numerous individuals, including the undersigned, witnessed the activities in paragraphs 2 and 3.

> [signed]
> CHARLES I. HALT, Lt Col,
> USAF
> Deputy Base Commander

This document clearly establishes that there was more than one significant encounter and further clarifies some of the confusion that surrounds the testimonies. Although the alien beings suspended or floating in a beam of light coming from the craft are not mentioned, the document reveals the following:

• A team of security police had gone into the forest in response to sightings of an object crashing [in the early hours of December 26, 1980] and pursued a strange craft through the trees before it outran them and left.

• Ground traces [three indentations in the earth forming a triangle] and excess radiation found inside these holes were landing marks left by the UFO and discovered at dawn by investigating officers.

• It tied in with Warren's testimony. A team of USAF personnel in the woods the next night, December 27, investigated the strange lights that created a disturbance among local farm animals, also witnessed by Halt.

In October 1983 banner headlines in Britain's top-selling newspaper, the *News of the World,* reverberated around the world and provoked questions of the British Parliament. Jenny Randles reported that Ralph Noyes, though retired at the time of the Bentwaters incident, was the man who headed the British department receiving UFO data from air bases and police. Noyes made the statement, "We now have evidence, I blush to say of my own Ministry of Defense, that they have lied about this matter—they have covered it up."

In 1986 the Armed Forces minister, Roger Freeman, was forced to put his comments on public record: "Clearly there was no threat to the American unit [at the Bentwaters base]. . . . There is, perhaps, doubt in the mind, certainly of the officer who reported the incident, what the occurrence was. But there are things which happen every day where you cannot necessarily explain what has happened or why." And as Jenny Randles says, "In other words, it was a UFO."

Lord Peter Hill-Norton, a brilliant military tactician and former head of Britain's naval fleet, was briefed about the UFO case by esteemed investigator-author Tim Good. [See Tim Good's excellent book *Above Top Secret.*] Insisting that this incident *did* indeed have defense significance, Lord Hill-Norton pursued answers receiving only that "the Ministry of Defense was content that the Rendlesham [Forest] incident was of no defense significance, because whatever was witnessed was not apparently hostile."

This puts the question in our minds of how so many released statements from high officials can be so certain that whatever was witnessed was not hostile. Several of the witnesses said they saw high-ranking officers working side by side with "the aliens" to repair the UFO. If this is so, then both add up to previous contact with the aliens in order to be so sure they were nonthreatening. Could the "secret deal" with the aliens be true?

On a chilly eve of November 1989, several *gendarmes* [policemen] reported sighting a strange triangular craft in the skies over Belgium. Hundreds of witnesses came forward—all describing the same triangular object. Belgian radar had also tracked the mystery object. But that wasn't the strangest part—that eve marked only the beginning of the continuing wave of similar sightings that are still going on.

On July 11, 1991, an extraordinary press conference was held. High-ranking members of the Belgian military briefed the media about a UFO, which Air Force jets attempted to chase down and had remarkably recorded on their radar screens. They were so deluged by thousands of similar sightings that a unique approach was taken to coordinate and decipher the reports. A research organization has been established and funded by scientists, the Belgium military, and private citizens—all working hand in hand to set up lines of communication to determine procedure for future encounters.

It all began just outside the town of Eupen, which is less than seven miles from the German border, when two officials from the *gendarmerie* were on a routine patrol. Their attention was drawn to an unusual sight. They saw a light shining down on a field that lit it up like lights on a football field would—but this was not a football field and there were no lights in that area to illuminate it like that.

Wanting to see what was causing the lights, they pulled over to the side of the road to get a closer look. "There was a *huge* triangular platform and underneath it—*strong* headlights. In the middle of it was this blinking—pulsating—orange light. The whole thing was just floating in the air," said Eupen *gendarme* Heinrich Nicoll.

The two officials immediately called in the report to Albert Creutz, the dispatcher for the Eupen *gendarmerie*. Creutz said, "They were telling me they were seeing a strange light in the sky and that it made no noise. We joked about it in the dispatch office—saying it might be Santa Claus trying to land." Nicoll didn't think that was so funny. He insisted it was serious; that something weird was in the sky. He asked Creutz to call the military to see if they were on maneuvers or if there was a secret project being tested.

Remaining skeptical, Creutz recorded the report in his journal. The *gendarmes* followed the UFO as it soared across the Belgian countryside toward Eupen. Moments later, a strange light flashed across the window of Creutz's office in Eupen. Creutz reported that off in the distance he could see something bright, but he didn't know what it was—then all of a sudden something like a laser beam shot out of the light and then went back to the light.

In the meantime the officers reported that the object they were following seemed to circle over the city of Eupen, then appeared to head toward the forest. The officers were mesmerized, but began to suspect that this "visitor" must have some special purpose.

Nicoll described that on each side of the triangular-shaped object a kind of laser light projected to the ground and a ball came out of the center of the object—leaving the object, going down to the ground, and then back up to the object—as if the ball were trying to measure something.

When Nicoll again called his dispatch office, he found that Creutz had contacted four local airports, each of which reported no unusual activity in the sky. Yet for a full thirty minutes, the *gendarmes* watched the object as it hovered silently in the same place—not moving.

Then a most unexpected thing happened. Suddenly another spacecraft appeared out of nowhere. They were more than a little frightened by another bright light that came out of the sky while the other one still hovered in the same spot. Then one tilted slightly. "You could see it was the shape of a triangle with bright lights—one bright one in the middle. It was exactly like the first object. We could see some kind of dome on the top of two or three small windows—and there was a light inside the object. By the time we realized what it was, the object flew away," said Nicoll.

Moments later Creutz saw through his office window a "strange machine" floating about 500 feet away. He described it as looking like a large ship floating in the air. "It drifted in front of me for a few seconds—then it flew away in the direction of Lacarmaine."

Six minutes later two other *gendarmes* eight miles to the north in the small village of Lacarmaine saw a similar object. They had heard their colleagues talking about a flying object. At first they thought it was some kind of a joke—until *they* saw it, and then it wasn't a bit funny! "Both of us had a funny feeling—it was impossible to explain what the object was," said the officer. At first they thought it was a new kind of plane, but soon realized they had no explanation for what was above them—except it was real and right overhead!"

The two officers told of another object that seemed to be leaving the main object. They described it as a red light—a red pulsating light that descended vertically from the object, then made a right-hand turn and moved off behind a building. Suddenly the officers saw the entire triangular craft transform into a single beam of light and completely disappear!

All four of these spectacular sightings occurred within twenty miles and one hour of each other. On that same day eleven other *gendarmes* and more than 100 private citizens came forward with similar reports. Belgium was literally buzzing with UFO reports and talk of UFOs.

In March 1990 the next wave of sightings began. Captain Jaque Pinson of the *gendarmerie* had been called to a home where a dinner party had been interrupted by strange lights in the sky. The guests and Pinson [when he arrived to check out the disturbance] described seeing an array of lights in the sky. They described the main colors of the lights as reddish or yellow, while others were green. The lights erratically began to travel short distances.

Meanwhile, thirty miles away at a NATO tracking station, radar tracked an unknown object at the exact same location where the dinner guests had reported seeing the strange lights. On radar it showed up as a small circle with a tail in the lower quadrant of the radar screen.

Lt. Col. Pierre Billen, the commander at the NATO radar station said that they phoned the other civilian and military radar bases to see if they were picking up anything. They were reporting the precisely same echo at the same place! Billen said they were not able to identify whether the echo showing up on radar was "friendly." He also stated that it wasn't clear if the object was an aircraft.

With four confirmations from four different bases, the Belgian Air Force was now on alert. Something very unusual was in the skies over Belgium! Two F-16 fighter jets were immediately deployed from the Belgian Air Force on a mission to locate and identify the object. The pilots soon locked on to the object with onboard radar. They gave chase, but after five seconds the object bolted out of range at what the pilots reported to be "blistering speed."

Maj. Gen. W. J. L. DeBrouwer of the Belgian Air Force said, "We measured some exceptional accelerating which cannot be related to conventional aircraft—that is clear." For the next hour the pilots reported that the UFO seemed to be playing a high-tech version of cat and mouse. Each time they achieved lock-on with the UFO, it darted out of range.

Lieutenant Colonel Billen said the pilots confirmed it was completely impossible for them to accelerate as quickly as the target.

An examination of the onboard radar footage astonished the military. When the pilots first locked on the UFO, it was at 7,000 feet in altitude. Then in seconds it climbed to 10,000 feet—and incredibly within seconds plummeted to just 990 knots—more than 1,000 miles an hour or one and a half times the speed of sound! This phenomenal combination of acceleration and deceleration would have been *fatal* to a human pilot.

Even though the craft exceeded the speed of sound, no one on the ground reported hearing a sonic boom.

Skeptics report the phenomena were due to mass hysteria and the echoes due to atmospheric changes. In response, Billen says, "Thousands and thousands of witnesses are undaunted by comments like this. They know what they saw. I think it is our job to find out if there really is something, *what* this thing is and *where* it comes from and what its *intentions* are. Indeed there *is* something going on in Belgium which is beyond our control!''

Beginning in July of 1991, thousands of UFOs have been sighted over Mexico City. Some believe this to be the largest, most documented UFO sighting in history—the beginning of an alien invasion predicted more than 3,000 years ago.

The sightings began on July 11, 1991. On that date there was a total eclipse of the sun. Mexico City was one of the best places to view the eclipse. Thousands of people had their home video cameras pointed at the sky, poised to capture the total eclipse on film.

It's not surprising that modern scientists and astronomers know the exact date that a total eclipse will occur. What might seem surprising to some though, is that ancient scientists predicted 3,000 years ago the exact date for this eclipse in the Mayan calendar! Also predicted was that on the exact date of the eclipse a new Age of Enlightenment would begin. It is referred to as the ''Prophecy of the Sixth Sun.''

Archaeologist Armando Nicolau, of the University of Mexico, says, ''The legend of the sixth sun, the eclipse that occurred on July 11, 1991, signified what the legend refers to as the opening of knowledge. The sixth sun legend speaks of precisely the very moment of its arrival.''

Strangely, on the day of the eclipse at 1:29 P.M. [July 11, 1991], something *did* arrive. Lee Elders, author and UFO researcher, was there and reported to the crew of the *Sightings* TV show: ''Exactly at the time of the full solar eclipse, a craft appeared over the city—hovering for over thirty minutes. Seventeen people I know recorded the object with their home video cameras—that has never happened before in UFOlogy!''

In fact, hundreds of home video cameras—aimed to capture the eclipse—got something quite unexpected on their cameras—UFOs! So far, reports of more than 110 video films have been verified to contain footage of unexplained, unidentified craft.

The UFO sightings are a common topic of discussion on Mexican radio and television shows. Jaime Maussan, one of the most respected TV journalists in Mexico City is editor general of a Mexican version of *60 Minutes*. He says that just about every afternoon in a city of almost twenty million people you can see a UFO. A former skeptic, now a believer, Maussan says, "Thousands—hundreds of thousands—of people have witnessed UFOs. What I feel is important as an investigative reporter is the fact that the evidence presented was never questioned. The credibility of the witnesses was attacked—not the *proof* presented!"

People from all walks of life recorded wave after wave of UFOs hovering in the sky. One of the first to come forward was a respected dentist. His opinion was that he observed that all the other witnesses of the UFOs were definitely not afraid or nervous about the strange appearances. He noted that people actually seemed to like the idea of UFOs and felt that these appearances could actually benefit Earth.

Once the first videotapes were publicly released in Mexico City, more and more people came forward with their videos, sightings, and photographs.

Just outside of Mexico City in the town of Atliso, a police chief had captured something on film that he could not explain. He had been in charge of taking surveillance photographs, not filming the eclipse. The surveillance was set up to capture a drug smuggler's plane. The police chief didn't notice anything unusual at the time; but when the film was developed, a startling, unexplained image appeared instead of the drug-smuggling plane.

The police chief was extremely irate, thinking it was a mistake of the film developer. Taking the photograph to the commandante (state police), he said, "Look what this guy brought me!" The commandante thought they should have the photograph blown up to see if anything else would show up. When the picture was enlarged—still no drug-smuggling plane, just a series of strange white lights in a semicircle.

To rule out the possibility of these UFOs being conventional or experimental aircraft or an organized hoax, the crew of *Sightings* had videotape footage analyzed by David Froning, a retired propulsion expert and chief scientist at a major aerospace firm.

Froning's opinion was that the pictures of inflight videos were as good as any he'd ever seen, and that they demonstrate a field propulsion and technology far beyond any capability currently available. Froning said, "Most scientists look at these things not as something that is violating the laws of physics, but as just some phenomenon that our known laws cannot explain right now."

Many television cameras and crews, reporters, and investigators from all over the world have launched their own invasion of Mexico City to evaluate the mass sightings. Certainly opinions and evaluations should be in soon as to whether the UFOs could be alien spacecraft from an unknown planet or from a civilization that visited here long ago—as many believe—and are returning at this time—according to the Mayan prophecies—from an enlightened civilization to enlighten ours.

CHAPTER 16

UFOs, The New World Order, and the Great Conspiracy

The November 1993 issue of the *Journal of Abnormal Psychology* contains the results of a study conducted by psychologists at Carleton University of Ottawa, Canada, which states that people who think that they have seen a UFO or a space alien are just as intelligent and psychologically healthy as other folks.

According to the authors of the report, "Our findings clearly contradict the previously held notions that people who seemingly had bizarre experiences, such as missing time and communicating with aliens, have wild imaginations and are easily swayed into believing the unbelievable."

Dr. Nicholas P. Spanos, who led the study and administered a battery of psychological tests to individuals who claimed to have undergone a wide variety of UFO experiences, said that such people were not at all "off the wall." In fact, he affirmed, "They tend to be white-collar, relatively well-educated representatives of the middle class."

Such comfortable reassurances from academia that one may experience a UFO encounter and not be analyzed as crazy will come as no small comfort to many students of the phenomenon who have suddenly found themselves enmeshed in a veritable maelstrom of bizarre and unexplainable occurrences.

The very essence of the dangers and hazards inherent in UFO research were effectively summarized in a 1993 story that appeared in the daily newspaper of a medium-sized midwestern city just a few days before Halloween. According to the perplexed yet intrigued reporter, a minister told her that he had spent the past twenty-three years running from UFO beings, angels, or aliens. The minister said that he was no longer certain just what the beings were, but he was certain that they were from another world or dimension.

After he had experienced a UFO sighting in the late 1960s, the clergyman became aware that something—some form of intelligence related to the flying saucer that he had seen—was following him.

On a Halloween night in 1978, the minister had a close encounter in his own home with the aliens or angels or whatever they actually were. They allowed him to photograph them with his Polaroid camera, and they freely demonstrated their ability to assume whatever physical form they chose. He saw them change shape, glow in the dark, or disappear right in front of him.

Feeling somehow secure in his photographic proof of the physical reality of the entities, the minister believed that he was now in the possession of some kind of cosmic trump card that would keep the things away from him.

A bit later some friendly police officers appeared on the scene, explaining that they had heard about his remarkable photographs. They examined his photographs very seriously—and they informed the minister that such solid proof of alien entities should be published in the media.

Seemingly well informed about such constructive public relations campaigns, the sympathetic police officers said that they would use their credentials and expertise to help him get the pictures published. Together the officers and the minister would prove to the world at large that such creatures did walk among humankind.

When they met with the clergyman on the following night, however, the officers confiscated his photographs, taped his hands behind his back, and pulled a stocking cap over his face. After the phoney policemen drove him around for a while, they finally released him.

Although the minister felt fortunate that he was still alive, he realized that his proof of the alien entities had been taken from him by the men—or the entities—who had posed as police officers. A few months later he began to notice strange side effects, which he blamed on his close contact with the policemen—

whom he now understood actually were the extraterrestrials assuming yet another disguise. The upper portion of his torso became scaly. His vision became blurred, and from time to time, he was temporarily blind.

When the journalist interviewed the clergyman, he was receiving emotional support from other ministers and praying continually that the UFO beings, the shape-changers, the angels, or the demons had decided at last to leave him alone for good.

The tale of the hapless minister epitomizes in so many ways the bizarre and chaotic psychological and physical nightmares that may await careless investigators of the UFO controversy. Whatever we are up against, both the actors and the eerie scenarios are very, very old—but each generation of humankind is challenged to participate in a seemingly crazy cosmic contest that we sometimes label the "Reality Game."

And yet in spite of such studies demonstrating the basic psychological soundness of UFO percipients as the one cited at the beginning of this chapter, a goodly number of psychiatrists and psychologists maintain that there are other explanations for tales of alien abductions and sexual assaults by disrespectful extraterrestrials. During an early peak of the abduction "fad" that had been set in motion largely by Whitley Striber's bestseller *Communion* and Budd Hopkins' *Intruders,* an article by anthropologist Dr. Elizabeth Bird in the April 1989 issue of *Psychology Today* sought to explore other possibilities that might explain the abductees' trauma.

Critical of UFOlogists who use hypnosis to help alleged abductees recall their harrowing experiences, Dr. Bird states that "while hypnosis may elicit remarkably detailed accounts, they are no more accurate than normal memories. Indeed, suggestible people produce notably less accurate accounts under hypnosis."

Perhaps most relevant to the discussion at hand was Dr. Bird's citing of the comparisons that folklorist Bill Ellis, assistant professor of English and American Studies at Pennsylvania State University, made between UFO abduction experiences and the accounts of the phenomenon known in Newfoundland culture as the Old Hag:

"A person who is relaxed but apparently awake suddenly finds himself paralyzed in the presence of some nonhuman entity. Often, the sensation is accompanied by terrifying hallucinations—of shuffling sounds, of humanoid figures with prominent eyes. Often the figure even sits on the victim's chest, causing a choking sensation."

Our own research led us years ago to accept the multiple manifestations of the UFO controversy as evidence that we humans are part of a larger community of intelligences, a far more complex hierarchy of powers and principalities, a potentially richer universe of interrelated species—both physical and nonphysical—than we could ever imagine.

In many old traditions, especially in the British Isles and Scandinavia, the fairy folk were supernormal entities who were said to inhabit a magical kingdom beneath the surface of the earth. Fairies were considered to be akin to humans, but they were known to be something more than mere mortals. Reluctant to resign them to the realm of spirit, ancient texts declared fairies to be "of a middle nature, betwixt Man and Angel."

One factor that has been consistent in fairy lore is the annoying attribute of the "middle folk" to meddle continually in human affairs, sometimes to do them good, other times to do them ill.

In tale after tale we learn that the fairies have the power to enchant humans and to take advantage of them. It was often related that they could cast a spell on a comely lass or lad and have their way sexually with them. From time to time they would wisk a mortal off to the fairy kingdom, where an entirely different system of time seemed to exist. At their nastiest, fairies often kidnapped human children.

On the other side of this bizarre coin, it was said that fairies could materialize to help a poor farmer harvest his crop before a storm or aid a browbeaten housemaid clean up a soiled kitchen. If they so chose, fairies could guide humans with their ability to foresee the future. They could stand by at the birth of favored human children and guide and protect them for the rest of their lives.

As we have seen throughout this book, UFOnauts have been reported to hypnotize or "enchant" men and women in order to make Earthlings more malleable. There have been many reports in which people claim that the UFO beings had sexual intercourse with them in what would appear to be an attempt to create a hybrid species. There are numerous cases in which it seems that men, women, and children were abducted and taken aboard UFOs. And UFOnauts have been reported working closely with scientists, doctors, and inventors—aiding, advising, and perhaps sharing their advanced technology.

Fairies, elves, Grays, angels, bearded inventors—we may not yet know what the UFO intelligences really look like. They may have the ability to influence the human mind telepathically and project what appear to be three-dimensional constructs to the percipients of UFO encounters. The actual image perceived may depend in large part upon the preconceptions, fears, and hopes that witnesses may have about extraterrestrial or supernatural life or energy forms.

Norio Hayakawa, author of *UFOs—The Grand Deception and The New World Order* [Inner Light, New Brunswick, NJ], warns of a global UFO conspiracy linked to a "sinister occult force" that is manufacturing the "Grand Deception of 1995."

Hayakawa believes that this worldwide plot is designed to "stage a counterfeit extraterrestrial contact-landing to simulate an extraterrestrial 'threat' of invasion in order to urgently and ultimately bring about a delusive New World Order." In his view the actual guiding force behind the staged event may be "highly intelligent, but deceptive, ultradimensional negative entities conveniently materializing in disguise as extraterrestrial 'aliens.'"

Hayakawa, the regional director of the Civilian Intelligence Network, foresees the Grand Deception of 1995 occurring concurrently with a series of shocking, incredible events beginning with the Russians backing an ill-fated invasion of Israel by the Arab Confederacy.

"This dramatic invasion and the ensuing catastrophic conflagration in the Middle East will immediately be followed by unprecedented [worldwide] earthquakes, a [global] financial crisis, and a sudden mysterious 'evacuation' [or 'removal,' depending on one's viewpoint] of a segment of the population worldwide—all of which will culminate in an urgent, official declaration of a totalitarian New World Order that will last for seven years upon its inception," Hayakawa states.

Such a shocking series of global events will place millions of people in "an absolute stupor for weeks," Hayakawa states, during which time "an ingeniously executed, extremely effective 'multi-leveled' mind control program will be activated to calm the stunned populace."

At this point in the scenario envisioned by Hayakawa—while the leadership of the New World Order struggles to assume complete control over the global populace—a "dynamic, charismatic leader" will arise out of the European community [by then known as the United States of Europe], appear in a worldwide television broadcast, and offer a brilliant explanation to sedate the public. Hayakawa believes that this dynamic leader is currently around twenty-nine years old and is residing somewhere in Western Europe, "just waiting to begin his 'official' mission."

Political theorist, futurist, and social analyst Michael Lindemann reached a point in his own research into the UFO controversy where he became convinced that "an alien presence" on Earth was being "selectively revealed to the public with the blessing and sometimes direct involvement of government authorities." Further investigation by Lindemann caused him to arrive at two basic conclusions why the government had been conducting a process of selective revelation.

"First," Lindemann states, "the evidence is now so voluminous and widely perceived into the public sector that official strategies for suppressing it have been superceded by a new priority: To nuance or 'spin' the facts of alien presence for political advantage, in order to recapture control over the pace and direction of alien revelations which the government might otherwise lose in the cascade of unauthorized and unanticipated revelations now occuring. At issue is the maintenance of social order in the face of potentially disruptive new realities."

The second reason for the "selective revelation" of alien presence that Lindemann perceives is that the architects of the New World Order, whom he refers to as "the Olympians," have an understanding that the world as we know it is "careening toward environmental and economic catastrophe."

In Lindemann's view the intentions of the Olympians is "to chart a course through a time of tremendous upheaval during which millions or even billions of people might die, and to emerge from that time still in power and with greatly enhanced prospects for an 'ideal' society of their own design. Their ability to succeed in this strategy will depend on controlling the perceptions and behavior of the citizens of the most-developed nations.

To do this, they will rely—as leaders always have—on the organizing potential of a terrible enemy. The enemy, I propose, will be alien. The threat might be entirely illusory, but it could be very persuasively presented.''

Apparently—from what we can ascertain from ancient records—angels and/or UFOnauts were far more open in their terrestrial comings and goings in less technologically sophisticated times. In fact, according to Roman Catholic scholar Matthew Fox, the number-one cosmological question in the Mediterranean area in the first century A.D. was whether or not angels were friends or foes.

With today's accounts of UFO beings presenting accurate prophecies, performing miraculous healings, and offering benevolent guidance on the one hand—and participating in cruel abductions, conducting genetic experiments, and plotting our planet's destruction or enslavement on the other—UFO researchers in the 1990s must still ask: Are the UFO entities friends or foes?

The "great UFO cover-up," the "grand UFO deception," has been going on since the first intellectual stirrings of human civilization. Whether the UFOnauts are extraterrestrial or multidimensional beings, they appear to have had our planet under surveillance for millions of years—and they have chosen to conduct their activities in secret for reasons that remain as yet undetermined by the general populace of Earth.

Sometimes it seems as though we are dealing only with multidimensional tricksters who deliberately seek to confuse us and to mislead us concerning their true purpose on our planet.

In other instances there appear to be dramatic clues indicating that we are dealing with paraphysical entities that may have always coexisted with us and are somehow participating with us in some grand evolutionary design.

Still other fragments of evidence would indicate that we are in occasional contact with superscientists from "somewhere out there" who created our species and many of the other life-forms on this planet, and who continually hover over their handiwork, shepherding their biological field project.

Sometimes it has seemed to us as though the intelligence

behind the UFO controversy has always been provoking humankind into higher spirals of intellectual and technological maturity, guiding us to mental and spiritual awareness, tugging our entire species into the future.

Throughout our history it seems that the UFO intelligence has always been there to show us that the impossible can be accomplished, that the rules of physics are made to be broken. In decades past they have demonstrated the possibility of air flight, radio communication, television, and a host of technological extensions of all of our senses. Today their baffling maneuvers might be demonstrating the possibility of dematerialization, invisibility, and rematerialization. Perhaps they are somehow showing us that the best way of dealing with space travel over megadistances is not to travel through space but to avoid it altogether.

In an earlier work we suggested that the UFO intelligences might be working at the gradual redefining of our concept of reality by challenging us in the teasing fashion of a Zen riddle. It may be that humankind has been invited to participate in a bizarre kind of contest with some undeclared cosmic opponents. We may have been challenged to play the Reality Game; and if we can once apprehend the true significance of the preposterous clues—if we can but master the proper moves—we may obtain a clearer picture of our role in the cosmic scheme of things. The rules of the Reality Game may be confusing, extremely flexible, and difficult to define, but play we must—for it is the only game in the universe.

Dr. J. Allen Hynek's UFO Classification System

Close Encounters of the first kind: A UFO observed at a close range.

Close Encounters of the second kind: The UFO produces a physical effect.

Close Encounters of the third kind: Involves contact with UFO occupants. [In the popular movie, *Close Encounters of the Third Kind,* many of the events were based on actual UFO reports filed with Dr. Hynek's center. The title was taken from Dr. Hynek's terminology. Dr. Hynek was technical director to and made a brief appearance in the film.]

Summary of Significant Events in the 1940s From a UFO Perspective
1940s Throughout WWII, mysterious craft witnessed by pilots

General MacArthur shocked by number of UFO reports by his troops in Tokyo

December 5, 1945
Five Avenger planes disappear off Florida with 14 men on board
Martin Mariner search-and-rescue plane disappears with 13 men

December 1945
Central Intelligence Group (CIG) created by Truman

Early 1947
CIG becomes CIA with General Vandenberg/head
U.S. Army Air Corp becomes U.S. Air Force (based with AC at Wright-Patterson, Ohio)
Department of Defense created
NSA created

June 23, 1947
Strange objects spew silver slugs onto Dahl's boat, injuring the son, killing dog, in Washington State

June 24, 1947
Man in black threatens Dahls at Maury Island, Washington

June/July 1947
Dahl tells Crisman

June 24, 1947
Pilot Kenneth Arnold reports 9 glowing saucerlike objects in Washington State
ATIC—Air Force applies for research funds
Air Force Intelligence officers: Lieutenant Brown and Captain Davidson appointed to research mysterious craft and interview witnesses
Crisman contacts Ray Palmer
Palmer contacts Arnold
Dahl boy disappears
Arnold contacts Lieutenant Brown, Captain Davidson (ATIC)
Brown/Davidson arrive: interview Dahl/Crisman and leave with samples
ATIC plane crashes, killing Brown/Davidson
Two newspaper men working with Arnold on his sightings story mysteriously die
Ken Arnold's plane almost crashes
Dahl boy, Charles, shows up 1,000s of miles away—with amnesia
Ray Palmer's office broken into—only thing missing was shoebox full of metallic samples from Dahl case

Palmer ordered by publisher to drop Dahl case
Palmer resigns *Amazing Stories* . . . creates *Fate* magazine
General MacArthur draws up 10-page document/report based on sightings in Japan, concluding they were from outer space and were hostile
ATIC draws up "top-secret" estimate of the situation, concluding that flying saucers were from outer space
Both ATIC documents (MacArthur's and top-secret estimate go to highest branch of government: sent by Air Force chief of staff to General Vandenberg, new head of CIA
General Vandenberg explodes; orders new approach to subject of UFOs: creates Project Grudge

July 2, 1947
UFO sighted over Roswell, N.M.

July 3, 1947
Rancher Brazel and family discover scattered wreckage on their farm, near Roswell, call sheriff
Sheriff Wilcox contacts Roswell Army base, Maj. Jesse Marcel
Brazel incarcerated, ordered to secrecy
Army moves in, collects debris, taking to Roswell Army Air Base
U.S. Air Force orders under Col. Blanchard to fly debris to Wright-Patterson Air Force Base, Ohio
Maj. Jesse Marcel on orders was diverted to Fort Worth, Texas

July 8, 1947
Press release issued by Roswell Army Air Base that they had a flying saucer

July 8, 1947
As the message was about to air on ABC radio, the wire service was ordering *not to transmit*

July 8 or so, 1947
G. L. Barnett reports UFO crash seen near Socorro, N.M. . . . damaged, but complete saucer reported discovered with dead alien bodies . . . carted away by Air Force (possible government diversion to Brazel's farm, where scattered pieces substituted for weather balloon for press cover story and retraction by Air Force

July 7, 1947
Secret operation set into motion to recover *UFO craft/pieces/alien bodies*

September 24, 1947
MJ-12 established as a special top-secret Research and Development Intelligence Operation responsible only to the president of the United States, special-classified by order issued under the executive order of President Truman, on recommendation by Dr. Vannevar Bush and Secretary James Forrestal

UFO Update

June 24, 1997 marked the fiftieth anniversary of UFOs in the modern era—and there can be no question that those fifty years of UFO sightings have certainly impressed the general public. A recent poll (December 1996) conducted by *George,* a popular magazine of politics and contemporary issues, found that

55% of Americans believe that life exists on other planets;
79% believe that extraterrestrials have visited Earth in the last one hundred years;
and 70% believe that the government is covering up the truth about UFOs.

In early May, 1997, a "USA Snapshot" conducted by a Fox News/Opinion Dynamics poll for *USA TODAY* stated that 44% of all registered voters in the United States believe that there is intelligent life on other planets.

Interestingly, more men [54%] than women [33%] believe in the reality of extraterrestrial life.

The U.S. Air Force Solves the Mystery of the Roswell UFO Crash

With belief in UFOs at an all time high, it could hardly have been a coincidence that the U.S. Air Force chose June 24, 1997, to conduct a special press conference to hype their own answer to the Roswell rumors, *The Roswell Report: Case Closed.* The new, official, updated explanation for the alleged UFO crash in the desert was that the alleged flying saucer fragments were really pieces of a balloon that was used in a highly classified intelligence gathering operation known as Project Mogul. The operation had begun almost immediately after World War II as a device with which to spy on the Soviets and to keep a close watch on their efforts to construct nuclear weapons.

And what about those alien bodies that were reported scattered around the flying saucer crash site?

Ladies and gentlemen, those were dummies that were dropped in 1953 to test parachute effectiveness.

Ah, excuse us. The Roswell crash occurred in July 1947. If these dummies you speak of were dropped in 1953, how do you account for the six-year discrepancy?

Simple. There is an interesting mental phenomenon known as "time compression." The witnesses in the Roswell incident became confused about the actual time period during which they saw the alleged alien bodies, and they "compressed" their memories of the 1947 crash into their recollection of the smashed parachute dummies in 1953 into the same scenario.

Such official government explanations as the one cited above make the results of a recent poll all the more self-evident. In a survey conducted by Princeton Survey Research Associates for Pew Research and published in *USA Today* on September 12, 1997, only 6% of adults in the United States express a degree of trust in the federal government.

What Can We Show for 50 Years of UFO Research?

Fifty years of UFO sightings also means fifty years of UFO research. So much has happened in those five decades—the alleged UFO crash at Roswell in 1947; the mysterious lights over Lubbock, Texas in 1951; the Washington, D.C., overflights in 1952 and 1965; the landing at Socorro, New Mexico in 1964; the UFO abduction of Betty and Barney Hill in 1961; the Condon Report of 1968; the Air Force's Project Bluebook—surely, one might assume, we are closer to the truth about UFOs.

Yes, well, talk to any group of UFO researchers, and you will soon find that the "truth" about the UFO enigma appears to be in the mind of the beholder of the mystery, for you will certainly find no unanimity, no central hypothesis that is embraced by all investigators.

To get a feel of the variety of UFO experiences and the multitude of interpretations thereof, imagine that you are a journalist assigned to do a feature article on the status of UFO research in 1998, a consensus of those investigators who have pursued the phenomenon for fifty years. Here are some responses that you might receive as you wander about a UFO conference with your tape recorder and notebook in hand:

You recognize three fairly prominent UFO researchers seated in a lounge area of the hotel where the conference is taking place. They appear to be having a rather lively conversation, and they are not particularly annoyed when you interrupt them with a request to gain their thoughts about the source of the UFO phenomenon.

"Where do you think UFOs come from?" is your first question.

"They Come from Outer Space," the three answer almost in unison. The so-called flying saucers are piloted by beings who come from one or more extraterrestrial civilizations. They appear to have had Earth under surveillance for centuries.

"If the UFOs come from an extraterrestrial source," you ask, "why haven't the UFOnauts as representatives—as ambassadors if you will—from another world, landed on the White House lawn? Why have they chosen to conduct their activities largely in secret?"

One researcher will tell you that it is because the space beings are benign; and in the best *Star Trek* tradition, they follow a policy of noninterference in a planet's evolutionary development.

The second researcher corrects his colleague by informing you that the UFO beings are indifferent toward humankind. In classic academic procedure, they follow a policy of noninterference because they are dispassionately observing and studying our planet's struggles. If our planet should be destroyed because of the stupidity, greed, and innate destructiveness of the human psyche, they will probably film the cataclysmic event as an object lesson in self-programmed species obsolescence for use in their college core programs.

The third researcher speaks up and warns that the UFOnauts conduct the bulk of their activities in secret because they are hostile to earthlings. They are in the final stages of conducting tests which will determine whether or not they will destroy our planet, exploit it ruthlessly, or totally enslave it under the domination of a hybrid breed they have been creating from the fetuses and sperm of abducted humans.

Colonel Corso's Controversial *Day After Roswell*

As you walk about the conference area, you hear all about the hot new topic regarding Roswell. In excellent timing for the 50th anniversary celebration in Roswell, New Mexico, Col. Philip J. Corso (U.S. Army, ret.) published his book *The Day After Roswell*, which details how, during his years at the Pentagon, he was given "personal stewardship" of artifacts recovered from the extraterrestrial spaceship that made a crash landing outside of Roswell in July 1947. It was Corso himself who saw that government contractors were given alien technology that led directly to breakthroughs in the development of integrated circuits, fiber optics, lasers, and a host of other Star Wars mechanisms.

Or did he? Another UFO investigator suspects the colonel's book is a deliberate work of disinformation, part of the overall government conspiracy. According to this researcher, Corso's book is filled with all kinds of contradictions.

And then there is the alleged Alien Autopsy, which the Fox Network did its very best to depict as a real-life episode of *The X-Files*. While researching film material for a music documentary, Ray Santilli claimed to have discovered footage shot in 1947 of an autopsy conducted on an alien cadaver by Air Force medical personnel. The cameraman, now in his eighties, was said to have been with the Army Air Force and special forces from 1942 to 1952.

Cries of hoax from one group of investigators have prompted equally vociferous shouts of defense from those who believe the film truly depicts the autopsy of an alien, rather than a deformed human. And as we progress into 1998, other snippets of film depicting alleged aliens being interrogated or sliced are being shown at UFO conferences and on network television.

As you move on in your research and walk into an area of the hotel where vendors are selling UFO books, magazines, tapes and other alien-type artifacts, you encounter another researcher who scoffs at the other theories you've just heard in an openly contemptuous manner.

With complete assurance, this investigator tells you that All UFOs are classified military aerial vehicles; that for the past fifty years, have been mistaken by the credulous for extraterrestrial spaceships. Alleged UFO occupants are actually solid terrestrial astronauts who have been spotted conducting secret military manuevers with classified aerial vehicles.

"What military branches have been responsible for these secret aerial vehicles?" you ask.

The answers stagger you: Probably the U.S. Navy . . . or Red China . . . or the Third Reich attempting to rise again . . . or scientists who worked in secret in the old Soviet Union . . . or Bell Telephone . . . or maybe Walt Disney Productions.

And then still another researcher walks over to you and butts into your conversation with an allegation that is spoken in an unnecessarily loud voice: "Yes, some UFOs are secret military aerial craft—but the military and the secret government have cut a deal with the aliens and they are using extraterrestrial technology!"

And you are hearing once again the familiar stories of underground bases and hordes of U.S. service men and women being slaughtered by superior alien forces. Colonel Corso's revelations are being offered as proof that such tales are frighteningly true.

* * *

By now you are likely to be getting the idea of the remarkable disparity of opinion to be found among any collected group of UFO investigators.

And by the time you leave our imaginary conference with your notebook filled and your tape recorder on the verge of a meltdown, you would no doubt have encountered the following additional theories about the true source of the UFO mystery:

UFOs Are Instruments of Programmed Deceit and Delusion

According to this theory, both UFOs and their alleged occupants are not real at all, but are something similar to holographic projections or elaborate special effects created by some unknown agency for an ulterior motive. Proponents of this particularly paranoid plot scenario generally name a secret branch of the government or the military as the villains in an insidious program to brainwash the masses. What they hope to gain from this program of lies and deceit—civil war, total dominance, a dictatorship—is somewhat vague.

UFOs Originate in Other Dimensions

Proponents of this theory insist that the evidence indicates that the UFO beings come not from a physical planet in our solar system or in any other, but from an adjacent Space/Time continuum, actually coexisting on Earth with us, but on another vibrational level.

Discussions of warping the normal confines of time and space also touch upon the Time Traveler Hypothesis to explain UFOs. In this school of thought, the UFOnauts are our own descendants from the future, studying humankind in our era and using the past as a kind of living, historical museum.

UFOs as an Expression of a Planetary Poltergeist

Author John A. Keel once termed our world a "haunted planet" in a book by the same name. In this view of the UFO enigma, the phenomenon is the result of some as yet unknown physical law that can at times activate or be activated by the unconscious human mind. This energy might not itself be intelligent, but it would be able to absorb, reflect, and imitate human intelligence.

UFOnauts as Images and Symbols

Researchers Jerome Clark and Loren Coleman once speculated that certain of humankind's basic and psychic needs are somehow able to tap psychokinesis (mind over matter) and other psi energies and fashion apparitions of fairies, holy figures, and UFOs—archetypes which humans can experience only as images and symbols. The forms that these manifestations assume are *ancient* in the sense that they have always been intrinsic aspects of the human psyche, *modern* in that we perceive them in the context of ideas the conscious mind has acquired.

John W. White is one theorist who has suggested that UFOs and their occupants may be quasi-real objects manufactured by the human "collective unconscious."

White interprets Jungian archetypes as "energetic thought fields" accessible through "dreams, meditations, and other altered states of consciousness." He suggests that these may be "larger, previously unrecognized dimensions of physical events" in which highly evolved beings exist on a grander, paraphysical scale and "influence and guide human affairs."

UFOnauts as Paraphysical Beings

A good number of UFO researchers have theorized that the various manifestations of the mystery could be the result of the "magical" machinations of those paraphysical beings that we have often called "elves," "fairies," or "leprechauns" throughout our societal and cultural evolution. Perhaps these entities have coexisted with humankind as members of a companion species and are somehow participating with *Homo sapiens* in a far grander evolutionary design than we have previously been able to envision.

According to some theorists, the UFO intelligences are the same entities as the Angels, who are described in the scriptures of so many world religions as the messengers of God. These beings remain concerned about the inhabitants of Earth as part of their divine mission of guidance and/or salvation.

Or as a few researchers have suggested, they remain interested in our evolution because they are, in fact, our creators.

* * *

So now you have a much clearer picture of what fifty years of UFO research has produced: A veritable smorgasbord of concepts and theories—any one of which will be passionately and vociferously debated and defended by its exponents.

Bibliography

Books

Adamski, George. *Behind the Flying Saucer Mystery (Flying Saucers Farewell)*. New York: Paperback Library, 1967.

Adler, Bill (ed.). *Letters to the Air Force on UFOs*. New York: Dell Publishing, 1967.

Asimov, Isaac. *Is Anyone There?* New York: Ace Books, 1967.

Barker, Gray. *They Knew Too Much About Flying Saucers*. New Brunswick, NJ: Inner Light, 1992.

Beckley, Timothy Green. *Subterranean Worlds*. New Brunswick, NJ: Inner Light, 1992.

———. *Jimi Hendrix: Starchild*. New Brunswick, NJ: Inner Light, 1992.

———. *The American Indian UFO-Starseed Connection*. New Brunswick, NJ: Inner Light, 1992.

———. *The UFO Silencers*. New Brunswick, NJ: Inner Light, 1990.

Binder, Otto. *What We Really Know About Flying Saucers*. New York: Fawcett, 1967.

———. *Flying Saucers Are Watching Us*. New York: Tower, 1968.

Bowen, Charles (ed.). *The Humanoids*. Chicago: Henry Regnery, 1969.

Brownell, Winfield S. *UFOs Key to Earth's Destiny*. Lytle Creek, CA: Legion of Light, 1980.

Bryant, Alice and Linda Seeback. *Healing Shattered Reality: Understanding Contactee Trauma*. Tigard, OR: Wild Flower Press, 1991.

Clark, Jerome and Loren Coleman. *The Unidentified.* New York: Warner Paperback Library, 1975.

Clarke, Arthur C. *Voices from the Sky.* New York: Harper and Row, 1965.

Commander X. *Nikola Tesla—Free Energy and the White Dove.* New Brunswick, NJ: Inner Light, 1992.

————. *Ultimate Deception.* New Brunswick, NJ: Inner Light, 1992.

————. *Underground Alien Bases.* New Brunswick, NJ: Inner Light, 1991.

Condon, Edward U. (project director). *The Scientific Study of Unidentified Flying Objects.* New York: Bantam Books, 1969.

Constable, Trevor James. *The Cosmic Pulse of Life.* Santa Ana, CA: Merlin Press, 1976.

Cooper, Milton William. *Behold a Pale Horse.* Sedona, AZ: Light Technology, 1991.

Crystal, Ellen. *Silent Invasion.* New York: Paragon House, 1991.

David, Jay (ed.). *The Flying Saucer Reader.* New York: New American Library, 1967.

Downing, Barry H. *The Bible and Flying Saucers.* New York: Avon, 1970.

Drake, W. Raymond. *Gods and Spacemen in the Ancient West.* New York: New American Library, 1974.

Edwards, Frank. *Flying Saucers—Serious Business.* New York: Lyle Stuart, 1966.

————. *Flying Saucers Here and Now.* New York: Lyle Stuart, 1967.

Erskine, Allen Louis. *Why Are They Watching Us?* New York: Tower, 1967.

Esoteric Publications. *I Am Ishcomar.* Cottonwood, AZ: Esoteric Publications, 1978.

Evans, Hilary. *Visions, Apparitions, Alien Visitors.* Wellingborough, Northhampshire: Aquarian Press, 1984.

Fawcett, George D. *Quarter Century of Studies of UFOs in Florida, North Carolina and Tennessee.* Mt. Airy, NC: Pioneer Printing, 1975.

Fawcett, Lawrence and Barry J. Greenwood. *Clear Intent: The Government Coverup of the UFO Experience.* Englewood Cliffs, NJ: Prentice Hall, 1984.

Fry, Daniel. *The White Sands Incident.* Madison, WI: Horus House, 1992.

———. *To Men of Earth*. Elsinore, CA: El Cariso, 1973.

Fuller, John. *Incident at Exeter*. New York: G.P. Putnam, 1966.

———. *Aliens in the Sky*. New York: Putnam/Berkley, 1969.

Good, Timothy. *Above Top Secret—The Worldwide UFO Coverup*. New York: William Morrow, 1988.

———. *The UFO Report*. New York: Avon, 1989.

Ginsburgh, Irwin. *First Man, Then Adam!* New York: Pocket Books, 1978.

Gladden, Lee and Vivianne Cervantes Gladden. *Heirs of the Gods*. New York: Rawson, Wade, 1978.

Goldsen, Joseph M. (ed.). *Outer Space in World Politics*. New York: Frederick A. Prager, 1963.

Greene, Vaughan M. *Astronauts of Ancient Japan*. Millbrae, CA: Merlin Engine Works, 1978.

Hamilton, William F. *Cosmic Top Secret*. New Brunswick, NJ: Inner Light, 1991.

Hayakawa, Norio F., *UFOs—The Grand Deception and the Coming New World Order*. New Brunswick, NJ: Civilian Intelligence Network/Inner Light, 1993.

Hynek, J. Allen and Jacques Vallee. *The Edge of Reality*. Chicago: Henry Regnery, 1975.

Hynek, J. Allen and Philip J. Imbrogno, with Pratt, Bob. *Night Siege*. New York: Ballantine, 1987.

Jung, C. G. *Flying Saucers: A Modern Myth of Things Seen in the Sky*. New York: New American Library, 1967.

Keel, John A. *Strange Creatures from Time and Space*. New York: Fawcett, 1970.

———. *The Mothman Prophecies*. New York: Saturday Review Press, 1975.

Kent, Malcom. *The Terror Above Us*. New York: Tower, 1967.

Keyhoe, Donald E. *Flying Saucers from Outer Space*. New York: Henry Holt, 1953.

Lewis, Richard S. *Appointment on the Moon*. New York: Viking Press, 1968.

Ley, Willy. *Missiles, Moonprobes and Megaparsecs*. New York: New American Library, 1964.

———. *Rockets, Missiles and Men in Space*. New York: Viking, 1944.

Lorenzen, Coral and Jim. *Encounters with UFO Occupants*. New York: Berkley, 1976.

Lovell, A. C. B. *The Individual and the Universe.* New York: Harper and Brothers, 1958.

McWane, Glenn and David Graham. *The New UFO Sightings.* New York: Warner Paperback Library, 1974.

Menger, Howard. *From Outer Space to You.* New York: Pyramid, 1967.

Michel, Aime. *The Truth About Flying Saucers.* New York: Pyramid, 1967.

Palmer, Raymond A. *The Real UFO Invasion.* San Diego: Greenleaf, 1967.

Pawlicki, T. B. *How to Build a Flying Saucer and Other Proposals in Speculative Engineering.* Englewood Cliffs, NJ: Prentice Hall, 1981.

Randle, Kevin D. and Donald R. Schmitt. *The Truth About the UFO Crash at Roswell.* New York: M. Evans, 1994.

Randles, Jenny. *Out of the Blue.* New Brunswick, NJ: Global Communications, 1991.

Rimmer, John. *The Evidence for Alien Abductions.* Wellingborough, Northamptonshire: Aquarian Press, 1984.

Ruppelt, Edward J. *The Report on Unidentified Flying Objects.* New York: Doubleday, 1956.

Sagan, Carl and Thornton Page. *UFOs—A Scientific Debate.* Ithaca/ London: Cornell University Press, 1972.

Santesson, Hans Stefan. *Flying Saucers in Fact and Fiction.* New York: Lancer, 1968.

Saunders, David R. and R. Roger Harkins. *UFOs? Yes! Where the Condon Committee Went Wrong.* New York: New American Library, 1968.

Science & Mechanics (eds.). *The Official Guide to UFOs.* New York, Ace, 1968.

Shapley, Harlow. *The View from a Distant Star.* New York: Dell, 1967.

Shklovskii, I. S. and Carl Sagan. *Intelligent Life in the Universe.* New York: Dell, 1968.

Sitchin, Zecharia. *The 12th Planet.* New York: Avon, 1978.

Stanton, L. Jerome. *Flying Saucers: Hoax or Reality.* New York: Belmont, 1966.

Steiger, Brad, *Strangers from the Skies.* New York: Award, 1966.

———. *Atlantis Rising.* New York: Dell, 1973.

———. *Mysteries of Time and Space*. Englewood Cliffs, NJ: Prentice Hall, 1974.

——— (ed.). *Project Bluebook*. New York: ConFucian Press/Ballantine, 1976.

———. *The Gods of Aquarius: UFOs and the Transformation of Man*. New York: Harcourt Brace Jovanovich, 1976.

———. *Alien Meetings*. New York: Grosset & Dunlap, 1978.

———. *The UFO Abductors*. New York: Berkley, 1988.

———. *The Fellowship*. New York: Doubleday, 1988.

———, Steiger, Sherry Hansen, and Alfred Bielek. *The Philadelphia Experiment and Other UFO Conspiracies*. New Brunswick, NJ: Inner Light, 1990.

——— and Sherry Hansen Steiger. *Starborn*. New York: Berkley, 1992.

——— and Sherry Hansen Steiger. *Super Scientists of Ancient Atlantis and Other Unknown Worlds*. New Brunswick, NJ: 1993.

——— and Hayden C. Hewes. *UFO Missionaries Extraordinary*. New York: Pocket Books, 1976.

——— and John White. *Other Worlds, Other Universes—Playing the Reality Game*. New York: Doubleday, 1975.

——— and Joan Whritenour. *Flying Saucers Are Hostile!* New York/London: Award/Tandem, 1967.

——— and Joan Whritenour. *New UFO Breakthrough*. New York/London: Award/Tandem, 1968.

——— and Joan Whritenour. *Flying Saucer Invasion: Target Earth*. New York/London: Award/Tandem, 1969.

Stevens, Wendelle. *UFO Contact from the Pleiades*. Tucson: UFO Photo Archives, 1982.

Stranges, Frank E. *My Friend from Beyond Earth*. Van Nuys, CA: I.E.C., 1960.

———. *UFO Conspiracy*. Van Nuys, CA: I.E.G., 1985.

Strieber, Whitley. *Communion*. New York: Beech Tree/William Morrow, 1987.

Sullivan, Walter. *We Are Not Alone*. New York: McGraw-Hill, 1964.

Trench, Brinsley Le Poer. *The Flying Saucer Story*. New York: Ace, 1966.

Tyler, Steven. *Are the Invaders Coming?* New York: Tower, 1968.

Velikovsky, Immanuel. *Worlds in Collision*. New York: Dell, 1967.

Walton, Travis. *The Walton Experience*. New York: Berkley, 1978.

Watkins, Leslie. *Alternative 3*. London: Sphere, 1978.

Weldon, John with Zola Levitt. *UFOs—What on Earth Is Happening?* Irvine, CA: Harvest House, 1975.

Wilkins, Harold T. *Flying Saucers Uncensored.* New York: Pyramid, 1967.

Wilson, Clifford. *UFOs and Their Mission Impossible.* New York: New American Library, 1974.

Woodrew, Greta. *On a Slide of Light.* New York: Macmillan, 1981.

———. *Memories of Tomorrow.* New York: Doubleday, 1988.

Periodicals

Beckley, Timothy Green and Harold Salkin. "Apollo 12's Mysterious Encounters with Flying Saucers," *Saga,* May 1970.

Binder, Otto O. "Is Shooting Humanoids Murder?" *Saga,* September 1968.

———. "Flying Saucer Mother Ships," *Saga,* December 1968.

———. "Eleven Scientists Prove UFOs Are Real," *Saga,* May 1969.

———. "Secret Messages from UFOs," *Saga,* June 1971.

——— and Joan Whritenour. "Flying Saucer D-Day," *Saga,* June 1969.

——— and Joan Whritenour. "Underground Network of UFO Bases," *Saga,* November 1969.

Bird, Elizabeth. "Invasion of the Mind Snatchers," *Psychology Today,* April 1989.

Bulantsev, Sergei. "Russia's Most Bizarre Unsolved UFO Cases," *UFO Universe,* October/November 1991.

Chulkov, Lev. "UFOs and Politics," *Aura-Z,* March 1993.

Darby, Christian. "World's First UFO Murder Case," *Argosy,* December 1967.

Douglass, Elaine. "Witnesses Claim They See Aliens at U.S. Bases," *Right To Know Forum,* September/October 1992.

Fredrickson, Sven-Olof. "A Humanoid Was Seen at Imjaevi," *Flying Saucer Review,* September/October 1970.

Friedman, Stanton T. and B. Ann Slate. "Air Force Study Proves Flying Saucers Are Real," *Saga,* May 1971.

———. "UFO Star Base Discovered," *Saga,* July 1973.

Gaddis, Vincent. "Are Flying Saucers Really Creatures That Live in Outer Space?" *True,* August 1967.

Goodavage, Joseph F. "Contact with Extraterrestrial Life," *Saga*, January 1973.

Guttilla, Peter. "UFOs—The Future of Civilization Is at Stake!" *Saga*, July 1970.

Hamilton, William. "Aliens in Dreamland," *UFO Universe*, July 1990.

———. "America's Secret UFO Program," *UFO Review*, #33, 1991.

Hewes, Hayden C. "The UFO Raid that Sparked a White House Alert," *Saga*, July 1972.

———. "UFOs After 30 Years," *New Realities*, June 1977.

Huneeus, Antonio. "An Alien–U.S. Government Liaison—A Matter Above Top Secret," *UFO Universe*, January 1990.

———. "Prof. Hermann Oberth—Confirmed UFO Believer," *UFO Universe*, February/March 1991.

———. "Spain's Non-Stop UFO Invasion Has Begun," *Unsolved UFO Sightings*, Vol. I, No. 2, 1993.

Imbrogno, Phil. "UFO Power Stations," *UFO Universe*, October/November 1991.

Keel, John A. "UFO Agents of Terror," *Saga*, October 1967.

———. "Strange Messages from UFOs," *Saga*, January 1968.

———. "Secret UFO Bases Across the U.S.," *Saga*, April 1968.

———. "The Secret UFO-Astronaut War," *Man*, September 1968.

———. "The Bedroom Invaders," *Male*, July 1969.

———. "UFOs and the Mysterious Wave of Worldwide Kidnappings," *Saga*, December 1970.

———. "Carlos Allende—UFO Mystery Man," *Saga*, September 1975.

Konrath, Jacob. "Flying Saucers and Their Occupants," *Real*, June 1967.

LaPorte, Wayne. "The Desert Craft of Dreamland," *UFO Universe*, Fall 1992.

Lasco, Jack "Has U.S. Air Force Captured a Flying Saucer?" *Saga*, April 1967.

Lore, Jr., Gordon. "UFO Pilots—Key to Space Mystery," *Saga*, October 1975.

Magor, John. "Playground of the Gods," *New World UFO Report*, Vol. 2, No. 3, 1971.

Mckay, Henry H. "UFO, Humanoid Reported in Ontario," *Skylook*, October 1975.

Phelan, James S. "Looking for the Next World," *New York Times Magazine*, February 29, 1976.

Randle, Kevin. "An Alien Survived the Roswell Crash," *UFO Universe*, Fall 1993.

Sanderson, Ivan T. "Visitors from Outer Space," *Argosy*, February 1969.

———. "Mysterious Salt Water Saucer Bases," *Saga*, June 1971.

Schurmacher, Emile C. "Mexico's Phantom Flying Saucers," *Saga*, November 1972.

Sherman, Carl. "Why Is the United Nations Censoring the Truth About UFOs?" *Saga*, December 1967.

Stark, Sherie and Vicki Cooper. "Panel Foresees Government 'Uncover-Up,' " *UFO*, Vol. 2, No. 4, 1987.

Slate, B. Ann. "Contactee Supplies New Clues to UFO Mystery," *Saga*, June 1975.

——— and Fritz Kron. "UFOs Are Alien Spacecraft," *Saga*, February 1971.

Steiger, Brad. "Flying Saucers on the Attack," *Saga*, September 1967.

———. "Flying Saucers Scorch Iowa Farms," *Male*, April 1971.

———. "Beam Me Aboard—UFOs and Astral Travel," *Saga*, December 1976.

——— and Sherry Hansen Steiger. "The Star People and the Pleiades Connection," *Connecting Link*, Vol. #5, 1989.

——— and Sherry Hansen Steiger. "Star People Are Amongst Us," *UFO Universe*, January 1990.

——— and Sherry Hansen Steiger. "UFOs: Friend or Foe?" *UFO Universe*, October/November 1991.

———and Sherry Hansen Steiger. "The Incredible Ancient Astronauts of Peru," *Unsolved UFO Sightings*, Vol 1. No 2, 1993.

——— and Sherry Hansen Steiger. "Beware of the Tricksters from Outer Space," *UFO Universe*, Fall 1993.

——— and Joan Whritenour. "Unidentified Underwater Saucers," *Saga*, June 1968.

Willms, Judith. "Close Encounters Update," *UFO Universe*, Fall 1992.

Zigel, Felix. "A Soviet Scientist Speaks Out on the Alien Agenda," *UFO Universe*, March 1990.

UFO publications are notorious for their transiency. As a service to the reader who wishes to acquire current information about the UFO mystery, the alleged government coverup of UFO sightings, abduction cases, contactee channeling, and so forth, we have provided the addresses of a number of magazines and newsletters. The best policy is to send a stamped, self-addressed envelope with a brief letter of inquiry to determine if the periodical is still being published and what the subscription requirements may be.

Saucer Smear   PO Box 1709/Key West, FL 33041. This is the present evolutionary form of one of the oldest newsletters in the UFO field, *Saucer News,* and it is still being published by James Moseley, the original editor. This newsletter is directed more at UFO insiders and long-time researchers and is filled with gossip, internecine quarrels, and correspondence—all uniquely blended with the wit and wisdom of Moseley.

Just Cause   PO Box 218/Coventry, CT 06238. Lawrence Fawcett, Publisher; Barry Greenwood, Editor. Hard research data. Exposes government cover-ups. Covers new cases and updates of older reports.

Inner Light: The Voice of the New Age   Box 753/New Brunswick, NJ 08903. Timothy Green Beckley, Editor and Publisher, features informative articles together with advertisements for his latest book releases and national UFO conferences.

UFOReview   Box 753/New Brunswick, NJ 08903. Timothy "Mr. UFO" Beckley is also the editor and publisher of this publication; Similar in format to *Inner Light,* there is a greater emphasis on UFO information and materials.

UFO Universe   GCR Publishing Group/1700 Broadway/New York, NY 10019. A slick newsstand publication with four-color illustrations and fully developed articles by an international roster of UFO researchers and investigators. Edited by Timothy Green Beckley—now you see why he is called "Mr. UFO."

UFO   1800 S. Robertson Blvd./Box 355/Los Angeles, CA 90035. Subtitled "an international forum on extraterrestrial theories and phenomena," the publication is edited and shaped by Vicki Cooper and Sherie Stark.

Right to Know Forum   PO Box 2911/Hyattsville, MD 20784. This newsletter and its staff is dedicated to ending all official secrecy concerning UFOs.

Contact Forum   c/o Wildflower Press/PO Box 230893/Tigard, OR 97281. The staff seeks to offer a vehicle for the open exchange of ideas and information concerning all aspects of the UFO controversy, with perhaps an emphasis on contactees and abductees.

The Steiger Questionnaire of Mystical, Paranormal, and UFO Experiences may be acquired by sending a stamped, self-addressed #10 business envelope to Timewalker/PO Box 434/Forest City, IA 50436.